GRAVEYARDS
of the
PACIFIC

Japanese planes attacking Pearl Harbor, Hawaii

GRAVEYARDS
of the
PACIFIC

FROM **PEARL HARBOR** TO **BIKINI ATOLL**

ROBERT D. BALLARD

WITH MICHAEL HAMILTON MORGAN

NATIONAL GEOGRAPHIC

WASHINGTON, D.C.

CONTENTS

Stephen E. Ambrose

WHEREVER BOB BALLARD IS, HE IS IN COMMAND. WHETHER AT A GATHERING with his fellow Explorers-in-Residence at National Geographic headquarters for a photo opportunity, an awards ceremony, dining with associates in a restaurant, or seated in the control room of his support vessel while two of his manned minisubs explore what is in the depths below, or even down there himself at 17,000 feet—he commands. Everyone else obeys. He speaks softly and thoughtfully, but when he indicates that this or that is what he wants done, you do it. This is because the order is reasonable and necessary. As a commander of men I'd rank him with my three favorites: Meriwether Lewis, William Clark, and Dwight D. Eisenhower.

He writes, "I'm an underwater explorer, not a historian." And of course his fame comes from his deep dives and startling discoveries. But despite his disclaimer, he is definitely the leading archaeologist-historian. He has found and described both ancient ships and modern ships, including *Titanic,* U.S.S. *Yorktown,* the German battleship *Bismarck,* and many others. In the process he links present and past, both telling a story and creating his own, thus adding to our knowledge of who we are and where we have been. "The deep ocean," he writes in his book, *The Eternal Darkness: A Personal History of Deep-sea Exploration,* "is the world's largest museum." He has carried out explorations in the Pacific Ocean, which form the core of this volume, the Atlantic, the Mediterranean, the Black Sea, and elsewhere.

Sunken ships from three centuries ago or from the 20th century are, Ballard writes, "sitting there like time capsules." When he finds and explores them, he uncovers their shapes, sizes, and capabilities—nautical history that cannot be found anywhere else. Further, as he observes, "virtually everything that humans have ever made has probably been carried across water on some sort of ship at one time or another." A former U.S. Navy officer who specialized in deep submergence, Bob Ballard has been fascinated by what is down there and devotes himself to discovery at the deep bottom of oceans. He has found and recovered or described trade goods of all kinds extending back over the centuries, including bits of pottery, tools, cargo containers, and much else that gently enhances our knowledge of the ancient and the modern worlds.

Burial at sea from the U.S.S. *Bunker Hill,* 1944

In November 2000, I spent a few days with Ballard as he searched for a Japanese midget submarine in the waters off Pearl Harbor. The Japanese launched five of these secret weapons in the vicinity of the harbor mouth on December 6-7, 1941. They had brought the midgets thousands of miles from Japan attached in cradles to the rear deck of much larger mother submarines. The midget subs sat pointed sternward of the larger submarine and were rigged so that as the mother ship dived forward beneath the surface, the midget sub could release itself in the opposite direction, proceeding on its mission independent of the tether that had until then provided for its needs, both electrical and communications. These two-man subs were intended to be the first wave of the attack on the U.S. fleet berthed at Pearl Harbor, firing their two torpedoes at targets in the shallow waters of Battleship Row and then returning—if they could—to their mother ships stationed several miles out at sea. All of the midget subs—but one—were later accounted for, sunk by American gunfire and depth charges or run aground without doing any damage to the ships in the harbor. The midget sub that's never been found was the one that Ballard was after.

Searching for this submarine was, for Ballard, an easy duty assignment. We went out each morning at 0800 on the research ship *American Islander,* which he had leased and outfitted with his usual assortment of underwater craft, which included ATVs, advanced tethered vehicles, ROVs, remotely operated vehicles, and also manned submersibles. And we returned to dock at 1800 hours. Ordinarily, Ballard is onboard a ship at sea for weeks at a time while doing his searches, but on this exploration he slept in a bed on shore every night. And, unlike what's true for most of his explorations, he went out with good maps of the sea bottom at the site, prepared by the National Park Service's Submerged Cultural Resources Unit, which, having located by sonar numerous possible locations for the midget sub, had never found it. Of course Ballard is known for finding what others have missed, and *Titanic* serves as the best example.

The area around the mouth of Pearl Harbor is relatively empty, except for what has been dumped there over the years, including all kinds of World War II weaponry and another Japanese midget sub captured somewhere else and abandoned there by the Navy after all its secrets were delivered. Inside the harbor, U.S.S. *Arizona* lies where it was sunk by the Japanese attack on December 7, 1941, a permanent memorial to all those American sailors who lost their lives that fateful Sunday morning.

With us were Ballard's crew, as well as a National Geographic television crew filming a documentary, other staff from the Geographic, and the ship's own crew. Ballard had brought along two small underwater search vehicles, each with a man aboard. They were minisubs he had helped outfit, with bright lights, videotape capabilities, and voice communications to *American Islander.* We could review the film they shot on screens in the surface ship once the minisubs had been hoisted back aboard. These minisubs were products of the highest technology, far advanced over the workings of the Japanese midget sub we were looking for, but still they were submarines, part of the long line of improvements to submersibles. As they searched, the two men in the two minisubs talked to us. They reported nothing to be seen, except the bottom of the harbor entrance. Ballard told them where to look next. They eventually discovered a downed American plane, which probably had run out of fuel and ditched in the drink, and lots of naval and airborne ordnance that had been dumped overboard by the Americans during the war. But no midget submarine—yet. However, looking but not finding is something Ballard has become accustomed to over the years. It took him considerable searching back and forth to find *Titanic*, and all the other sunken ships he has discovered. While I was onboard *American Islander* with him, it was, in Ballard's own words, "another day at the office in which nothing happened." But something did happen. I learned a great deal about the Japanese attack, about the midget subs, about the tactics, about the floor of Pearl Harbor and environs, and about how Bob Ballard works.

On our second day out, the minisubs discovered two torpedoes, side by side. They almost certainly were the torpedoes carried by the midget sub. We saw them on the video, but there were no signs of the submarine itself. We were gathered around the dining table on *American Islander*, watching on a television screen the video brought up by the minisubs. The National Geographic cameramen filmed the viewing. Ballard commented. He had maps of the harbor bottom, plus photographs of the midget sub, and books recounting the action. We were fascinated by the torpedoes and the upside-down plane, but downcast at this point by the failure to find what we were really looking for. Ballard raised our spirits. He said that the next day we would try here, there, wherever. His optimism was contagious. Dwight Eisenhower once said that he had learned during the 1942 invasion of North Africa that a commander's pessimism could spread throughout his staff, so after that he kept all his doubts for his pillow. That is one of the marks of a great leader. It is one part of Ballard in action.

He always will keep searching. He never gives up. We are all of us, around the world, forever indebted to him. Everyone who reads this book will understand that. Everything he has done, from exploring the ancient submerged sites of the Mediterranean and the Black Sea through the Pacific War sites, has benefited us all.

One night on Oahu we went out to dinner with his wife, Barbara, and the National Geographic staff. It was grand. There were eight of us, sitting at a round table. I can testify that where Ballard sat was the head of the table.

In this exciting book, Ballard clearly tells the complicated stories of what happened in the greatest naval battles of the Pacific, at Coral Sea, Midway, Guadalcanal, Truk Lagoon, the Philippine Sea, and Leyte Gulf, and about his underwater searches for those unlucky ships that didn't make it through these historic battles. He also recounts the horrible story, which begins on July 30, 1945, of what happened to the cruiser *Indianapolis* and her surviving crew. He relates as well the tragedy of the amphibious landings on beachheads such as Tarawa, Saipan, Iwo Jima, and Okinawa, which, nevertheless, rolled the Japanese back to their home islands and laid the groundwork for their unconditional surrender, following the atomic bombing of Hiroshima and Nagasaki. He ends with a thorough presentation of what took place at Bikini Atoll in July 1946, when the United States conducted the first postwar tests of later versions of the atomic bomb—with only a minimum understanding of the long-term effects of radiation on those participating.

His accounts of searching for sunken ships at the sites of historic naval battles, even when he wasn't successful in finding what he sought, make fascinating reading. As a historian and an explorer, as a storyteller and a commander of men, Bob Ballard is unique.

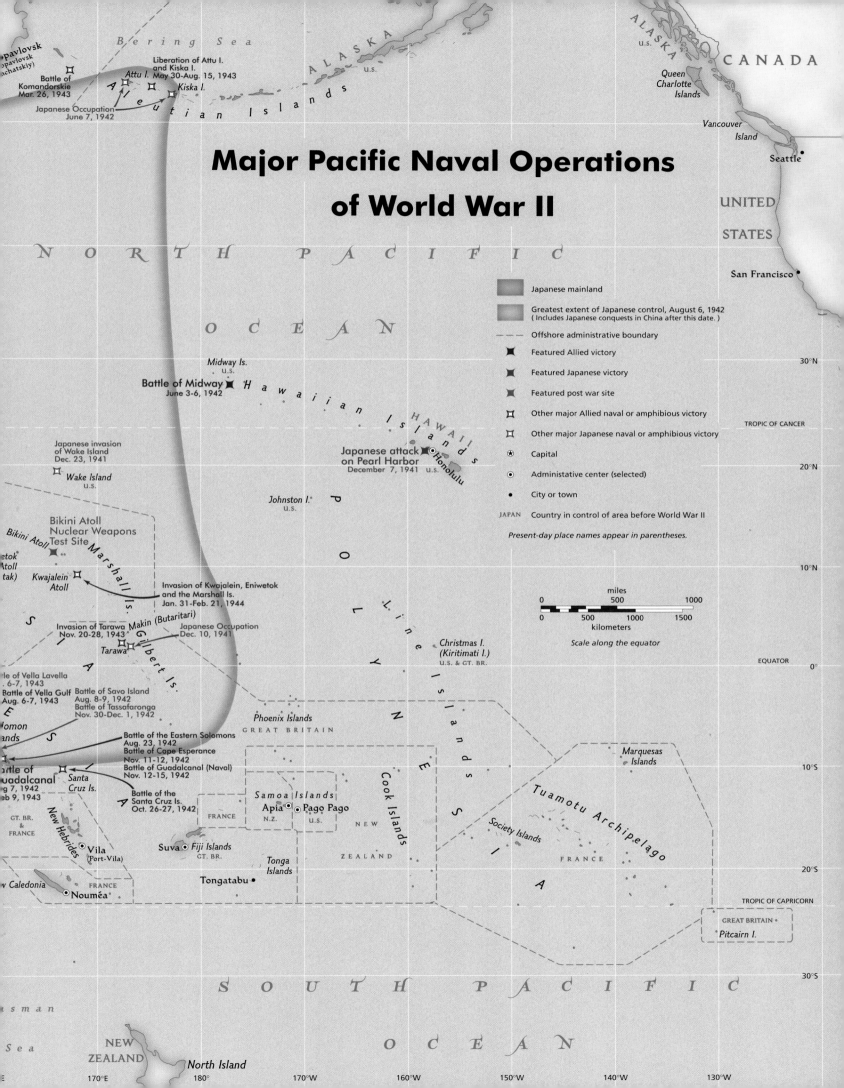

Major Pacific Naval Operations
of World War II

Legend:

▮	Japanese mainland
▮	Greatest extent of Japanese control, August 6, 1942 (Includes Japanese conquests in China after this date.)
– – –	Offshore administrative boundary
◆	Featured Allied victory
◆	Featured Japanese victory
◆	Featured post war site
⬡	Other major Allied naval or amphibious victory
⬡	Other major Japanese naval or amphibious victory
✪	Capital
◉	Administative center (selected)
•	City or town
JAPAN	Country in control of area before World War II

Present-day place names appear in parentheses.

Map labels:

- Bering Sea
- Petropavlovsk (Petropavlovsk Kamchatskiy)
- Battle of Komandorskie Mar. 26, 1943
- Liberation of Attu I. and Kiska I. May 30-Aug. 15, 1943
- Attu I.
- Kiska I.
- Japanese Occupation June 7, 1942
- Aleutian Islands
- ALASKA — U.S.
- ALASKA — U.S.
- CANADA
- Queen Charlotte Islands
- Vancouver Island
- Seattle
- UNITED STATES
- San Francisco
- NORTH PACIFIC OCEAN
- Midway Is. U.S.
- Battle of Midway June 3-6, 1942
- Hawaiian Islands
- HAWAII
- Japanese invasion of Wake Island Dec. 23, 1941
- Wake Island U.S.
- Johnston I. U.S.
- Japanese attack on Pearl Harbor December 7, 1941 U.S.
- Honolulu
- TROPIC OF CANCER
- 30°N
- 20°N
- Bikini Atoll
- Bikini Atoll Nuclear Weapons Test Site
- Eniwetok Atoll (Enewetak)
- Kwajalein Atoll
- Marshall Is.
- Invasion of Kwajalein, Eniwetok and the Marshall Is. Jan. 31-Feb. 21, 1944
- Invasion of Tarawa Nov. 20-28, 1943
- Makin (Butaritari)
- Japanese Occupation Dec. 10, 1941
- Tarawa
- Gilbert Is.
- 10°N
- Line Islands
- Christmas I. (Kiritimati I.) U.S. & GT. BR.
- POLYNESIA
- EQUATOR
- 0°
- Battle of Vella Lavella 6-7, 1943
- Battle of Vella Gulf Aug. 6-7, 1943
- Battle of Savo Island Aug. 8-9, 1942
- Battle of Tassafaronga Nov. 30-Dec. 1, 1942
- Solomon Islands
- Battle of the Eastern Solomons Aug. 23, 1942
- Battle of Cape Esperance Nov. 11-12, 1942
- Battle of Guadalcanal (Naval) Nov. 12-15, 1942
- Battle of Guadalcanal 7, 1942 Feb 9, 1943
- Santa Cruz Is.
- Battle of the Santa Cruz Is. Oct. 26-27, 1942
- Phoenix Islands GREAT BRITAIN
- Samoa Islands
- Apia N.Z.
- Pago Pago U.S.
- Cook Islands
- NEW ZEALAND
- Marquesas Islands
- Tuamotu Archipelago
- Society Islands FRANCE
- GT. BR. & FRANCE
- New Hebrides
- Vila (Port-Vila)
- Suva Fiji Islands GT. BR.
- Tonga Islands
- Tongatabu
- New Caledonia FRANCE
- Nouméa
- 10°S
- TROPIC OF CAPRICORN
- GREAT BRITAIN
- Pitcairn I.
- 20°S
- FRANCE
- SOUTH PACIFIC OCEAN
- 30°S
- Tasman Sea
- NEW ZEALAND
- North Island
- 170°E
- 180°
- 170°W
- 160°W
- 150°W
- 140°W
- 130°W

Scale:
miles
0 — 500 — 1000
kilometers
0 — 500 — 1000 — 1500
Scale along the equator

BURNING SHIPS AND A FLAK-FILLED SKY, PEARL HARBOR, HAWAII, DECEMBER 7, 1941

CHAPTER ONE

PEARL HARBOR

Japanese bomb Pearl Harbor, December 7

Sunday, December 7, 1941—Dawn

THE DESTROYER U.S.S. *WARD*, UNDER COMMAND OF LT. WILLIAM W. Outerbridge, was not supposed to be on sea duty, but mechanical problems on a sister destroyer had sent her back out again, to patrol the mouth of Pearl Harbor, which since May a year ago had been America's forward military base in the troubled Pacific. Crewmen Russell Reetz and Will Lehner, both reservists from icy St. Paul, Minnesota, had agreed that once the thrill of Hawaii's tropical clime and its lush scenery had worn off, they had become bored with their usual routine of sailing back and forth day after day, guarding a harbor where they knew most of America's Pacific fleet was now peacefully berthed.

Reetz recalls that having drawn the midnight to 4:00 a.m. watch on the morning of December 7, he was relieved from duty at 3:45 a.m. and had gone below to take a shower. But at 4:05 a.m., he was astonished to hear "general quarters" sounded. He remembers thinking, "Why at this ungodly hour?" Above deck again, he learned that the minesweeper *Condor* had reported sighting a periscope nearby. When nothing could be found on *Ward*'s sonar, the ship stood down from general quarters at 4:45 a.m. "Reveille" was sounded at the usual 6 o'clock, but scarcely half an hour later it was "general quarters" again.

This time, the transport *Antares*, towing a barge into Pearl Harbor, reported it had a submarine in its wake, presumably hoping to sneak in with *Antares* through the

A sleepy tropical military base awakens to chaos. A rescue boat tosses a line to a survivor in the water; others are trapped on the *West Virginia*.

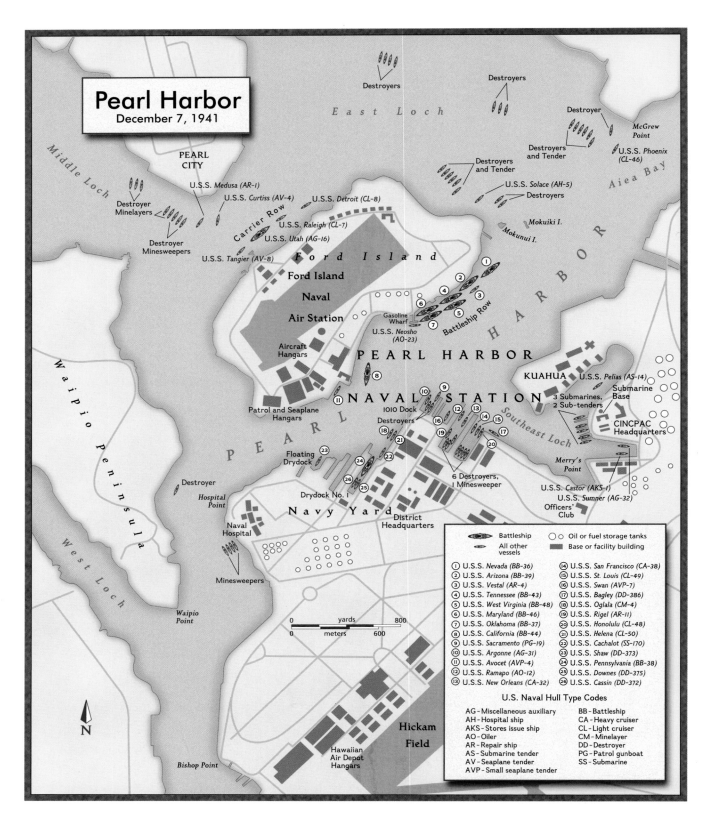

Pearl Harbor
December 7, 1941

East Loch

PEARL CITY

Middle Loch

U.S.S. Medusa (AR-1)
U.S.S. Curtiss (AV-4)
U.S.S. Detroit (CL-8)

Destroyer Minelayers

Destroyer Minesweepers

U.S.S. Raleigh (CL-7)
U.S.S. Utah (AG-16)
U.S.S. Tangier (AV-8)

Carrier Row

Destroyers

Destroyers

Destroyer

McGrew Point

Destroyers and Tender

U.S.S. Phoenix (CL-46)

Destroyers and Tender

U.S.S. Solace (AH-5)
Destroyers

Aiea Bay

Mokuiki I.
Mokunui I.

Ford Island

Ford Island Naval Air Station

Gasoline Wharf

Aircraft Hangars

U.S.S. Neosho (AO-23)

Battleship Row

HARBOR

PEARL HARBOR

KUAHUA

U.S.S. Pelias (AS-14)
Submarine Base

3 Submarines, 2 Sub-tenders

Patrol and Seaplane Hangars

NAVAL STATION

1010 Dock

Destroyers

CINCPAC Headquarters

Southeast Loch

PEARL

Waipio Peninsula

Floating Drydock

Merry's Point

U.S.S. Castor (AKS-1)
U.S.S. Sumner (AG-32)

Destroyer

Hospital Point

Drydock No. 1

Naval Hospital

Navy Yard

District Headquarters

Officers' Club

West Loch

Minesweepers

Waipio Point

| | Battleship | | ○ ○ Oil or fuel storage tanks |
| All other vessels | | ■ Base or facility building |

① U.S.S. Nevada (BB-36)		⑭ U.S.S. San Francisco (CA-38)	
② U.S.S. Arizona (BB-39)		⑮ U.S.S. St. Louis (CL-49)	
③ U.S.S. Vestal (AR-4)		⑯ U.S.S. Swan (AVP-7)	
④ U.S.S. Tennessee (BB-43)		⑰ U.S.S. Bagley (DD-386)	
⑤ U.S.S. West Virginia (BB-48)		⑱ U.S.S. Oglala (CM-4)	
⑥ U.S.S. Maryland (BB-46)		⑲ U.S.S. Rigel (AR-11)	
⑦ U.S.S. Oklahoma (BB-37)		⑳ U.S.S. Honolulu (CL-48)	
⑧ U.S.S. California (BB-44)		㉑ U.S.S. Helena (CL-50)	
⑨ U.S.S. Sacramento (PG-19)		㉒ U.S.S. Cachalot (SS-170)	
⑩ U.S.S. Argonne (AG-31)		㉓ U.S.S. Shaw (DD-373)	
⑪ U.S.S. Avocet (AVP-4)		㉔ U.S.S. Pennsylvania (BB-38)	
⑫ U.S.S. Ramapo (AO-12)		㉕ U.S.S. Downes (DD-375)	
⑬ U.S.S. New Orleans (CA-32)		㉖ U.S.S. Cassin (DD-372)	

U.S. Naval Hull Type Codes

AG – Miscellaneous auxiliary	BB – Battleship
AH – Hospital ship	CA – Heavy cruiser
AKS – Stores issue ship	CL – Light cruiser
AO – Oiler	CM – Minelayer
AR – Repair ship	DD – Destroyer
AS – Submarine tender	PG – Patrol gunboat
AV – Seaplane tender	SS – Submarine
AVP – Small seaplane tender	

| 0 | yards | 800 |
| 0 | meters | 600 |

N

Hickam Field

Hawaiian Air Depot Hangars

Bishop Point

Like a bull's-eye, Ford Island Naval Air Station sits dead center in Pearl Harbor. Ships of Battleship Row are neatly lined up. Navy officers thought the bay's waters too shallow for torpedo attack. Planes on Hickam Field, parked wingtip to wingtip, were devastated. Relief map (opposite) shows the bowl-like terrain of Pearl and the mountains over which the surprise attack came.

Japanese Air Assault on Oahu

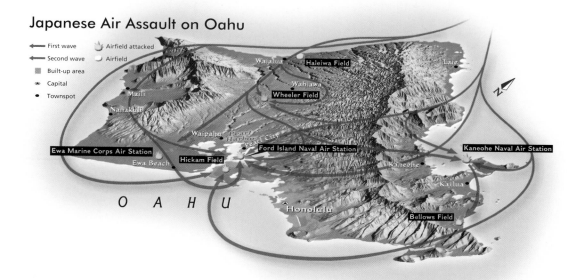

submarine gates that guarded the inner harbor. And the watch officer on the *Ward* confirmed a sighting of what he identified as a periscope behind *Antares*. At 6:37 a.m., Lt. William Goepner, bridge officer on the *Ward*, summoned the skipper when he spotted what he thought was the surface trail of a submerged vessel. Drawn to the scene by reports trickling in, an antisubmarine patrol plane circled the area, confirming the presence of a hostile submarine. Skipper Outerbridge ordered his crew to open fire on the intruder.

Will Lehner, at his battle station, says he got a good look at the sub from about a 50-foot distance. It had no markings, was "mossy green," and looked like it had been in the water for a good long time. But he'd never seen a sub so small. Reetz, on deck amidships, was also studying the sub. He heard No. 1 gun fire, but it looked like that shot was high, sailing over the conning tower now breaking the surface. When No. 3 gun fired, it appeared to have scored a hit on the tower, just above the base. Reetz says he saw the surfaced sub list to starboard, then right itself before beginning to go down. It was now 6:45 a.m., and both the *Ward* and the circling Catalina patrol plane dropped depth charges, the concussions of which jolted the *Ward*, and probably severely hurt the sub. The midget sub rolled over and went down, surrounded by lingering foam and spray from the depth charges. Other crewmates told Reetz they had watched the sub surface one more time a moment later, but those reports are unconfirmed. Lehner remembers thinking only that "at least now I've got something to write home about."

That very hour, 20 miles off the island of Oahu, Kichiji Dewa was diligently manning his radio. Near midnight on December 6, his vessel, *Submarine I-16* of the

Imperial Japanese Navy, had been operating only five miles off the entrance to Pearl Harbor. Part of a greater advance force that numbered 27 submarines, *I-16* was one of five mother ships that each carried one midget submarine, Japan's closest thing to a secret weapon. Armed only with a pair of lethal torpedoes, these tiny subs were destined to play the opening role in a grand drama. When they were cut loose, their mother subs withdrew to a safe rendezvous point, ready to recover the midgets if they could find their way back after completing their mission.

Dewa was first a radioman, but he was also in charge of maintaining the electrical systems, a circuit at a time, for the midget sub tethered to *I-16*. These skills went hand in hand, because he personally installed a switch that allowed the sub's telegraph to get power both from a special communications battery, as well as from the midget's main battery if need be. That midnight, when Dewa communicated by phone with the midget sub while it was still attached to the mother ship, he told Masaji Yokoyama and Sadamu Uyeda "goodbye" and to take care; he knew that they probably would not make it back alive. Like kamikaze pilots, who wore uniforms of brownish silk and leather caps, the crews of those midget subs, at first, had been deliberately marked for suicide missions. But eventually, the idea of using well-trained, intelligent sailors in one-shot, flame-out missions was considered wasteful. So, the mother subs would wait nearby, only a few miles out, to rescue the midget subs that could make it back.

And in that slow crawl toward dawn, Dewa did his duty at the radio, awaiting transmissions from the midgets, but at the same time monitoring world news as it came in. He began to think of the few things Yokoyama and

Uyeda had in their favor. Things like surprise. And a wire-cutter that would help get them through the American torpedo nets. And the fact that they had been trained to operate at night, giving them an advantage over their adversaries, who avoided action after dark. But he also had seen the horrendous conditions that midget-sub crews had to endure just to undertake routine missions, not to mention combat. Inside the cabin, the craft's narrowness was almost suffocating, and on top of that, sulfuric acid gas continually leaked from the storage batteries, filling the already polluted air with caustic fumes. In preparation for this mission he had checked through the sub's electrical wiring, and he had put the 600-horsepower motor into top shape, but it ran on batteries that had a life, at most, of only 25 hours.

And yet Dewa maintained a loyal kind of hope for his friends as his mother sub waited at the rendezvous point. Even if these two would not return, he thought, it was simply the price to be paid for the success of their mission. Still, he manned his radio patiently. Sometime around dawn, he heard the far off sounds of explosions. He considered that they might have come from depth charges, perhaps those directed at his own crewmates only miles away—at the front lines of a war that had not yet started. Much later that day, Dewa isn't quite sure when, he got an inkling of hope for them when a radio message came crackling through. He deciphered it as *kira kira kira*, not quite the agreed-upon code message of *tora tora tora*, signaling success, but it could have been altered by some kind of communication glitch. Nevertheless, despite this glimmer of hope, his crewmates never came back.

Although an outside observer might have seen these little submarines as supporting characters in the prologue to a larger drama not yet begun, in fact the midget subs had been awarded the leading role in the drama's first act. For even as the main striking force of Japan's Imperial Navy was still steaming south toward Pearl Harbor, and before any Japanese aircraft had taken off from the mighty carriers still hundreds of miles away, the first action in the war between Japan and the United States had been assigned to the midget submarines. These craft were held in such reverence by Japan's military hierarchy that their existence was kept top secret, their continued development given highest priority. It was clear that in war propaganda their crews would be lionized as great heroes.

However, on that partly cloudy midnight of Decem-ber 6, 1941, all future adulation was small comfort to those two-man crews as their midget vessels slipped from the relative security of their mother-sub tethers into the ocean's black depths off Oahu. As only they and a few of their commanders were authorized to know, these brave men were on a secret mission to single-handedly deliver the first in a series of staggering blows to a powerful enemy in its own home waters. And, in doing so, they would launch the U.S.'s involvement in World War II.

Monday, November 6, 2000—Dawn

A light rain had fallen during the night, but the wind had dropped off on the beach at Kailua, Hawaii, and the sunrise poking through cloud cover was as glorious as I've ever remembered it. That same sky on a morning not unlike this one, nearly 60 years ago, was full of Japanese aircraft attacking an American military outpost set in a tropical paradise. It was the beginning of the worst war that either America or Japan has ever seen. That lazy Sunday morning attack would bring on nearly 300,000 American and more than a million Japanese military casualties, millions more civilian deaths in Japan and other countries, hundreds of ships sunk, thousands of aircraft lost, societies all over the world destroyed outright or transformed beyond recognition, and it would culminate in the dropping of two atomic bombs.

At heart and by profession I'm an underwater explorer, not a historian. But I believe that my explorations beneath the seas have helped us see history up close, helped us find the physical evidence that confirms or rewrites the unavoidably imperfect accounts of tumultuous and confusing events that happened years or centuries ago. I've been doing this for a long time now—from the Atlantic to the Pacific to the Mediterranean to the Black Sea—peering through murky depths to see what history can tell us, getting a new and unique perspective on things that shaped our view of the world, and ourselves.

And that's why I'm here, on this beach, looking back in time. I'm conducting an underwater search for the target of that first American shot fired at Pearl Harbor on December 7, 1941: a two-man midget submarine that the Japanese sent at dawn to infiltrate the harbor and unleash its torpedoes in the shallows of Battleship Row. Hit by gunfire and pounded by depth charges, it sank out of sight, mortally wounded, or, perhaps, it fled out to sea. Another four midget subs had set out on similar missions that morning and were sunk or wrecked. Three were later found and accounted for.

But that first one, that tiny sub fired on while we were still a nation at peace, has never been found. By some accounts, as late as 10:44 that night it was still able to send a message to its mother ship signaling "mission accomplished." And so its whereabouts has captured the imagination of many: those on the *Ward* that day who fired the shots, historians in Japan and the U.S., and, of course, me.

Why me? Well, the one that got away, the one that sank beneath the waves, has always hooked me. It hooked me into looking for *Titanic, Bismarck,* Greek and Roman artifacts beneath the Mediterranean, and evidence of a cataclysmic flood in the Black Sea 8,000 years ago. And this one hooked me good, a midget vessel known only as *16-A,* which had sailed 4,000 miles of ocean to this site tethered to a mother sub identified as *I-16.* This little undersea boat had started a war, even though those who sank her didn't know the main attack was still an hour off, didn't know the worst war of human history was coming their way.

I wanted to find her and close the book. Even if my quest wasn't successful, my work might at least raise consciousness that, contrary to popular opinion, the first shots fired on Pearl Harbor Day 1941 were American and the first vessel sunk was Japanese.

Preface to Infamy: The Days Before December 7, 1941

Pearl Harbor has changed a lot in 60 years, but with a little effort you can imagine how it looked in 1941. Still a surprisingly beautiful meeting place of land, water, and sky, it seems an unlikely spot for military action, much less the site of a great battlefield and a hallowed graveyard. Out in the harbor you can look back and still see unspoiled land rising up into the highlands of Waianae Range on your left and Koolau Range to the right, both lush and green with tropical forest and almost always topped with clouds. Despite encroachments of modern life in the foreground, the high-rises of Pearl City to the north or Honolulu Airport to the east, you can very easily strip away all of that in your mind's eye. You can picture the pristine beaches that Western explorers sighted when they first came upon these islands in the 18th century. Even in 1941 American sailors and airmen found it a little-changed paradise when rising tensions between the U.S. and Japan yanked thousands of them from homes all across America and deposited them in this mid-Pacific outpost.

On the other side of the world, Hitler had been on the march since 1938, swallowing up continental Europe in swift gulps. By 1941 America's professed neutrality in this Old World conflict was clearly belied by streams of Lend-Lease convoys bound for England and points east. Japan had been on its own binge of militarism, occupying Manchuria and coastal China since the 1930s, which it governed through puppets, while augmenting its naval force so rapidly that by 1941, in the Pacific at least, it surpassed in size the U.S., British, and Dutch fleets combined. President Franklin D. Roosevelt had watched Japan's expansion with alarm, and, determined not to abandon American interests in China and Southeast Asia, threatened Japan with an embargo on American oil and other strategic supplies if it didn't pull back. When Japan moved on into Indochina in the summer of 1941, Roosevelt turned off America's oil spigot and froze Japanese assets in America. Japan was then faced with either bowing to U.S. demands or seizing new and reliable sources of oil and rubber in the resource-rich colonial bastions of the Dutch East Indies, British Malaya, and Burma—and, perhaps, America's own Philippines.

Japan's prime minister at the time, Prince Fumimaro Konoe, was constitutionally inclined to keep the peace and sought to pursue diplomatic negotiations with the U.S.—even as others in the cabinet continued working toward war. Unable to bring about a parley at the highest levels, Konoe resigned his portfolio in October 1941 and was replaced by the militarist Hideki Tojo, former army chief of staff in Manchuria and minister of war. Negotiations between the two countries continued on for another two months, but the diplomatic breakthrough never came. While America awaited more concrete gestures of compliance from Japan, it had given little thought to declaring war if those gestures were somehow not to materialize. However, the countdown to a war was already ticking away. By late November, what came to be known as the Pearl Harbor Striking Force had already set sail from the Kuril Islands.

Although the whereabouts of the Japanese fleet would

Honolulu's skyline and forested hills rise beyond the deck engineer, Mark DeRoche, and
Argus, a tethered submersible. In November 2000, Ballard led an expedition here to search
for the sunken victim of the first American shots fired—a Japanese two-man submarine.

remain unknown in Washington for weeks, tensions were such that repeated warnings had gone out to Pacific commanders to expect Japanese aggression in Asia at any time. No one in the American high command at Pearl Harbor, from Adm. Husband Kimmel, commander in chief of the Pacific Fleet, and his Army counterpart Lt. Gen. Walter Short on down, expected any direct air threat to Hawaii. It was simply too far from Japan, and U.S. surveillance flights, which went out 700 miles, would give plenty of warning that a naval force was on its way. And more important, would a small island nation directly assault the fortifications of a mighty industrial power? No, an unprovoked attack on Hawaii was not a logical threat.

A prevailing sense of American impregnability and security gave rise to what would become unfortunate security lapses at Pearl. The comings and goings of warships had been set to a clockwork routine for months, so that

uninterrupted dredging of the harbor could be carried on, and a potential enemy would have little trouble establishing which ships would be where, when. And because the water was judged too shallow for a torpedo to navigate accurately, no torpedo nets were deployed around vessels while in harbor. And because the greatest threat to aircraft on the island was believed to be sabotage from locals of Japanese extraction—not strafing from aloft—hundreds of airplanes were routinely arranged on the tarmac of Hickham Field wingtip to wingtip: like "sitting ducks," in a description that has become a cliché.

Even with those lapses, it still seems hard to believe that the Pearl Harbor tragedy unfolded as it did. Too many obstacles to a surprise naval attack had to be overcome: The likelihood of a huge fleet being reported by random ships or planes somewhere along the route of a 4,000-mile sea voyage, of not being able to coordinate the movements of this fleet without breaking radio silence and exposing its location, and of ultimately being discovered by Hawaii's air surveillance and radar too far from target to deliver the strongest card in Japan's deck—surprise. The second card was good luck. The third was no mistakes. In other words, all the cards had to come up right for this attack to work as Japan planned it. And with a few exceptions, they all did.

While those cards would be much harder for either side to play later in the war, in the first week of December 1941 they all worked to Japan's benefit. They were all played to fulfill a grand strategy drafted by Japan's Adm. Isoroku Yamamoto, commander in chief, Combined Fleet. What is so ironic in this moment of history is that a supremely daring plan was created by a man who did not want to go to war with America at all, much less direct an attack on such a large and powerful opponent. He knew America well, having studied (and played poker) at Harvard and later having served as a naval attaché in Washington, D.C.

He didn't relish going to war with America. But his superiors, particularly Prime Minister Tojo, believed that *Yamato damashii*, Japan's sense of discipline and national spirit, gave their country the fighting edge over what was seen as a lax, unmilitary, and materialistic democracy focused only on comfort. Convinced of America's innate weakness and incompetence, Japan's military dictatorship showed its troops Laurel and Hardy movies as clear evidence. Emboldened by their conquests of Korea, Manchuria, and coastal China, and watching the success of Hitler's blitzkrieg in Europe, these warlords were set on joining the Axis in a war against the Western democracies. Yamamoto so vociferously opposed Tokyo's militarist plans that, perhaps to protect this talented strategist from those who feared years in America had compromised him, he was sent to sea, as admiral of the Combined Fleet.

It was then that Yamamoto fatalistically realized war was inevitable and that to give Japan time to further its campaign to dominate Asia, he'd have to come up with a plan incredibly devastating to the U.S. presence in the Pacific—so devastating that privately he hoped it might lead to a negotiated peace. Yamamoto fought for his plan through much of 1941, threatened to resign if he wasn't put in charge of it, and finally got the go-ahead that fall. And what a plan it was! Yamamoto would direct a surprise attack on Pearl Harbor that would unleash the force of Japan's mightiest aircraft carriers, which he had long championed as the navy's greatest weapon. This man of Japanese honor who knew America so well, this accomplished poker player who feared the strength of the huge industrial power on the other side of the water, fully accepted that the only way his country had a fighting chance for success was through surprise, treachery, and betrayal.

Monday, November 6, 2000—10:00 a.m.

Following another magnificent dawn on the beach at Kailua, I headed for the docks in Honolulu. A bit behind schedule because of traffic, I arrived around 8 o'clock. After looking around, I spotted the *American Islander*, our research ship for the next two weeks, tied up at Pier 13, and my gang hard at work. Engineer Jim Newman and video engineer Dave Wright were testing out *Argus*, one of our new towed imaging vehicles based at my Institute for Exploration back in Mystic, Connecticut. Remotely operated vehicle (ROV) pilot Martin Bowen and deck engineer Mark DeRouche were busy in the tool van. Data management guru Dwight Coleman was working on the database, video engineer Jay Minkin was on the video decks, and my trusty operations officer Cathy Offinger was running around making sure all was being taken care of.

Argus was fresh from underwater duty in the Black Sea, where I'd been just a few months earlier. Cathy had seen to it that *Argus* made it all the way from Turkey, via Malta, to New York, then overland to Long Beach, and finally to Honolulu—all within eight weeks. One slip-up along the way and we'd have been sitting here with no undersea "eyes" and the National Geographic meter running with nothing to show for it. All the scheduling, logistics, contracts, and coordination are what keep the rest of us afloat, and that's Cathy's department. She was out here in August to make sure our vehicles would fit on *American Islander* and to negotiate the best deals for crews, equipment, and services. As you can imagine, undersea exploration doesn't happen for free. While in some cases, like Midway and Guadalcanal, we were able to use Navy craft and divers at a subsidized rate, this trip is totally out of pocket. *American Islander* would cost us about $13,000 a day, ship and crew. In the Black Sea, *Northern Horizon* was cheaper at $9,000 a day, but research ships out of Woods Hole can run $21,000 a day or more.

Continued on page 30

Noses to the wind, Japanese "Zero" fighters warm up on a carrier deck prior to the attack. Their pilots are breakfasting after a long and restless night. Japanese leaders were not unanimous in their approval of an attack on America's Pacific headquarters. Many argued that Japanese expansion should concentrate on southeastern Asia. Mastermind of the operation, Adm. Isoroku Yamamoto, though opposed to a protracted war with the U.S., thought a "fatal blow" might lead to the negotiating table, where Japan could win concessions.

In a photo taken from a Japanese newsreel, aircraft carriers steam toward Hawaii in the days before the attack. Far from standard shipping lanes, they encountered seas so rough that several sailors were swept overboard. Yamamoto centered his strategy on carrier-borne planes. Torpedo bomber pilots trained extensively on the Japanese island of Kyushu, at a bay similar to Pearl Harbor's, perfecting the new skill of dropping torpedoes into extremely shallow water.

Aboard the Japanese carrier *Kaga*, pilots study a map of Pearl Harbor chalked on the deck.
Targets for *Kaga* bombers were the *Tennessee*, the *West Virginia*, and the *Arizona*; its torpedo planes
also attacked the *Oklahoma* and the *Nevada*. *Kaga* was later sunk during the Battle of Midway.

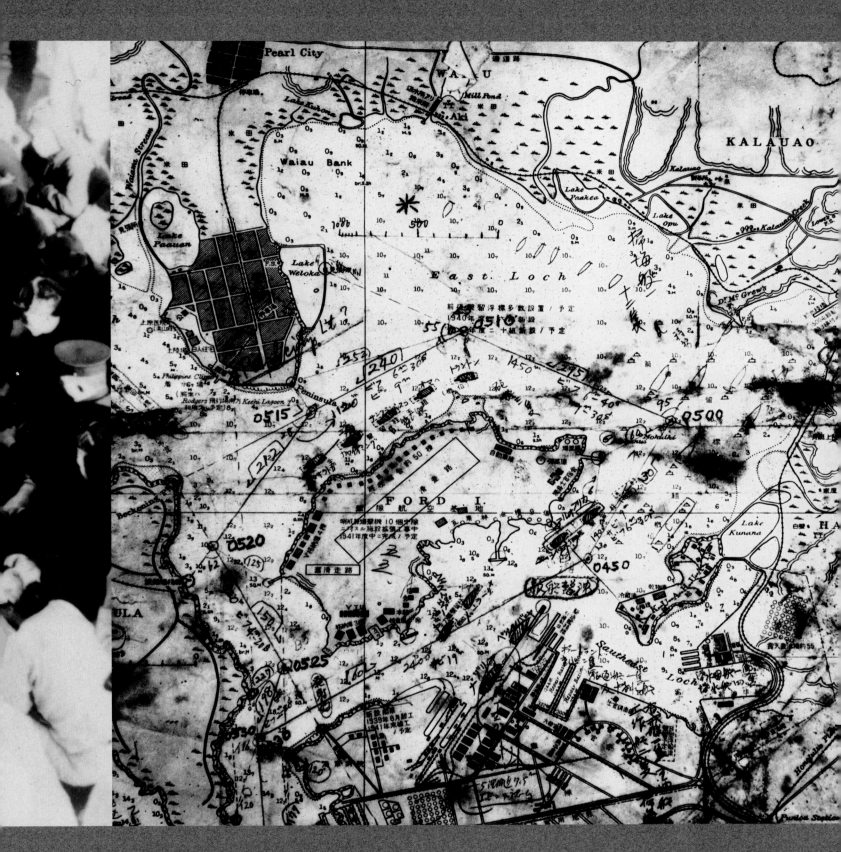

Annotated with notes on headings and depths, a map of Pearl Harbor was taken from a captured miniature Japanese submarine. Midget subs carried two torpedoes and were powered by scores of batteries. Five minisubs were used in the attack: One was sunk, one captured, and the others disappeared.

Beneath a fluttering Rising Sun, a Japanese "Kate" bomber takes off past cheering crewmen. Most of the planes that attacked Oahu were this type, which carried a crew of three and a 1,700-pound torpedo or the equivalent weight in bombs. Kates were relatively slow but could cruise 1,000 miles.

On his first visit to Pearl Harbor since 1941, Japanese submariner Kichiji Dewa (above) scans now quieter waters. He was last here as a radioman aboard mother sub *I-16*. Nbuo Fujita, the only Japanese pilot to bomb the continental U.S., poses in full gear beside his plane (opposite).

Continued from page 21

Everything seems to be working out—so far. No big equipment failures, no obstacles we can't overcome, but I'm not an idiot. I've done this so many times I know nothing ever works perfectly. There's something about being on a ship, on the ocean, that throws unpredictability into the mix. I expect unpleasant surprises now, so I try to build in the time for them—or at least some backup plans, some quick fixes. Just as in naval warfare, the greatest plans for undersea exploration can be undone by bad luck—or bad judgment. Each new expedition, just like each new combat engagement, is like starting all over again. It's test time, and you're on the line.

By afternoon I've assured myself that things are truly under way and there's nothing more I can do here today, so I head for my temporary home on the beach in Kailua. As I drive back, I'm imagining how Admiral Yamamoto must have felt on those fateful days in November and December as his grand plan, his master plan to win the Pacific War in one year, was taking shape. Talk about the potential for mistakes and screwups. In my quest, was I dreading anything like what he must have been 60 years earlier: a bad break from Mother Nature, like storm or adverse winds and seas, or premature discovery by a stray American merchant ship or a lone scout plane? Was he worried about the possibility of sending hundreds—or thousands—of his own men to their death?

If he was, he didn't tell anyone about it. He just plowed ahead.

Preface to Infamy: The Grand Plan

The tragedy of Admiral Yamamoto—starting a war he didn't want to fight, attacking an adversary he knew and feared and maybe even admired—is not at all out of character with Japan of 60 years ago. This was a people capable of the most exquisite refinement—haiku poetry, *sumi-e* painting, Kabuki theater—and in the

Rape of Nanking the most unspeakable butchery. Tragedy, stemming from the deepest national insecurity, could be said to have propelled this nation from feudal isolation to candidate for world power in only a hundred years. Tragedy was inherent in a cultural devotion to saving face over saving life, a subjugation of self to an absolute code of Bushido, Samurai honor, kamikaze missions, and ritual suicide before dishonor.

Already the dominant power in Asia in 1940, Japan's militarist rulers convinced the people that their power had to be absolute in what they called the Greater East Asia Co-Prosperity Sphere. If they did not rid Asia of colonial influences and grow stronger they would be choked by the greed of others and die as a nation. More than anything else, the Japanese were a people balanced between bending the world to their will and being subconsciously fascinated with their own death and destruction. The Japanese in 1941 were too much in love with death—even their own—to avoid a tragic end.

And so Admiral Yamamoto and his fleet officers, many of them as ambivalent as he was about a war with America, began in mid-1941 to further a plan to destroy the U.S. Pacific Fleet in one bold stroke. Then, as America reeled from such devastation and was impotent to retaliate, Japan would construct an impregnable mid-Pacific defense ribbon running from the western Aleutians in the north, down through Midway, Wake, and the Marshalls and Gilberts in the south. Even as French Indochina, the American Philippines, British Malaya and Burma and India, and the Dutch East Indies were being swiftly conquered for their raw materials, English-speaking Australia and New Zealand would be cut off from their Western allies and then strangled into submission.

If the Japanese could do all of this by early 1943, they believed that America would have to concede the Pacific Ocean and control of Asia to them. If, however, all of this was not accomplished on schedule, then all bets were off. Perhaps Yamamoto thought privately about the possibility that his plan might fail and what to do next, but for the political high command failure and defeat were not possibilities. The militarists believed they were on a sacred mission for a divine emperor, and destiny was on their side.

To carry off his bold plan, Yamamoto had created a mighty attack fleet with six aircraft carriers—*Akagi*, *Kaga*, *Hiryu*, *Soryu*, *Zuikaku*, and *Shokaku*—at its core. The debut of carriers in a major military operation—and naval warfare—would never be the same. These six carriers could bear as many as 360 airplanes: "Zero" fighters, "Kate" high-level or torpedo bombers, and "Val" dive bombers. The fleet also numbered battleships like *Hiei*, known to be Emperor Hirohito's favorite, the heavy cruisers *Tone* and *Chikuma*, and the light cruiser *Abukuma*. This armada was commanded by Vice Adm. Chuichi Nagumo, who also was personally opposed to attacking America, but his duty to country would overcome his reservations. Initially at least, few knew what they were going to attack. Among those few who had a need to know it, the fleet was called the Pearl Harbor Striking Force.

Yamamoto knew that a huge surface fleet could not sail intact from the home islands undetected, so he had the ships slip out in twos and threes from their various bases to rendezvous in the Kuril Islands, the mostly barren chain that stretches 700 miles between Hokkaido, Japan's northern island, and Russia's Kamchatka Peninsula. The exact gathering point was Hitokappu Bay, also known as Tunkun Bay, on Etorofu Island. By late November 1941, all of the attack force had gathered there. The carriers *Shokaku* and *Zuikaku* were so new that this was their shakedown cruise. In addition, a formidable group of 27 submarines, including 5 that carried two-man minisubs, was gathering separately. They had sailed on November 19 from ports in Japan, refueled in the Marshall Islands, and by December 6 would be only a few miles off Oahu, as prearranged.

On November 22, Yamamoto's plan and its target were revealed to senior officers, news that filtered down over the following day to flight officers, who began feverish preparations for their mission. On November 26, the surface fleet weighed anchor and steamed for Hawaii. Sailing east through the stormy North Pacific and north of shipping lanes to avoid detection, the fleet had orders to turn back if their presence was detected anytime before December 5. Their only encounter was with a Japanese merchant vessel, and miraculously no other ships or aircraft ever observed them. And, just as fortuitously, heavy seas at the beginning gave way to remarkable calm for most of the voyage—another good omen for Admiral Yamamoto.

By 9:00 p.m. December 6, the Pearl Harbor Striking Force was only 490 miles north of Oahu, nearing the tragic climax of its voyage at full speed ahead and in absolute radio silence. And now the time had come for psychological preparations, as patriotic orations were vehemently spouted from the bridges of all carriers and cruisers, whipping everyone into an anti-American frenzy. The captain of *Shokaku* exhorted his crew to "obey and die for your country, Japan! Whether you win or lose, you must fight and die for your country!" Work went on non-stop, with officers sleeping in their uniforms. They were all honor bound to fight to the death, to die rather than to surrender, to give their lives for the divine Hirohito and for Japan.

Tuesday, November 7, 2000

Just before we pulled away from the dock, we were boarded by three World War II veterans who would accompany us on our underwater search just off the mouth of Pearl Harbor. On December 7, 1941, Russell Reetz and Will Lehner were crewmates aboard U.S.S. *Ward* and Kichiji Dewa had been on Japan's mother sub *I-16*. We were also joined by Japanese military historian Katsuhiro Hara and an interpreter. I was particularly keen to have these veterans along because the midget sub that Reetz and Lehner had seen fired on that fateful morning— the one I'm hooked on finding—may have been the one launched by Dewa from *I-16*. Or, actually, it might have been another one deployed by mother sub *I-20* on the eastern side of the harbor approach. No one could be absolutely sure which unmarked sub the *Ward* had fired on that fateful morning.

Reetz and Lehner were both in their 80s now, but barely into adulthood when they and 82 other Naval Reservists from St. Paul, Minnesota, found themselves, in March 1941, at Pearl Harbor. All these guys from the same bone-chilling hometown, battered by a terrible storm on their way out from San Diego, had suddenly become crewmates in the tropics on the destroyer U.S.S. *Ward*. "Hawaii

was a dream come true when we first got here," the two Pearl Harbor survivors agree. "It was really quiet then," Reetz says. "There were only two major hotels in Honolulu, the Mauna Loa and the Royal Hawaiian on Waikiki Beach. Servicemen could stay nearby in the Prince for 25 cents a night."

Reetz is a fine-featured, precise, and meticulous man, who spent his life after the Navy back in Minnesota, teaching trade school at night and working by day in insulation and maintenance. Lehner is more of a rogue, an aging Donald Sutherland look-alike, still cracking jokes and engaging the girls in a little flirtation, much as he might have done as a 19-year-old reservist. He broke family tradition by returning to settle in Wisconsin after the war. Both Reetz and Lehner were inducted into the Navy as firemen third class, but Reetz gravitated to machinist mate and Lehner to cook. "I loved that time," says Lehner. His main duty was in the galley of the *Ward*, serving up steaming quantities of beans, potatoes, chili, and spaghetti to the more than 130 men aboard. "Occasionally we were able to serve pork or beef," he says. "But what we had too much of was mutton. For every allotment of beef, we'd get three of mutton. And it wasn't too popular with the men. So we'd throw it overboard, in hopes of getting more beef."

And what was their routine like in those early days, those last days of idyllic peace? "We were on guard duty outside the harbor," says Reetz. "So we sailed back and forth, back and forth, day and night. We'd stay out for a week at a time, then come back in. We took liberty when we earned it on Oahu and the other islands." Reetz served on the *Ward* until 1943, but Lehner stayed with her until she was sunk in Ormoc Bay, Philippines, in late 1944.

We got under way on schedule at 8:00 a.m. and headed out to sea in a good swell that I'd have to keep an eye on, making sure all the landlubbers had taken their seasick pills. Our first objective was to reach deep water so that we could safely pay out most of our fiber-optic cable and rewind it evenly onto the drum under tension. One of our advanced tethered vehicles, the already-mentioned *Argus*, works closely with *Little Herc*, our other remotely operated vehicle, or ROV. In fact, *Argus* is a kind of middleman, directly tethered to the search ship while *Little Herc* is tethered to *Argus*, which in a sense acts as a shock absorber for *Little Herc*. *Argus* can even provide the lighting for her sister ship and shoot video and stills of

Little Herc at work. Following our spooling test, we headed toward the search area, where we would be working in water about 1,200 feet deep. The sky was clear and winds were blowing more than 20 knots as we approached the site, but as we began picking up the lee of the island, the winds were cut and the seas started dropping off.

The search at Pearl Harbor is different from my other expeditions, Midway and Guadalcanal, *Titanic* and elsewhere, because Pearl already has been mapped so well. I came out today with charts showing one hundred potential targets, all found by Dan Lenihan of the National Park Service's Submerged Cultural Resources Unit. Dan and his crews have mapped Pearl twice in their efforts to find the lost midget sub, but with no luck. They've also done underwater searches in Micronesia and the Aleutians and at Bikini Atoll. The bottom here, though not as deep as at Midway, poses its own challenges. It's a mix of volcanic slope with coral reef growing on top. Believe me, coral outcrops are scary since they grow vertically.

My strategy in this search is to use our sonar to relocate the targets Lenihan found and then take a visual look at them. We'll rely on sonar and visuals from *Argus*, with her big lights, and then send *Little Herc* moving around our target like a dog on a leash. Of course in relying on sonar you've got to deal with the issues of range versus resolution. If you want maximum range—if you want to be able to see a great distance—then you need to use sonar at low frequency. If you want maximum resolution or definition—if you want your underwater image on sonar to be a clear silhouette of your target—then you use high frequency. Each is a trade-off.

My plan is to run a systematic series of lines through the search area, using *Argus*'s low-frequency sonar to relocate all one hundred targets. Then I plan on attaching our new remotely operated vehicle *Little Herc* to *Argus* and using its high-frequency sonar to close on the target until it can be seen by *Little Herc*'s high-resolution color video camera. Once the minisub is found, I can then position *Argus* over the sub and illuminate it with *Argus*'s powerful lights while *Little Herc* gets close up, to obtain detailed images of the sub.

This strategy will work in 90 percent of the search area, but it won't work in the northernmost area where steep overhanging coral cliffs preclude operations by *Argus* and *Little Herc*. Here, I plan on using the two one-man submersibles.

With this strategy in mind, we launched *Argus* and began tuning the system. In relocating the targets, we were going to run a series of east-west lines 250 meters apart within our search area, which measured one mile north to south and one-and-a-half miles east to west. Running at an attitude of 7–8 meters, our visual search swath was about 20-plus meters. Unfortunately, I learned that on *American Islander* the slowest we could run lines and maintain course was about two knots. Though slow, even that would be too fast for *Little Herc* to keep up unless we decreased our towing speed to one knot.

When we recovered *Argus* from the depths, I was beginning to relax, but just as the vehicle broke the surface the ship's hydraulics on the winch failed. *Argus* became a wild monster hanging out over the water, swinging back and forth with the ocean swells. There'd been some glitches earlier, none insurmountable, but this one was major. We had to get this thing under control before it got shaken too badly, or worse, hit the ship and ended our mission before it even started. We quickly secured its stern with two lines, stopped the swinging, then added more lines as it became clear that the ship's engineer was going to need time to bring the hydraulics back on line. With the rest of the day shot, we finally decided to head back into port with *Argus* hanging from the A-frame. It's particularly exasperating when a low-tech problem like hydraulics interferes with high-tech vehicles and a major discovery. But undersea quests are just like space missions, since launches can fail as often from a bad fuse or loose connection as from a flawed computer chip.

As we headed back to the docks, and to get my mind off bad equipment I couldn't do anything about today, I talked with Kichiji Dewa, the Japanese veteran. A thoughtful, compact man in his 80s, he was serious to the point of being impassive, almost like the village elder or wise man. Not yet recovering his sea legs, he was clearly intrigued with the sea and ships, and submarines in particular. Long retired from an electric utility in Japan, he says he still misses submarine life. This he and I have in common: We're a special breed, we underwater sailors. Though from a small town near Osaka in western Japan, in a country never distant from the sea, he didn't come from a seafaring family. He volunteered for the navy, went straight to submarine duty, and never looked back.

I ask him direct questions about how he felt back then, about the possibility of war, about the possibility of going

As helpless as a beached whale, a two-man midget Japanese submarine rocks in Oahu's surf on the day of the attack (opposite). The boat was later salvaged and toured the U.S., encouraging Americans to buy war bonds. One of its crewmen drowned, but the other, Kazuo Sakamaki, became the first Japanese prisoner of war. He begged his captors to shoot him so that he might have an "honorable death." The destroyer U.S.S. *Ward* (left), painted by A. B. Chesley in 1976, fired the first American shots of the war, sinking one of the midget submarines at about 7:00 a.m. The *Ward* was later sunk in the Philippines by kamikazes. After the war, a painting on silk honored the Japanese midget submarine crewmembers lost in the Pearl Harbor attack (above), but Sakamaki's shame at being captured was considered so great that his portrait was not included.

to war with America. He's very honest and direct, saying he knew as early as October 1941 that he and his midget subs were going to attack the U.S. Not that anyone explicitly told him, but the charts he was using for exercises looked very similar to a well-known harbor on Oahu. In 1941, he, like most of his compatriots, hated America, because they were told we were choking them with our embargoes on oil and strategic materials. No matter that the embargoes were there to deter further conquests in Asia, to pressure Japan to depart from China. In that day and time, Japanese history and truth were being written by a jingoistic pen. Two years after Pearl Harbor his sub was sunk off Saipan. He swam for six hours to the island, and survived. Dishonored for not going down with his ship, he was flown back to Japan with American prisoners of war.

All that is in the past, Dewa says. He has learned the truth about America, about his country's martial customs, and about war. He's a determined pacifist now, hoping that the world will become peaceful, that countries will learn more about one another, so as to avoid conflict. He and I nod in agreement on peace. But, later, when someone shouts that an American fast attack sub can be seen to starboard, headed out to sea, he and I are the first to the rail to watch it slide past. We realize that while neither of us likes war, we both like our submarines.

Wednesday, November 8, 2000

Today was a perfect day at sea, with less wind and less chop on the water. The sea was that transparent tropical blue of the tourist brochures, so different from the dark water of the Black Sea where I had worked only a few months earlier. But the clarity and blueness here are a factor of the tropics, where warm water holds less nutrients, supports less microscopic life, and thus is less green. Plus, this far out in the Pacific, there's just less continental sediment to darken the water. Ironically, the murky Black Sea and the green North Atlantic nourish more marine life than these beautiful waters off tropical Hawaii.

Early in the day my mind wandered off to the fact that, unlike many of my other missions, on this ship we don't have dynamic positioning (DP)—side thrusters and a global positioning satellite (GPS) link—to keep us in a fixed spot. With data wizard Dwight Coleman telling us where we are and where we need to be, it's up to the skipper to keep us there with fancy footwork on the throttles and rudders. I wish we had DP, but we'll just have to make do the old-fashioned way.

We spent the entire day running a series of seven search lines east-west across our area, but no midget subs popped up on sonar. We saw plenty of ordnance, including two torpedoes, lots of what looked like 16-inch shells, and a variety of objects we just couldn't identify—UUOs I call them, Unknown Undersea Objects. We also found a Cessna of more recent vintage, lying upside down, as well as a seaplane. Crewmen on the *American Islander* speculated that the Cessna was a day charter that went down back in the 1980s. We also found our share of rock outcrops, sand waves, slump blocks, and other geological features one would expect in this kind of terrain. But we saw very little marine life.

Our three veterans seemed more at ease today, more comfortable on their sea legs, but more important, they were all eager to help us find that midget sub. Honestly, I'd love to have them pinpoint the exact spot where it went down, but that seems unlikely. Adm. Jay Cohen, the chief of Naval Research, spent the day with us, talking with the veterans about what they remember of that morning so long ago and speculating on what actions the midget sub commander might have taken after coming under attack. Our consensus is that the search needed to be expanded to the north, toward the entrance of the harbor. The veterans feel they were closer to shore that morning than we are operating, and the sub was pointed that direction when attacked.

On the way back to the docks, I spent some time with Lehner and Reetz, trying to get to know them a little better and to pick their brains. While Lehner likes to play the crusty rogue, he's very devoted to his wife back in Wisconsin, who every few days requires a dialysis trip to the hospital. It's quite a challenge for someone his age, not only moving her to and from the center, but helping her recover from the exhaustion of each session. I know it took some juggling for him to do this with us, and I hope he enjoys the break. Reetz was able to bring his wife, Loretta, although she couldn't make it out on the ship with us. She walks with a cane, and pitching and rolling on this deck would have been misery for her.

These two guys are getting along quite well with Kichiji Dewa, as well as with Katsuhiro Hara, the military historian, despite the language barrier. These three ancient mariners from two warring nations nearly crossed paths right here on that morning 60 years ago. They went their separate ways, and now they're back at this point where their own lives were changed forever, where history was changed forever. It makes you think. Did Lehner, who worked during general quarters as loader on No. 4 gun, help chamber the shell that hit the midget sub from Dewa's mother ship? Maybe not. According to Reetz, the shot we think hit the sub came from No. 3 gun. Better yet, did Reetz, who witnessed the hit from his amidships damage repair station, who saw the midget sub right itself and then go down, have the exact position of the sinking somewhere deep in his memory? Only hypnosis could dredge that up, I conclude. And that's our dilemma as we move closer to the docks and I content myself with listening to Reetz and Lehner reminisce about the hours leading up to dawn on December 7, 1941, and the first shots fired by the U.S. in World War II.

These veterans of the destroyer *Ward* remember nothing especially threatening in the days leading up to their dawn brush with history, but those farther up the chain of command had received repeated warnings of possible Japanese aggressive action. So much so that there were those in Washington greatly concerned about sending a constant stream of alerts that didn't materialize, for fear of dulling a quick response in the Pacific when the real thing came along—the "boy who cried wolf" syndrome. And this partly explains what happened when, at about the same time of the sub encounter, an Army radar station at Opana picked up a large group of aircraft 132 miles distant, at a bearing of 3° and closing at 180 miles an hour. When the sighting was reported to Fort Shafter at 7:20 a.m., it was pretty much ignored as nonthreatening, since it was known that a large group of American B-17s was to be ferried in sometime that day. However, at 7:25, the commandant of the 14th Naval District ordered the destroyer *Monaghan* to get under way and investigate the submarine contact reported by the *Ward*. Just in case.

Sometime later that morning—Lehner is unsure but Reetz thinks it was at the beginning of the second wave of Japanese air attacks, around 9:00—a group of aircraft flew so low and close over the *Ward* that the crew could see the faces of the pilots. Bombs were dropped, but they didn't hit the *Ward*. Much earlier the two sailors had heard explosions and could see smoke rising from the inner harbor. "That damned Army practicing again," thought Lehner. At 7:56, with the first wave of the Japanese attack well under way, Ford Island Operations Center radioed the message to all stations that Pearl Harbor was being bombed by enemy airplanes, that this was no drill but the real thing!

The day of infamy had begun.

Thursday, November 9, 2000

Despite the delay with a morning devoted to hydraulics repair, we were able to shove off for our search area just before noon. We did three east-west search lines in the northernmost region, extending our original coverage farther inshore toward Pearl Harbor and across the channel. It was there, the *Ward* veterans were convinced, that the midget submarine was sunk, and it also made sense from my reading of the historical records. In conducting the survey of those northern lines, we detected two linear targets that clearly deserved a closer look. I decided to come back to them next week with our one-man subs and video cams to investigate up close. Two southern lines completed our overall coverage of the enlarged study area and wrapped up this phase of the expedition.

At this point, we had a whopping 72 targets on sonar as possible candidates for examination. Not bad for four days. But there's no guarantee that midget sub *16-A* is among them. I'm beginning to appreciate how busy this particular piece of underwater real estate has been. Aside from the attack and the ensuing war, this stretch of sea bottom has been affected by dredging and dumping and all sorts of activity as befits the mouth of a major naval base adjacent to a large port city and world-class beach resort. We know the Navy used this area as a glorified dumping ground for years, so we're more likely to find old refrigerators and tires than what my usual searches produce hundreds or thousands of miles from a continent, much less a city.

As we plot up all the targets, the patterns suggest that two regions in the eastern and western portions of the search area appear to have numerous rock outcrops. You never know for sure whether it's man-made or Mother Nature until you've put a camera on each one. So, before heading in for the day, we decided to look at two of our targets situated in the southwest corner. It's here, we were

The author helps prepare *Deep Worker,* a one-man untethered submarine capable of descending to 2,000 feet, for a dive. *Deep Worker* will search for a Japanese midget submarine. Ballard and his team had maps prepared by the National Park Service showing some 100 hard-target hits in the harbor—any of which might have been the sub.

told, that we could find another midget sub taken captive elsewhere, brought to Pearl for study, and then hauled offshore and dumped. And after some fair amount of maneuvering we located the sub and shot good clear images. We spent a long time studying the central section of this trophy, still complete with conning tower and periscope. Finding this one so easily made me feel better, at least for the moment. But then my "what-ifs" started: What if a Navy dredging operation had later covered our *16-A* or *20-A* with sand and rubble? What if the damaged midget had been able to limp south toward the mother ship for a mile or two—or five? What if, his bearings lost, the skipper headed somewhere else: east toward Waikiki, or west of Barbers Point? Or even worse: What if the

combination of shelling and the crushing pressure of depth charges had caused the midget sub to disintegrate into little pieces of nondescript junk?

It was then that I began to wonder if this seemingly tame and easy search—more of a vacation in some ways than what I usually do—might prove much harder than I'd thought? Was this one like looking for the Loch Ness monster and less like looking for the *Yorktown*? After all, we were searching for something 72 feet long, possibly in very little pieces. This wasn't a case of finding a huge *Titanic* or *Bismarck* or *Canberra*. Much smaller than those, this one was more likely to have wandered from the point it was last seen. After all, that's what submarines are supposed to do, damaged or undamaged. A sinking surface ship goes only one way: straight down. A damaged midget sub might go in any direction.

And now this train of thought took me through the naval officer's litany of worries. While Napoleon and Hitler had been defeated in Russia by "General Winter," naval officers, certainly in World War II, were just as much hampered by the tactics of Admirals Blunder and Bad Luck. Those two had done as much to alter the course of war as grand plans, or even superior armament and numbers. I started thinking about how, at Pearl Harbor, Japan's grand plan was assisted as much by our own Blunder and Bad Luck as by its brilliance. There were all those things that didn't go wrong for the Japanese but could have:

A massive fleet with six aircraft carriers not being detected as it trekked 4,000 miles across the biggest ocean in the world.

Not being fouled up by bad weather or serious equipment failure.

In the final hours, not being spotted by the American planes.

Having the vaunted American code-breaking and intelligence capabilities not quite come together in deciphering that an attack was coming, and that Pearl Harbor was the target.

Having assorted hints that dribbled in days and hours before the strike that were ignored or lost in the communications chain, like the decoded diplomatic message asking all Japanese naval intelligence agents to report which U.S. ships were in port at key places around the Pacific, including Pearl.

A misinterpretation of the radar sighting of the first wave of Japanese planes half an hour before they arrived, which was thought to be American B-17s expected from California.

Having the Navy assume that Pearl Harbor was too shallow for enemy torpedoes and not to deploy torpedo nets around our battleships.

Above all, having the American commanders gamble that Pearl was just too secure or far from Japan to be threatened—so that all those precious aircraft at Hickham were tied down wingtip to wingtip, like sitting ducks.

And what about all that fishy submarine activity just outside the harbor entrance, going on for hours before the main attack, why was it ignored for so long?

Of course hindsight is deceiving. Like just about everybody else in the world, we Americans learn much more from our mistakes and failures than from our successes. A certain degree of naval blunder is unavoidable, since the ocean is by nature featureless and fluid and unpredictable, a more hostile environment than land. Error was already with us since we had never faced such an enemy on such a scale, and we still assumed that an adversary would have the same concepts of fair play we did. And bad luck, bad weather, bad timing, being in the wrong place at the wrong time all happen. The only way to overcome this is to envision and plan for a thousand possibilities. We sometimes forget about possibility number 1001.

My expeditions are designed to leave as little to luck as possible and to avoid the blunders. In other words, if somehow I don't find midget sub *16-A* on this expedition, I want to make it as certain as possible that this is because it limped ten miles out to sea and fell into an abyss, or disintegrated into bits of sea junk. Not because I made a mistake. Not because I had bad luck.

The Attack: First and Second Waves

And then it came, the surprise that had been planned for many months. All of Japan's militarist dreams and its resentment of the only Pacific power that could stop her were expressed in a single destructive moment—just before 8:00 a.m. on Sunday, December 7, 1941.

At a little before 6:00 a.m., only a few hundred miles north of Oahu, Japan's mighty carriers had turned abruptly into the wind to launch their forces of destruction. But lifting off took longer than was planned, for the

skies had turned overcast and heavy seas rocked the carriers. More than 180 aircraft—representing the first attack wave of Zeros, Kate high-level and torpedo bombers, and Val dive bombers and torpedo bombers—were launched from the decks of the carriers *Akagi*, *Kaga*, *Hiryu*, *Soryu*, *Shokaku*, and *Zuikaku*. The fleet then turned south again and steamed on for about an hour.

At just after 7:00 a.m., the fleet wheeled once more into the wind, and the second wave of nearly 170 aircraft, including Kates configured for high-level bombing rather than torpedo-launching, lifted off from the carriers. Once takeoff was completed, the fleet resumed sailing south, to a rendezvous point 180 miles north of Oahu. There, Admiral Nagumo would wait for his returning birds, many of which he expected would receive damage from American antiaircraft fire and fighter response.

At 180 miles an hour, the first and second waves flew south. A few moments after a strange cluster of approaching aircraft had disappeared from the U.S. radar screen at Opana, which had first spotted the planes, the commander of the Japanese air unit radioed back to his superiors *tora tora tora*, signifying that total surprise had been achieved.

According to later accounts by Japanese pilots, the scene they flew into was uncannily tranquil, almost surreal in its disconnection from their own heightened battle fever. Oahu spread out before them in all its tropical grandeur, the sea going from cobalt onshore to indigo farther out, the patchwork of pineapple fields and farms, the winding roads rolling down from the dark green highlands into the little town of Honolulu. But the most surreal thing of all was that America's greatest Pacific fortress was literally disarmed, still lost in dreams of peace and security. American decks were being swabbed, American bands were just tuning up for ceremonies, American sailors were sunning or shining their shoes. Many were just getting up and preparing for a day of shore leave, while others slept off the weariness of the graveyard watch.

In the event that such total surprise was actually achieved, the Japanese plan called for the torpedo-carrying Kates to strike American ships first and to launch their shallow-water torpedoes before smoke from the bombing obscured targets. But in a misunderstanding of their orders, the Japanese dive bombers attacked first, hitting Hickham Field and Pearl Harbor Naval Air Station. The first destruction occurred there. And it was only then and there that Lt. Comdr. Logan Ramsey understood that this was no drill. This was the real thing, and Japan had struck the U.S. on its own defensive perimeter, not in its distant colonial holdings in the Philippines.

Even as this high drama was unfolding from the air and the first bombs were falling on the airfields, most Americans on Oahu were still blissfully unaware of what was about to happen. They had not known of the flurry of odd events outside the harbor or the reports of strange radar sightings filtering in. What they knew was that it was an idyllic morning in the tropics, like so many before it. The forenoon watch was still on duty, and their relief was just now eating breakfast. Only one out of four guns was manned, and the live ammunition was locked up.

On Battleship Row, the pride of the Pacific Fleet was moored stem to stern, an array reminiscent of what you'd find in a shooting gallery. Of the 94 American ships anchored in the harbor, only one had cast off and was under way. The others would need precious time to get moving even under normal circumstances, but this morning there was no time to be had. During a surprise attack, nothing could be done but send men running to battle stations or for cover, and amid all this try to get off a few telling shots.

Even as the moments ticked by toward 8:00 a.m. and the Japanese attack on the airfields intensified, many on the ground still didn't know that the first wave of destruction was now upon them. Having first concentrated on destroying U.S. air power by bombing Bellows Field, Hickham Field, Ford Island Naval Air Station, Wheeler Field, Ewa Marine Air Corps Station, and Kaneohe Naval Air Station, the Japanese aviators were now at the point of strafing and chasing individual American servicemen down the streets, machine guns blasting away.

From his vantage point in the Ford Island barracks, survivor Ralph Lindenmyer saw the attack begin: "I looked out the window. The plane came over and I saw the meatball on the fuselage and the wing. I could look into the pilot's face and almost see him grinning as he flew around. They flew in and they were so close to us, but we didn't have time to think about it. We had to get to our battle stations. And so amid the explosions we all ran from our bunks down to the main floor. We couldn't get outside because the planes were bombing and strafing. So what we had to do was wait. We went out one at a time, trying to get to our battle stations. But this was amid the strafing. After they dropped the bombs and the torpedoes, then they started shooting at anybody who was walking, anybody who was going anywhere. As they pulled out of their dives they were firing their machine guns and strafing. So it wasn't good for us to be going out as a group.

"They were firing .50-caliber bullets at anybody who was alive, anybody who was running. Boy, were they firing. We didn't know where to run, where to hide. We were under attack and were just running, trying to get to some kind of protection. Who knows what we were trying to do? While the bullets came down, there were probably 50 or 100 men running around trying find some place to hide or someplace to go. It's hard to say if anybody got hit. It's a miracle there were no deaths on Ford Island. Nobody died."

Even as American air power was being neutralized by the Japanese, the awful torpedoing of the ships was beginning. The loss of the aircraft was frightful, but the destruction of the ships burned itself forever into America's collective memory. Screaming Kate bombers dropped their specially designed torpedoes into the shallow waters of Battleship Row, also attacking the ships moored at Ten Ten Pier and along Ford Island. Immediately *West Virginia*, *Oklahoma*, and *California* were hit. By 8:05, the old battleship *Utah* was also hit and listing at 30 degrees. Then the light cruiser *Raleigh* was hit. *Utah* rolled over at 8:10, only the bottom of her hull showing, a useless wreck.

And along with the torpedoing of the ships came the bombing, starting at 8:00. *Arizona* was hit first, then hit again by a lucky shot that detonated her forward magazines at 8:05 and turned the ship into a billowing inferno, a symbol more than anything else of the day's tragedy. Now *Oklahoma* capsized, going over into the harbor mud even as *West Virginia* was slowly sinking, but through counterflooding was kept upright as it settled onto the bottom. Even so, *West Virginia* was hit hard and lost 105 men out of 1,500. *California* took two torpedo hits, and also began listing, but like *West Virginia*, deliberate counterflooding kept her from capsizing.

On the support ship U.S.S. *Argonne*, Charles Christensen had gone to bed on December 6 after an idyllic night of shore leave, which he thought would be followed by another day of leave on Sunday with a beautiful Japanese-American girl he had just met. "When I went to bed that night everything was peace and quiet. I had a weekend pass and had come back and gone to bed. Because I had relatives living in Honolulu, I was able to

A Japanese torpedo, its warhead carefully removed, lies submerged in *Argus*'s lights in Pearl Harbor. Open access ports on the side suggest it was examined and disarmed by the Navy prior to dumping. Historians can't be certain, but it may be an air-launched torpedo that didn't go off.

get a weekend pass. My relatives Fern and Idel and their daughter Judy were matchmaking for me with this little Japanese girl. She had come over the night before and cooked a nice big Japanese dinner for us. Then we talked. She loved to roller skate and she knew of beautiful waterfalls back in the hills, and we were going to go there on Sunday morning.

"I went back to the ship on Saturday night, December 6, slept there, and had breakfast on Sunday morning. I'd gone to bed late, slept all night, and I got up early because I was ready to go ashore at 8:00. I had my dress white pants and my civvy shirt on. I was carrying my little suitcase where I kept my roller skates, and I was all set to go ashore, at five minutes to 8.

"Then I heard an explosion, and the ship just vibrated. I thought, 'That didn't sound good. What happened?' On the *Argonne* we didn't have a PA system, we only had the

master-at-arms who would sound the alarm with a bugle and then get the men to pass the word. And they passed the word, 'Fire on Ford Island.' I thought I'd better go take a look.

"So I went up to the next deck and opened up the porthole cover. Then I stuck my head right out, and, oh boy, was there ever a fire on Ford Island. I thought, 'Something is really blowing up over there,' and with that I heard a plane, like he was throttled way down. I didn't have him in view but could hear that he was coming in from the side. I just kind of glanced over. Just as I did, he came in almost straight across me at a slight angle. And he had his wings up because he must have been turning a half circle. I could see the red ball insignia.

"With that I knew it was a Japanese plane, and I could see his torpedo underneath, ready to be dropped. I was watching the pilot as he was coming along Pier 1010

Continued on page 50

A waterspout blossoms from Battleship Row on the east side of Ford Island. The climbing plane to its right probably made the attack. The *California*, the *Oklahoma*, the *Maryland*, the *West Virginia*, the *Tennessee*, the *Nevada*, and the *Arizona* were all moored here. All were sunk or badly damaged. A Japanese photographer caught this image of the attack. Though the Japanese repeatedly strafed Ford Island, there were miraculously no fatalities there. And, ironically, on the Saturday morning preceding the attack, Ford Island service personnel were roused early to take part in a simulated attack from saboteurs; danger, instead, would come from the skies.

Stunned servicemen watch in horror as the destroyer *Shaw* explodes beyond wrecked and burning aircraft on Ford Island. As at all the airfields, planes were vulnerable to attack from the air because they had been parked close together to protect them from saboteurs.

Japanese-eye view of Battleship Row shows shock waves from torpedo attacks; the dive bombers have not yet arrived. *Arizona* is the larger of the two at the top. Enduring symbol of "a day which will live in infamy," the badly listing *Arizona* (opposite) burns out of control.

A million pounds of exploding ammunition sink the *Arizona* in just nine minutes. A Japanese bomb dropped from high altitude pierced the ship's forward deck, setting off the explosion. A thousand men died aboard her. When the *Arizona* exploded, men in cement barracks on Ford Island felt their building shake "just like a California earthquake," one remembered. The dead of the *Arizona* account for more than half the total at Pearl Harbor that day. This film still is the only surviving color picture from the attack on Pearl Harbor.

Continued from page 41

(as in Ten Ten), which is pretty wide, and he was coming at an angle. It looked like he was making sure he didn't drop that torpedo on Ten Ten Pier. He was maybe 30 feet off the water, which put him at eye level or a little higher for me. I could actually see the pilot's face. He had his helmet and his goggles on, and he was looking over the side. When he leveled that plane out, he dropped his torpedo. And I thought 'Oh my God, look at that.' And the torpedo just went as straight for the *Oklahoma* as it could go. Just about the time it went off, we had a bell on the *Argonne* for general quarters. *Bong, bong, bong, bong, bong.*

"At that point I closed the porthole and ran up one flight to the poop deck. I was the first one up there on No. 5 gun. All the others came running, and the officer in charge said, 'Secure aft ammunition. Our surface guns are just built for shooting at ships, so we ain't got anything to fire at. Stand by for working parties.' So we stood by for the working parties. They were getting a launch ready, because I looked over at the *Oklahoma* when I first got up there, and it had already started capsizing. It was going over. I remember thinking at the time, 'My friends are over there.' I'd badly wanted to serve on one of the battleships, and I had friends from boot camp, friends from the Ford Motor Company on those battleships. I didn't know for sure, but I feared they were trapped inside—*Oklahoma* just rolled right on over. And there it was keel up.

"Even as all this was going on, I wasn't as much terrified as I was amazed at what was happening. I couldn't believe that all of this carnage was going on right before my eyes. And that wasn't the only thing that was going on. We were finally starting to fire back, from the destroyers *Jarvis* and *Mugford*, and from the cruiser *Sacramento* right beside us. Then there were all the cruisers, *St. Louis* and *Honolulu* and *New Orleans*. They were all beginning to fire. I saw the fellows come out of the Mugford with just their shorts on. They didn't even have time to put on pants. They started firing right away. They had their 50s, .50-calibers, and the five-inch antiaircraft guns. They were really firing. It didn't take long.

"One of the torpedo planes come from over by the *California* and torpedoed the *Helena*. The blast wave from that burst the hull of *Oglala*, and she started to sink. I had a front row seat for all this, only 50 yards away. The ideal place to watch all this was right at the end of Pier Ten Ten, because you could look down and see the *Oglala*, the *Helena*, the *Pennsylvania*, the *Cassin*, the *Downs*, the *Shaw*.

And then when the *Nevada* got under way, it passed between us and the *California*. Over by the *California* you could see the oil tanker *Neosho*, and then the *Oklahoma* and the *Maryland*. For nearly two hours I watched 350 Japanese planes coming and going. Once they dropped their torpedoes, I saw the dive bombers come in. When they finished their dives, then they came down and machine-gunned us.

"We had really started firing back by the time I got down to the pier. Shrapnel was just bouncing all over Pier Ten Ten. I remember going over to pick up a piece of shrapnel and it was still hot, and I dropped it. But the shrapnel was coming down and I just wasn't scared. The only time I got scared was when a high-altitude bomber came over. When I saw the bomb headed for me, I thought my time had come. But I couldn't run. Where are you going to run? You might run over here or run there, and that's where it ends up hitting. You just have to stand there and watch it, and hope it misses.

"And as I watched all this I was just amazed at it. I don't know why I wasn't scared. I was just excited. Everything was going off at once, everything was just blowing up right in our faces. Some of the most beautiful ships we had in the Navy—there they were, they were nothing, they were on fire. The oil leaked out of them. It caught on fire. The big oil slick that started there on Sunday morning burned all day Sunday, all Sunday night, until Monday morning.

"Later in the morning on December 7, I was assigned to help with the wounded on Pier Ten Ten and take them to the hospital. Most of them had come out of the oil slick. They were swimming in the fire and the oil. They were trying to swim out of it. They'd just come up, and they were trying to get their breath. Their eyes, the whites of their eyes, were just as red as they could be. The skin on their faces was just falling off. And the black sailors were coming in, their skin just laying down, hanging down, the flesh underneath snow white. On top of all of this, everybody was just soaked in oil. Their hair and their ears and their eyes, all just drenched in oil.

"And the doctors were there on the pier with boxes of hypodermic needles, giving morphine shots. We didn't have any ambulances. The only ambulance we had was a dump truck. We also had two or three automobiles, little Ford coupes that belonged to some of the officers. A lot of the wounded we had to put on stretchers in the dump truck, we took others in the Fords. The wounded were being brought to us in motor launches and in whale boats. We had no military vehicles, no fire engines. Just these three officers' Fords. I think I went over to the hospital about three times.

"I was a young man. I'd never seen any violence like this. It was beyond my imagination. I never saw any panic. I was always proud of the Navy after that. The men were well trained, the officers were well trained, and they were giving orders and the orders were being carried out. And everything was going smoothly even in all this carnage; it was just going smoothly.

"I was a little different in handling grief. Others were in shock or in grief, but I understood that this was the way it was and I accepted it. There was nothing I could do to change that. My adrenaline was flowing. I didn't feel like crying. No, I had something to do, and in the Navy you do what you're told. If they tell you to go down there and get the wounded out and take them to somewhere, that's exactly what you do. You don't have time to do anything else. And I think that's what we were doing. We were doing the job."

According to *Utah* survivor Clarke Simmons, the sinking of that proud old ship may have been a case of mistaken identity. "On Friday, December 5, we sailed in early in the afternoon. And we went into what we call Box 11, which is on the west side of Ford Island. The carrier *Lexington* had moved out that morning, and we moved into the berth where it had been originally. So apparently the Japanese had planned on carriers being on the west side of Ford Island based on their reconnaissance and spy reports.

"On that Friday and Saturday I had taken a launch to shore from the ship, tied up, gone to the beach at Honolulu, done some shopping for the officers, shopping for myself, and come back to sleep at night. We had what we called 'Cinderella liberty,' which meant that we had to be aboard ship by 12:00 that night. So I came in about 11:30, quarter to 12, and went to sleep.

"Sunday morning a young guy on duty came down and said that something was happening and we were under attack. And he thought the ship in front of us had blown up. But what really had happened was that the Japanese had attacked us, and the first torpedo that they sent into the *Utah* had gone through the bulkhead and run up on the beach. And when this young man

came down, there were several of us in the compartment. I looked out the porthole on the port side, toward Pearl City. It's where the old Pan American Clipper used to anchor en route to China. It would come from the States, and that was the only civilian air transportation Hawaii had to the mainland.

"And as I looked out the port I saw a plane making a run on my *Utah*. As she dropped her torpedo, the wing dipped and then she straightened up, and the torpedo headed for the *Utah*. And another one right behind it did the same thing. As they hit the ship we felt a jar, but the torpedoes didn't explode. They went right into the hull and let water in. And at that time the bugler sounded 'man your battle stations.' My battle station was below deck. I went down to find water coming through the ship. It was knee-deep. When I first went down, we were all frightened. We didn't know what was going on. But we knew the ship was taking in water and there was no way to close the watertight doors, so we knew that it was just a matter of time before the ship sank. And it took only eight minutes. In only eight minutes the ship was history. She had turned turtle in eight minutes.

"During those eight minutes, the next command I heard was 'abandon ship.' I was already familiar with the officers quarters because this is where I worked. I knew by going up to the officers area I'd be above the water that was pouring in. And maybe I'd be able to find a life jacket and get off the ship if it was beginning to sink.

"As I got to the captain's cabin, which was on the starboard side, I and two others went through three portholes, each about 18 inches in diameter. We all managed to crawl out. And the fortunate thing was that none of us had put on the life jackets—big kapok life jackets, very different from what they have now—because otherwise we'd never have gotten through the portholes. By that time the ship was listing so much the furniture was beginning to break loose. So we crawled through, out onto the walkway outside the captain's cabin. By now the ship was listing so badly that the lines tying the ship down were beginning to snap, She had about a 40°-45° list. She was turning over. We just went over the side and swam for Ford Island where the rest of our surviving crew was gathering.

"Sometime while I was still in the water or coming up on the beach I was hit, either by shrapnel or a gun wound. I was hit in the head, the shoulder, and the leg. And one of the corpsmen noticed I was bleeding and began to patch me up a little with a first aid kit he'd brought ashore. He said, 'We better get you to the hospital.' So I went to the first aid station on Ford Island, and from there they transferred me to the submarine base hospital."

The situation on *Oklahoma* went from bad to worse in rapid time, according to survivor George Smith. Smith was only 17 on December 7, the youngest sailor on board and already a veteran of the *Oklahoma* brig for not following orders. "I finally served my 30 days in the *Oklahoma* brig and was released about December 3. Meantime a couple of other sailors were still in there for reasons I don't know. And they were still there on December 7 when the ship took the Japanese torpedo. The brig was located in the carpenter's shop, and when the torpedo hit, it broke the carpenter's workbench loose and pinned the guard against the bulkhead, so he couldn't release the other men. They all drowned. The marine's name was Black. I can't recall the other guy's name. I'd have drowned right along with them had I not been released.

"On the morning of December 7, I had the 4:00 to 8:00 watch on the starboard machine gun. I was awakened at 3:00 to take over the watch, stood my watch, and got relieved at a quarter to 8:00. I went down to my mess deck and I asked the guy about breakfast. He said he couldn't serve me, because he didn't know I was on watch. 'I didn't save you anything,' he said. 'To hell with it,' I said. 'I'm going to shore anyway.'

"So I went down to my locker and started taking off all my clothes, because I was going to shower and then put on my whites and go ashore. Just then the loudspeaker announced, 'All hands man your battle stations.' We'd known we were going to have drills because we had admiral's inspection on Monday. Well, I said, 'Aw bullshit,' and then I didn't hurry to my battle station. All of a sudden a guy came over the loudspeaker and just says, 'No shit, move it.' Right about then we took a torpedo.

"Altogether we got nine torpedoes that morning. I don't know if we got any bombs or not. After the seventh torpedo we were given orders to abandon ship. It was really terrifying. I didn't know what to expect. I was so scared I didn't know what the hell was going on. But when they said 'abandon ship,' the only way we could get out was through the casemate window. We didn't have far to jump out of the ship, because the ship was listing badly, rolling over, and we were coming down closer to the water. I guess we only jumped about five feet into the water.

But once outside, when you turn around and see this thing coming down on top of you, this massive ship about to fall on you, then you swim for all you can swim and as fast as you can swim. We knew we had to get around the big gun turrets, rolling on down on top of us.

"So we got around them, went around the bow, and then we were free because the ship kept going the other way, listing over to port. We swam over to the battleship *Maryland*, and they threw cargo nets over the side so that we could climb aboard the ship. We all climbed up there, so that there were so many men on it from the *Oklahoma* that they ordered us to leave the ship as soon as the first raid was over, and to go over to Ford Island. So for the second time we jumped back in the water and swam to Ford Island, just a couple of hundred feet, not that far away. We got onto Ford Island just as the second wave of bombers was coming in. We all were laying on the side of a hill.

"As far as I know now, 429 of us died that morning. I didn't know that at the time. That afternoon they took us over to the Army base, and we started bringing ammunition down to the ships. That night, when we drove down from the mountains, because of the blackout I sat on the fender on the passenger's side and another sailor sat on the driver's side, human headlights. We came down the mountain, yelling 'Over to your right, over to your left.' We had no lights coming down the mountain all the way. When we got closer to Pearl we could see the fires, so much so that the fires were throwing light over the area. We unloaded our last ammunition about 12:30 at night and we reported to the receiving station. Then we went to bed. But at about 2:00 air-raid sirens started to blow. They were our own airplanes coming in, but at the time we didn't know it. So we shot some of them down. We went back to bed, and then they woke us up and said they needed 50 volunteers. From there they took us to the battleship *California* and had us pulling dead bodies off the ship. I got sick from doing that, so they sent me back to the receiving station. I had never done that before in my life, and so they sent me back to the receiving station where we got something to eat and a bath. Then we got to go to bed again. And I slept for about 24 to 30 hours straight. When I got up from there, I realized then this was Tuesday morning.

"Then they called us all out in front of the receiving station, counted us out, and I was reassigned to the U.S.S. *Prebble*. When I went to bed that night, I cried. I kept

Silenced by half a century on the floor of Pearl Harbor, 14-inch guns attract divers from the National Park Service. In addition to the *Arizona*, the Pearl Harbor National Historic Landmark includes the remains of the *Utah* as well as aircraft lost during the attack.

saying to myself, 'What the hell am I doing here? I could be home in Seattle going to high school with my buddies.' I quit school to join the Navy for this? I was scared. I didn't know what to think, what to do. I couldn't stand being on the ship, I couldn't stand looking over there, seeing *Oklahoma* upside down. And I saw people working on it, heard rumors that they were cutting through the hull. I heard that when they cut through with the torches, they killed a couple of men because the fumes suffocated them. They finally had to use chipping hammers to get through.

"The second morning after the attack, the Navy told us to send a postcard home to our parents letting them know everything was all right. I got one of the last postcards out of there, and I sent it home on December 9. My mother didn't get that postcard until the first week of February. She didn't know if I was alive or dead. But when the mailman got the card at the post office, he closed down and ran all the way to my house. He woke my mother and stepfather up at 6:00 in the morning and told them, 'Your son's ok. Here's a card.'

"I didn't get to see my mom for two-and-a-half years after she got the card. I was on different ships in different places, but she hung the card in the window of our radio business, a store where we repaired and sold radios. She outlined it so everybody could see. She even had a big sign made up that said. 'He's ok.' So it was great in that sense. When I finally came home, I got a great welcome."

Stuart Hedley, dodging bullets on *West Virginia*, had a spectacular view of *Arizona* as she was hit. "I'd just taken off the sight caps on the guns. Talk about strafing, we could hear the bullets bouncing off the side of the turret while we were inside. And just as soon as we took off the sight caps, probably about 7:58, the *Arizona* got hit and we saw about 32 men fly through the air.

Continued on page 60

Workmen clamber atop the overturned hull of the *Oklahoma* on the day following the attack. Struck by multiple torpedoes, the huge battleship shuddered, according to sailors aboard her, then quickly capsized and settled on the bottom, trapping scores of men inside. She was within some 20° to 30° of being perfectly upside down. Rescuers broke through the ship's double hull and pulled out 32 survivors.

A tangle of wrecked ships fills Dry Dock Number 1 following the attack. Destroyers *Cassin* (left) and *Downes* rolled together when their munitions exploded; battleship *Pennsylvania*, beyond them, was in dry dock when struck by a bomb during the second wave of attacks.

Riddled by friendly fire, a civilian Packard five miles from Pearl Harbor holds the bodies of three men slain by shrapnel from Navy shells. The Japanese didn't bomb Honolulu, but the city sustained considerable damage and several casualties from inexperienced gun crews and defective fuses.

Pride of the fleet, American battleships steam majestically through unthreatening seas (above). Soon they would lie ablaze on Battleship Row (opposite) or in crumpled ruin like the *Arizona* (below.) The success of the surprise attack provoked heavy criticism of military leaders. Both Adm. Husband Kimmel and Gen. Walter Short, the Navy and Army commanders at Pearl Harbor, were relieved of duty. Of the battleships, all but *Arizona* and *Oklahoma* were repaired and eventually returned to service.

Continued from page 53

And even as I was watching this, the stern end of the *West Virginia* lifted up as we took two torpedo hits."

Ralph Lindenmyer could see—and feel—the *Arizona* explode from Ford Island: "When *Arizona* exploded it rocked the whole Ford Island. Our barracks were two blocks long, three stories, and solid cement. When *Arizona* went, my barracks shook just like a California earthquake. And I tell you we thought that the ceiling was going to come down and bury us right there. We were saying our prayers."

Miraculously, several hundred men did survive on *Arizona*. Carl Carson was out on deck on that beautiful Sunday morning, when all hell broke loose. "I was out on deck doing the morning chores that you did every morning, and I was working on Admiral Kidd's hatch, shining brightwork and so forth. And all of a sudden this plane came along, but I didn't pay much attention to it, because planes were landing at Ford Island all the time. But this was different. The chips started flying all around me, and I realized that this same plane was strafing me.

"When they flew between the ship and Ford Island, I could look up and see the meatball on the wings and I could see the pilot sitting up there. Now somebody hollered to get under cover. So I ran forward and tried to get under cover. The officer on deck, one of my division officers, ordered me back out to close the hatches. So I was out there closing the hatches when another plane came around about the same direction and strafed us. But I don't think anybody that was out there working at the time got hit.

"Then I went forward and inside the ship and started back to my battle station. At that point a bomb went off. I learned later it was back about turret No. 4, about where I'd been working only ten, fifteen minutes before. Evidently it knocked me out, ruptured both my lungs, and I suffered smoke inhalation. All the lights went out, and I don't know how long I laid there. But when I woke up I picked up a flashlight, which I guess had fallen out of somebody's hand. And so again, I started down into my battle station. But at this point they wouldn't let me in the door, the watertight door you're not supposed to open in battle conditions. But I managed to wait for what seemed like it was about 20 minutes. And I finally outlasted the guy on the other side.

"When I got into the turret it was totally dark except for my flashlight. And one of my division officers, Ensign J. B. Fields said 'You're a good boy, Carson.' And he said that's exactly what we needed. Strangely, there was no

panic down there or anything, despite the smoke and water knee deep. And a bosun's mate by the name of Tucker took the flashlight and ordered me up the ladder to open the hatch into the upper handling room.

"But now I started to feel pretty sick, so they had a guy come up to hold me, to keep me from falling off the ladder until I got the hatch open. And then we all made it out of the lower handling room into the upper. We'd only been up there about ten minutes when Ensign Miller, the senior division officer, stuck his head through the escape hatch in the rear of the turret and told us to all come out on deck and help fight fires. But there was nothing we could do. The ship was a total loss. So Commander Fuqua and Ensign Miller both said we might as well abandon ship.

"Before I did, I ran into a friend of mine who was crying and asking me for help. I looked at him in horror. The skin on his face and his arms and everywhere else was just hanging like a mask. And I took hold of his arm. His skin all came off in my hand. And there was just nothing in this world I could do for that boy. That has bothered me all my life. Of course he died. He died later.

"Now they gave the word to abandon ship, and because the ship was sinking so low we practically stepped off the quarterdeck into the water. I was planning to swim over to Ford Island, but I'd forgotten how badly I'd been injured, in my lungs. So I swam out there about ten feet and I guess I must have passed out. I went down in the water, and everything was just as peaceful and nice that it would have been so easy to just let go. But I saw this bright light you hear about, and something made me come to. So I got back up to the surface of the water only to find oil all around, oil in my eyes and my teeth, just as fire was burning across the water toward me. I got back to the quay. Miraculously a man saw me down there just as the fire was approaching me. It wasn't more than two feet from me, and this man reached down and pulled me up out of the water. This man saved my life. I think he was a man from the Fourth Division. About now a motor launch came along, and I either jumped or fell into the motor launch, because they said they couldn't stop on account of the fire. And they took me over to Ford Island.

"At Ford Island, I walked down to the barracks with the rest of the crew. About the time I got down there I must have passed out again, because my friends and shipmates took me over to the sick bay at Ford Island. They laid me alongside the bulkhead. While I was unconscious there a

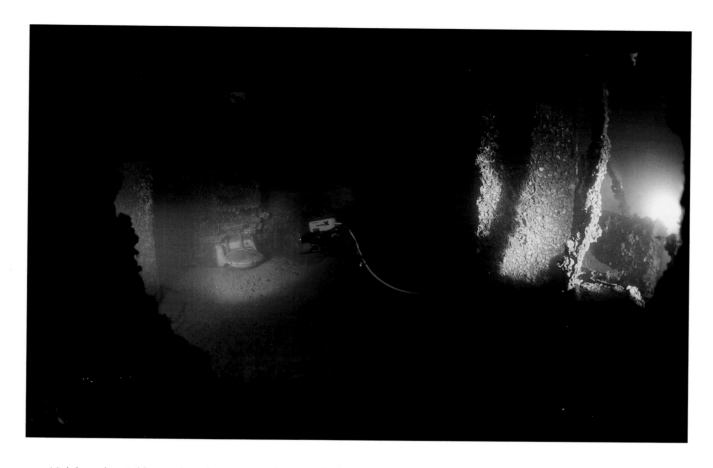

Mobile and portable, a tethered surveyor explores inside the sunken *Arizona*. Dozens of brothers as well as a father and son were among the victims aboard the *Arizona*, which took more crewmen down with her than any other ship in U.S. Navy history.

dud Japanese shell hit right in the center of the sick bay. The impact brought me to and I looked over. Another of my shipmates was laying across from me, and I realized he was holding his intestines in with his hands. And he looked up at me and said, 'War sure is hell isn't it, shipmate?' And I said, 'Yeah it is.' Then I discovered I wasn't bleeding anywhere, so I got up and walked out of there."

As the awful morning wore on, *Arizona* turned out to be the most disastrous loss. Her fires, explosions, and sinking killed 1,103 officers and men out of her total crew of 1,400, and the total death toll finally reached 1,177. The casualties on *Arizona* accounted for more than half of the 2,403 deaths suffered by the U.S. at Pearl that day.

And as if in a mockery of bad timing and bad luck, at 8:10 that group of B-17s being ferried in from California finally did arrive, unaware of what was happening below. Defenseless, they thought the Japanese Zeros

around them were a welcoming committee. Then they found themselves under fire from American antiaircraft guns too, which couldn't tell the difference in the planes at that moment of crisis. So with both sides firing at them, the B-17s searched frantically for somewhere to land before they were shot down.

As the smoke cleared, one stroke of good luck for the Americans emerged. The Pearl-based carriers *Enterprise*, *Saratoga*, and *Lexington* were all away from port. *Enterprise* was ferrying aircraft to Wake Island, and *Lexington* was ferrying to Midway. Eighteen-year-old Portland-born Quartermaster Don Yeamans was on the heavy cruiser *Astoria* escorting *Enterprise* to Midway Island when the reports of the Japanese attack began to filter in. Instead of turning back to the burning home port, the two ships were ordered to search for the Japanese fleet. "It's a good thing we didn't find them," Yeamans recalls. "Who knows what would have

With all eyes on a monitor, expedition members view videotape brought to the surface by *Argus*. A Japanese interpreter stands at Bob Ballard's shoulder; historian Stephen Ambrose is behind Kichiji Dewa, and a veteran from the *Ward* is on Dewa's left.

happened? It was a lucky stroke that we weren't at Pearl, either. We'd left there just two days before, on December 5. As it turned out, we didn't come back until January 13, because we were still searching for the attackers."

But *Enterprise* was on its way home on December 7. At the same time the Japanese were launching their first wave, *Enterprise* sent up a routine patrol of Dauntless scout bombers to fly ahead, but without breaking radio silence to tell Pearl of the ship's arrival. And so these hapless pilots also flew right into the Japanese and American buzz saw. While some made it through, others went down in flames.

By 8:30 a.m., the first wave was over, and a wretched calm settled in, like within the eye of a hurricane. At 8:37 a.m., the destroyer *Monaghan*, the first to get under way after the attack, managed to fire on another Japanese midget sub, the only one that actually got into Pearl Harbor proper,

and then ultimately rammed it. The *Curtiss* also claimed to have made a direct hit on its conning tower, and in another small victory for America on that dark day, the midget sub sank at 8:44. Another midget ran aground near Bellows Field. One of its crew drowned, the other, Kazuo Saka-maki, became the first Japanese prisoner of war.

But at just before 9:00 the lull ended, and the second wave began. Luckily, the Americans were now awake and on the alert, and their antiaircraft fire was much more effective. The second wave was made up of 50 Kates, 80 Val dive bombers, and 40 Zeros. These focused most of their destruction on Hickham Field, and also pummeled battleship *Nevada*, damaged in the first wave and making a desperate attempt during the lull to get out to sea. The attempt was in vain; after being hit, *Nevada* was ordered aground, out of the battle, and sank. Destroyers, which had been anchored in East Loch rather than Battleship Row, and cruisers docked in Southeast Loch were now able to get under way.

By 9:45, the attack was over, and all Japanese planes were en route back to their fleet in the north. The American death toll by that point already stood at over 2,008 Navy men, 218 Army, 209 Marines, and 68 civilians. The death toll would grow in coming days, but the worst was over. Yet that afternoon and night Americans weren't at all sure that of that, fearing now that worse was yet to come, and jumping at the wildest rumors: that an invasion force was preparing to come ashore and that Japanese-Hawaiians would welcome them, that Japanese-American sabotage was now about to erupt with a vengeance. Everyone was on edge as the fires continued to burn, the dead and wounded rolled into hospitals, and the damage toll rose higher. And the Americans still didn't know where the Japanese attack force now was, misinterpreting radar information to think they were south, not north, of Oahu. So all those able to counterattack went off in the wrong direction, perhaps missing an opportunity for some vengeance, or maybe saving themselves from further losses.

To cap off a terrible day, that evening the U.S. shot down four of its own dive bombers based on *Enterprise*, which had gone out that afternoon to search for the enemy. As they flew back to Pearl that night, communications screwups failed to alert American antiaircraft gunners, who thoroughly blasted them.

Although they missed most of the action after their dawn encounter with the midget sub *16-A, Ward* veterans Reetz and Lehner watched this morning drama of destruction from a distance, still on patrol outside the harbor mouth. They'd seen the aircraft swirling over the island and the smoke from the fires on Battleship Row and Hickham Field. At about noon, they even came into West Loch to pick up ammo. But they didn't steam back into the harbor proper until Tuesday, December 9, and it was only then that they appreciated the full impact of the attack—and their relative good fortune. Lehner was truly shaken at the sight of the bombing damage. He even began to think the U.S. didn't have enough firepower to hold off Japan, and secretly he wondered if a war that had come on so suddenly might be over in six weeks.

The losses were indeed grave, but, as the days passed, not so great as they seemed at first. After the shock wore off, the sober assessment was that it could have been much worse. The final toll stood at half the aircraft on the island destroyed, seven battleships capsized, resting on the bottom or out of commission, and three destroyers eliminated.

But on the positive side, while surprise, good luck, and lack of mistakes had run with the Japanese, as the flames ebbed and the explosions quieted, it became apparent that Admirals Blunder and Bad Luck had not totally ignored the Japanese. The attackers had missed the submarine force anchored at Pearl, and so it was untouched. Also, as noted, Pearl's aircraft carriers were at sea and unharmed, and it was they who would prove more important in stopping the Japanese advance than the battleships lost in the day of attack. In addition, the bulk of U.S. destroyers, cruisers, and support craft were unhurt.

The Japanese also missed the Pearl fuel tank farms, having abandoned a third wave of attacks. By losing them, the U.S. fleet could have been hobbled for months or longer, perhaps even long enough for Japan to build its impregnable defense ribbon. And the fact that the U.S. ships were sunk in shallow water of 40 feet meant that almost all of them could be raised, repaired, and sent back to battle. Just as important, the base's machine shops were unhit, and so they could get to work immediately on repairs. And the fact that no ship had been caught and sunk in the narrow harbor entrance—the most vulnerable feature of Pearl Harbor—meant that ships could come and go as they needed, immediately after the bombing.

A year later, after all this destruction and its subsequent repairs, it turned out that the U.S. had to write off only three major ships: *Arizona, Oklahoma,* and *Utah. Utah* was already obsolete, so its loss was not major. The refloated *Oklahoma* sank in the Pacific while being towed to the West Coast for scrap. The *Arizona,* after much consideration, was left where she lay, the core of a future memorial to the day of infamy, hundreds of men still entombed in her hull.

Friday, November 10, 2000

A few minutes after 8:00 a.m. we headed out to our search area. Our plan today is to look up close at as many of our targets as we can, beginning with the two we located just the day before in shallow water inside the channel. Once on site, we launched *Argus,* but before we knew it our vehicle had wandered into very scary terrain. We were in danger of dragging *Argus* up a

Like eggs in an incubator, Japanese midget submarines lie in dry dock in the Kure Naval Base in Japan in October 1945. Carried to the vicinity of Pearl Harbor by mother subs, the midgets were expected to slip into the harbor undetected and wait for the air attack before beginning their own. None managed

to do any damage. The destroyer *Ward* spotted one trying to enter the harbor and attacked. "We have attacked, fired upon, and dropped depth charges upon submarine operating in the defensive sea area," it reported, the first action of the day. The Navy salvages one of the subs (above) in 1960.

vertical coral scarp, but she cleared the top at the last minute, and none too soon. Had she hit the wall, that could have been the end of this expedition. And wouldn't you know it, after this scare, both targets proved to be just rock outcrops the size of a midget submarine. The rest of the day was spent looking at one disappointing rock after another—great for a geologist, but not for a military historian. Our spirits lifted a bit, however, when we came across a large sunken barge and landing craft, vintage unknown. Though interesting, most of this stuff we saw was dumped by the Navy in the years following the war.

And as we sorted through this junkyard of history, I thought about the needle in this underwater haystack where we now floundered, the real graveyard we sought, the grave of our little 72-foot sub *16-A* and its crew of two, Yokoyama and Ueda, or was it *20-A* crewed by Akira Hiroo and Yoshio Katayama from mother ship *I-20*? Whichever one it was that *Ward* hit, where the hell was it? Would this historical footnote, this memorial to the first shots fired, forever remain a mystery? Without the physical evidence, would we ever be able to write history that no one would question?

As I went down that road, I saw about two million paths of possibility forking off into the dark waters. We as a people try to understand who we are, where we've come from, and where we're going, but it's a miracle we can agree on anything. Shifting memory, differing perceptions, confusion, mistakes, speculation leading into fabrication—even simple typographic or transcription errors—abound. Compound that by the potential for confusion in a military engagement, when people maybe didn't get enough sleep or were worried about a girlfriend back home or a shell or torpedo coming through the hull, and we wonder how anyone knows what really happened. With our veterans and survivors passing from the scene each day, physical evidence is all the more important. As I looked at the radio log for *Ward* 's report of the sub encounter, I was dismayed to find that the Navy typist had recorded the year as 1942, a full year off the truth. Somebody else had later handwritten the correction, but had the other scribes and logkeepers who recorded the brief encounter even gotten the positions right?

Now I tried to put myself in the shoes of the crew of *16-A*—or *20-A*. If I was skipper of *20-A* that morning, at 6:45, and it was my ship that took the hit in the conning tower and suffered the concussion of at least four depth charges, would I have been killed? Would my head have been blown off or a shell have cut me in two? Had the force of the depth charges done brain and internal damage, so that I was dead and gone in a flash? Or was I instead choking on a flood of seawater blasting in like from a fire hose? Might I have been injured but still aware, cut and bleeding from pieces of the hull as they shot inward? Or might my body and my life have been spared, only to leave me with jammed controls, taking in water, and inexorably settling down to a lightless bottom 1,200 feet below, where I would die a quick—or extended— death, depending on how much oxygen was left?

But maybe it was *16-A* that survived all this. If some records are correct, Yokoyama or Ueda were alive as late as 10:44 that night, long enough to radio back to Dewa what he deciphered as *kira kira kira* but interpreted to be *tora tora tora*, meaning the attack was successful? Why no more messages later that night, or the next day? Why no more Morse code to Dewa, sitting back there expectantly on *I-16*, messages like I'm hit, I'm taking water, I'm injured, I'm going down? Or, having missed the rendezvous point, I'm just plain lost?

Was I afraid to break radio silence and trigger another round of depth charges? Or was I alive but without power, my batteries dead at midnight, their 25-hour capacity drained now, without light or radio or any hope at all, breathing sulfuric acid gas? Were the circuits gone, leaving me in wet blackness? In those final minutes of December 7 did I and my partner miraculously limp along, headed south, or just plain headed away? Did I even know for sure which direction I was going, or if I was leaking and sinking? Did I think about trying to surface and swim for shore or for a rescuing boat, even if it meant triggering more gunfire, more depth charges? Was I upside down as the water finally came in, choking and washing over me locked in this coffin reeking of battery acid and machine oil, of cold wet steel, 1,200 feet down? Was I dying of hypothermia, in chilled steel surrounded by 35°F water?

Was I questioning my faith in the emperor, in the justice of our cause? Did I have time to regret anything, miss anything, think of parents and girlfriends and family back home? Did I whisper a prayer as I died?

Who would ever know but the ones who lived this, the ones who died? And as we pulled into Pier 13 and my little historical fantasy drew to a close, I thought of all the tens of thousands of other Americans and

Japanese who had died on the water in this war, mostly reduced to statistics as impersonal and sanitized as computations of the gross national product. Eleven hundred here dead, 1,000 there gone to the bottom in five minutes, 100 gone up in smoke in a firestorm somewhere else. The wrecks on the bottom were the only remains we would ever find of them, for the guys who had animated those ships were forever lost. By locating the midget sub, *16-A* or *20-A*, and the *Bismarck* and the *Yorktown*, we would find all that survived of the fear and creativity and magnitude of those heroic and awful times. And, if we couldn't find them, we would lose a part of our memory, of our heritage, a piece of ourselves.

Saturday—Sunday, November 11–12

Today we plan to use *Little Herc* for the first time. To test our capabilities, I decided to find and examine a torpedo we had spotted the other day with *Argus*. It's situated out in flat, sediment-covered terrain, a good safe place to experiment with joint *Argus/Little Herc* operations for the first time on this expedition. My primary concern is whether *American Islander* will be able to move slowly enough to permit *Herc* to maneuver safely. After a bit of getting used to working the ship in the wind and seas, we discovered that we could stall *Islander* long enough for our two underwater vehicles to accomplish something together.

We located the torpedo and obtained some excellent images from both our vehicles. Hara, our Japanese historian, is convinced the torpedo is Japanese, and of the same type carried by their midget submarines. I hope this isn't wishful thinking on his part, just to make me feel better, for I know how hard it is in the Japanese culture to disappoint someone. I know how hard it is for the descendants of Samurai to just say no. They would rather defer to a committee or never give an answer at all. However, the torpedo's location fits the scheme, in that it's close to the official sinking site and about where one might find a torpedo fired after the sub was hit by *Ward*.

We spent the remainder of the day locating various other targets, most of which turned out to be rock outcrops. But we did find a landing craft, imaged it, and ended the day at the dumped midget submarine in the southwestern extreme of our search area. A great day for

imaging, but we've now been at this for a week and still haven't found our missing sub. Are we going to come up empty-handed?

On Sunday we spent the entire day traveling from one target to another, gradually eliminating all of the possibilities in the eastern and western region of outcrops. The weather was the best we've had during the entire trip, and I hope it holds up when we begin joint submarine operations on Tuesday. We'll be taking Monday off, but next week is the test. We're truly now down to the wire. The expedition is on a set schedule that can't be extended. *American Islander* has other projects coming up after next week. The crew has other commitments. I have other commitments.

Is this going to be another Nessie expedition for me? I hope not. An entirely different kettle of fish, the monster Nessie came wrapped in myth and superstition. Nothing we knew in science ever supported our finding a plesiosaur or mosasaur or some other marine reptile in the depths of that cold loch. But that doesn't mean the quest was an impossible one. Science constantly expands through accidental discoveries—and surprises. In the case of the midget subs, we know they existed. We know how and why they were built. We've seen them. While all the crews are dead, we've found a guy who knew them firsthand, who maintained the subs. Hundreds of credible witnesses saw the midget subs in action, but we still are not absolutely sure which one *Ward* hit at 6:45 a.m. on Sunday, December 7, 1941.

Dewa says, late on that Sunday night *16-A* was still at large. At 10:41 he received its message of success. Was it a case of glorified Japanese politeness? Though all the midget subs had failed in their missions, was it better to tell the commanders back on the mother ship what they wanted to hear, even as the last midget sub crew faced certain death in the dark water? Was their last message a polite social convention? Or a way of saving face, even when the senders knew they were going to die?

Pearl Harbor Aftermath

In succeeding days and years, those hours of horror on December 7, 1941, changed the world. The Japanese believed they had scored a great and lasting victory, and in the following weeks their troops swept south, expanding their empire beyond Manchuria, Korea, and

China into Indochina, Malaya, the Philippines, and the Dutch East Indies. Just as Hitler had swallowed continental Europe, they had swallowed much of Asia. And just as that first surreal panorama of Pearl Harbor asleep and undefended had amazed Japanese pilots from the Striking Force, the ease of Japan's other conquests amazed the troops even more, validating the conviction that they were on the divine path to victory.

As for the Americans, those bombs and torpedoes launched at Pearl Harbor did more than wake them from a great sleep. Rather than so demoralize and defeat America that she would allow Japan to consolidate its conquests, the American public rose up in raging fury at what had happened. Voices in the U.S. who had opposed our military participation in World War II either changed their tune or grew silent. The surprise peacetime attack on Pearl Harbor gave President Roosevelt the mandate to wage all-out war on the perpetrator and brought the full industrial might of the U.S. into the war effort.

In a narrower sense, this debacle deeply jolted the American military, still entrenched in its antiquated, uncoordinated structure and concepts. It ended once and for all the idea that there were still lessons to be learned from the earlier world war. The divisions and rivalries between the services and the existence of independent fiefs in intelligence gathering were now understood (at least by some) to be threats to national survival. And the battleships that once controlled the seas and won the wars were now seen to be secondary players. With Pearl Harbor, the name of the game became mobility, speed, and flexibility, all to enable the projection of military power across thousands of miles of ocean and land. Carriers were now the masters of the sea, and aircraft ruled the skies.

The Japanese strike, characterized as "idiotic" by historian Samuel Eliot Morison, did achieve certain tactical goals, like surprise, psychological shock, and immobilization for several months of the U.S. battleship fleet in the Pacific. But the U.S. carriers, which were the real keys to modern naval success, had remained untouched and were ready for the next battle, which would be in the Coral Sea six months later.

Pearl Harbor, still in shock and reeling with pain, quickly resumed its role as the home port or stopping place for just about every American ship or aircraft that would play a part in subsequent battles of the Pacific. Ships like *Ward, Enterprise, Yorktown*, all the surviving warships from Battleship Row and Ten Ten Pier, and others like *Indianapolis* went on from Pearl to the Coral Sea, Midway, Guadalcanal, and the Solomons, the Philippine Sea, Truk Lagoon, and Leyte Gulf. Each ship and plane in its own way helped fill out the mosaic of what grew into a titanic, bloody, and often confusing military struggle.

While the attack on Pearl was violent and shocking, it was not the worst that Japan had in store for the Allies in late 1941 and early 1942. Despite ample warnings and a fair amount of armament and men on scene, the U.S. by mid-December had suffered a much worse defeat in the Philippines, as did the British in Hong Kong and Singapore, and the Dutch in the East Indies. Months of American preparation and strategizing needlessly went up in smoke beginning December 8, as Japan roared south, bombing American aircraft positioned once again like "sitting ducks," sinking ships that had no air cover, mining strategic harbors and straits, and invading cities. The defeat was needless because tangled chains of command, bad decisions by commanders including Douglas MacArthur, and outright incompetence allowed the Japanese to take the offensive and totally rout their opponents. Once hostilities had commenced, the long-standing American plan was to swiftly dispatch B-17s from the Philippines to bomb Japanese airfields on Formosa. In fact, hours went by after reports of Pearl Harbor came in, as the American military did nothing, allowing Japanese bombers to take off and pulverize the Philippines, followed shortly by their ships and troops.

The loss of the Philippines was an appalling debacle, a strategic and geopolitical disaster that would take three-and-a-half years and tens of thousand of lives to reverse. But it had happened. The Allies were now in a terrible box, and the only way out was through very hard work and the ceaseless expenditure of weapons and material that America would supply in spades.

For the Japanese, in early 1942, the task was to consolidate their vast conquests, seal off Australia and New Zealand from the Allies, and build their

Stars and Stripes waves at the Arizona Memorial, where casualties' names are inscribed on a marble wall. About 900 crewmen were never recovered. Pearl Harbor's final toll: 2,403 dead, 1,178 wounded, 169 aircraft destroyed, 3 ships destroyed, and 18 ships damaged.

defensive ribbon down the mid-Pacific, from the Aleutians to the South Seas. For the Americans, the imperative was to block all those strategies, and then, having built up sufficient forces and supplies, to begin rolling the Japanese back to their home islands. No easy task for either side.

To get going, the Americans had to rally their forces from the ashes of defeat and obstruct the unfolding Japanese plan. But an American recovery mustn't take too long, because the clock was ticking and, at least for now, Japan had the advantage. The Japanese plan had been years in the making, while America had thought she was forced to wait for Japan to make the first moves before shaping a strategy in response.

America's tale of defeat and retreat was to continue for some more months, until the right opportunity could be found, an opportunity that did not present itself until May 1942, 3,500 miles southwest of Hawaii, in the Coral Sea east of New Guinea. American moves there were initially uncertain, a U.S. counteroffensive strategy still in the making, but for the first time since Pearl, U.S. sailors could do more than just fire back as they retreated, or as they lay unprepared and defenseless, losing another critical piece of real estate to Japan. And the American heroes of Coral Sea would prove to be two Pearl-based carriers, *Yorktown* and *Lexington*. Only one would survive the Battle of the Coral Sea; the other would go down, to rest forever in the depths of the next Pacific graveyard.

U.S.S. *LEXINGTON* FLIGHT DECK IN TROUBLE, MAY 8, 1942

CHAPTER TWO

CORAL SEA

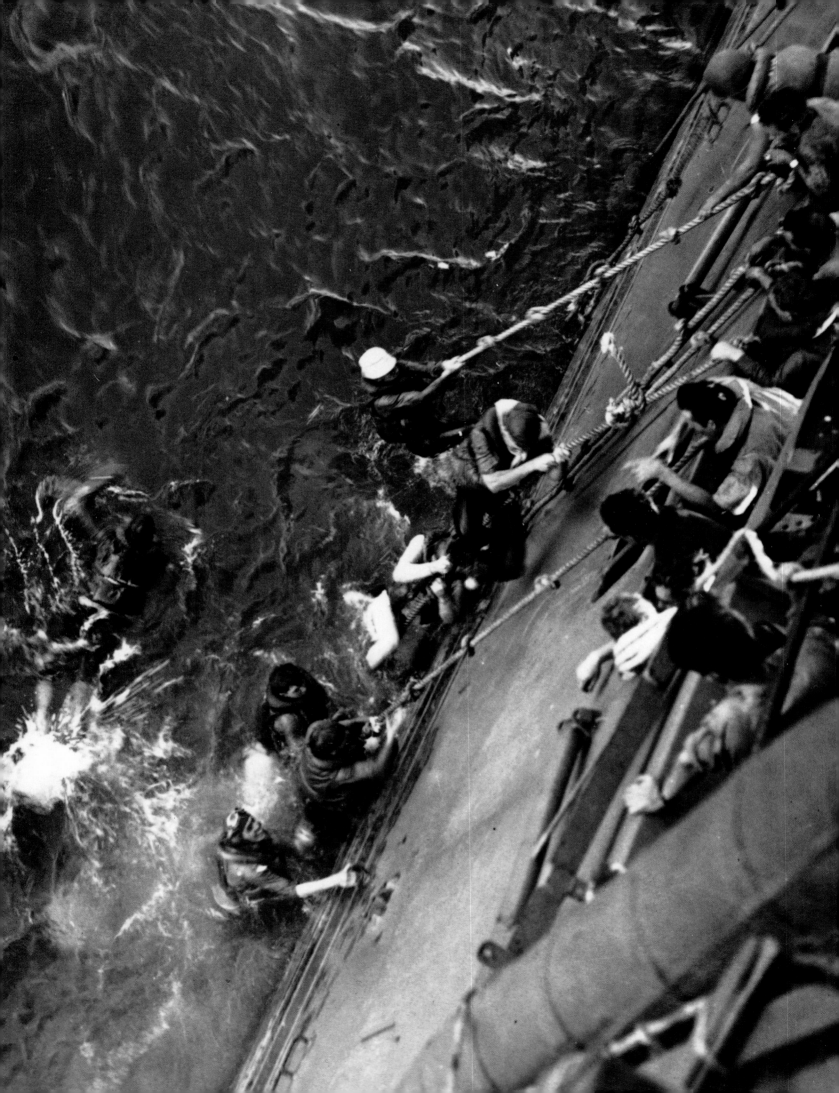

U.S. wins Battle of the Coral Sea May 1942

Graveyard Coral Sea, May 3–8, 1942

THE MIDGET SUBMARINE THAT'S NEVER BEEN ACCOUNTED FOR AND THE attack on Pearl Harbor itself are compelling stories. They are dramatic and concise and easily understood. But without diminishing the sacrifice of all those who died at Pearl, both the midget subs and the surprise attack are only preludes to what came after: The subsequent battles of the Pacific War, the losses that dwarf all that was lost at Pearl—all those planes shot down, all those mighty ships sent to the bottom, all those lives snuffed out, often in horror that can't be re-created. I'm concerned about all the other graveyards, as well as Pearl, graveyards that are all we have left to mark where the great battles took place, the mighty confrontations that redefined what naval warfare is in the modern era. In the great Pacific War, the numbers in every category just went up—the cost in men and materiel, the size and complexity of the ships, the variety of weapons, the distances covered, as well as the fires, the explosions, and the tally of casualties.

There are so many Pacific burial grounds that contain untold stories. Two of them, Midway and Guadalcanal, I've been fortunate enough to explore. Others remain shrouded for everyone in watery silence. These Pacific graveyards are linked to Pearl Harbor, even

---

Survivors of the stricken *Lexington* scramble up the side of a cruiser, probably the *Minneapolis,* after abandoning their ship. The *Lexington* was lost during the Battle of the Coral Sea, the first naval engagement in history fought without the opposing ships ever making visual contact. Victory here stopped Japanese forces from occupying Port Moresby on New Guinea.

Their eyes set on Port Moresby, the Japanese hoped eventually to cut off Australia from the Allies. American forces first struck a Japanese landing group at Tulaghi in the Solomons, then intercepted the Japanese in the heart of the Coral Sea.

to the point of now sheltering many of the same ships and men that passed through Hawaii on their way to battle. So, in the same order as the war unfolded, I'd like to contemplate these other underwater cemeteries that were once battle sites because they finish the story that was started at Pearl. Without the other, the midget subs lost at Pearl Harbor become only curiosities. Without consideration of the other graveyards, this mighty epic of war becomes a brief novella rather than a vast trilogy that carries truth and some lessons for us all.

The next major naval battle after Pearl, Coral Sea, could not have occurred as it did except for what happened at Pearl. The seeds for determining who would win the Pacific War were accidentally sown at Pearl but did not begin to come to fruition until six months later in the Coral Sea. And those seeds germinated not because of who was at Pearl Harbor on December 7, but because of the people not there on that cruel morning. I'm thinking about our proud carriers, *Enterprise*, *Saratoga*, and *Lexington*. By coincidence, they all happened to be far

enough out at sea so they were missed by the Japanese strike. *Lexington* and *Yorktown* joined forces in the Coral Sea six months later. And they came to embody that fateful battle.

Coral Sea was special, because it was the first time modern carrier fleets engaged one another. Breaking all the traditional rules of a naval battle, the opposing carriers never even saw each other during this vast operation; they were always separated by at least 70 miles of ocean. As in most battles, grand plans were radically revised to factor in the effects of errors in communications and identification, good and bad luck, and the steady attrition of aircraft, ships, and men in battle. The resulting graveyard is in water so deep and so far from land that it may never be mapped or photographed.

Although Admiral Yamamoto continued to have a healthy respect for the temporarily stunned U.S. Navy after Pearl Harbor, his superiors in Tokyo now succumbed to what one Japanese commander later called "victory disease." As they rolled across Asia in late 1941 and early 1942, the Japanese began to believe their own propaganda. Their convictions that they were a superior nation, a superior race, blessed by their divine mission, were all reinforced. They believed they could not lose. In fact, the Japanese military playbook dealt only with taking the offensive, with attacking, and with conquest. There were no plans on the books for defense, for retreat, or for defeat in any form.

Just as Japan had seemed predestined to succeed at Pearl Harbor, perhaps its subsequent arrogance also predestined Japan to lose the greater war. Over time, as Admiral Yamamoto had recognized early on, size and resources differences would tip the scale against his country. And the Japanese leadership grossly miscalculated how the U.S. public and leadership would react to being ambushed on a Sunday morning. But what about the very nature of Japan's authoritarian mind-set? Are rigid militarist minds more prone to being deluded—and ultimately defeated in battle against an equal opponent—than the somewhat more flexible military minds of a democracy like the U.S.? Perhaps it's best to say merely that America's more realistic, flexible approach was one more factor that eventually worked in favor of the U.S.

But whatever the ultimate outcome, the U.S. in early 1942, along with other Allies in Asia, was in retreat. Even "retreat" is an understatement; the West was being routed in Asia. Japan, late in 1941, following huge victories in the Philippines and elsewhere, capped off the slaughter at Pearl by taking Wake Island and capturing its Marine defenders. Several Marines were even beheaded for sport.

Under these adverse conditions, all the U.S. could do in early 1942 was mount hit-and-run missions against the Japanese. *Enterprise*, *Yorktown*, and *Lexington* supported bombing and attack missions directed at Kwajalein Atoll, at the growing Japanese base at Rabaul, New Britain, northeast of New Guinea, and on Japanese installations on the north coast of New Guinea.

Lexington's first action in the South Pacific had been south of Rabaul, where on February 20 she shot down 16 of 18 Japanese bombers that ambushed her. None of the ships in the carrier's fleet was hurt that day. On March 10, *Lexington* and *Yorktown*, in a daring surprise attack, launched their planes from the south side of New Guinea and sent them over the central mountains to bomb two Japanese ports on the north side of the huge island. They caught the Japanese unaware, and did appreciable damage to enemy ships. While these expeditions reminded the Japanese that they were not unopposed, such actions only harassed the Japanese advance but did not stop it. In April 1942, Jimmy Doolittle led his daring air attack on Tokyo itself.

One of the tactical advantages that the U.S. had gained early in 1942 was the ability to break high-level Japanese military codes. While this had not been achieved in time to alert the U.S. to an impending Pearl Harbor attack, it was now of growing and perhaps decisive help. Although the U.S. had broken Japan's diplomatic code, "Purple," years before, this new secret development was so important that it carried the code-named "Magic."

After the collapse of Indochina and the Philippines, the U.S. began to better understand Japanese strategy through code breaking, which helped us know that Japan now needed to neutralize the Allies by cutting off Australia and New Zealand. Code breaking revealed in spring 1942 that, from its new and growing base at Rabaul, the Japanese had decided to push farther south, to pursue the encirclement of Australia and New Zealand by conquering New Guinea and controlling the Coral Sea. More specifically, the Americans learned that Japan would use her naval forces to occupy Tulaghi in the Solomons, establish a seaplane base there, and invade Port Moresby, New Guinea. She would hold off Allied counterattacks

coming into the Coral Sea from the east with a carrier strike force that included Pearl Harbor veterans *Shokaku* and *Zuikaku*.

After reading the intelligence reports and decoded messages and understanding the stakes, Adm. Chester Nimitz, commander in chief of the Pacific Fleet, assembled Task Force 17, a two-carrier group led by *Lexington* and *Yorktown*, to stop the Japanese. Superior code breaking now became critical in helping offset the size of the Japanese force—more than twice what Nimitz was able to come up with. He sent *Lexington*, under the command of Admiral Fitch from Pearl Harbor, and ordered *Yorktown*, carrying fleet commander Adm. Frank Fletcher, to depart from the island of Tongatabu, where it was undergoing maintenance work. The carriers were joined by many of the ships of "MacArthur's Navy," later to become the Seventh Fleet, including three cruisers (H.M.A.S. *Australia*, H.M.A.S. *Hobart*, and U.S.S. *Chicago*) and several destroyers.

I know *Yorktown* well, at least what's left of her. In 1998 I found the wreck of this great carrier in 17,000 feet of waters off Midway Island, and in the next chapter I'll go into more detail. But the *Lexington*, like the elusive midget sub at Pearl, is still a mystery to me. I know only what survivors and other historians can tell me. She's almost as deep as *Yorktown* in this graveyard 3,500 miles from Midway, but still undiscovered.

U.S.S. *Lexington*, Lady Lex, had been launched as an aircraft carrier way back in 1925 and commissioned in 1927. She was 888 feet long, with a top speed of 34 knots, and on her final day she had 2,951 men on board. She could also launch 30–35 aircraft. By fall 1941 she was based at Pearl Harbor, although on that fateful day she was actually at Midway, delivering aircraft. When her commander heard news of the attack on home base, he had seaplanes launched to hunt for the striking force. After that, *Lexington* and *Saratoga* had been sent to help reinforce Wake Island, but when Wake fell later in December, the twin ships were called back to Pearl. Until April she took part in the hit-and-run and harassment missions in the Coral Sea, then went back to Pearl, and finally sortied from there on April 15 to rendezvous with *Yorktown* in preparation for the coming Battle of the Coral Sea.

What is the Coral Sea, then and now? It hasn't changed much since 1942, although many of the islands that were once European colonial holdings are now independent nations, with population totals and land areas more akin to counties than to countries. In 1942 those islands were jungle and wild and almost primeval, some not far removed from tribal warfare and head-hunting. The offshore waters were, and still are, turquoise and spectacular, a huge blue expanse reaching from Australia in the west to New Guinea and the Solomons in the north, to the New Hebrides on the eastern side. The Coral Sea covers a vast and broad basin averaging 10,000 feet in depth, topped by a million square miles of ocean. It is marked as much by the coral reefs and atolls of its name as by the volcanic upthrusts of the islands on its northern and eastern rims. It is these same inky depths that hold the Coral Sea graveyard, and these depths, so far from land and support services, make discovery of the wrecks difficult to undertake today.

The two American carriers sailed into this corner of the world forgotten by time. And it was in this tropical paradise—just as beautiful as Hawaii—that Japan accomplished its next objective, right according to plan. On May 3, Japan took Tulaghi, and there was no one there to stop her.

Now Admirals Blunder and Bad Luck began to have their way and to shift the one-sided Japanese steamroller toward a more balanced contest. Yet it was not so much a contest of brilliant equals as a standoff of mistakes made by both sides.

Yorktown on May 4 sent fighter bombers to hit Tulaghi, which they did with great fanfare. But when the smoke cleared, they hadn't hit very much. At this point the Japanese might have been expected to counterattack the retreating *Yorktown* and probably could have done so with punishing force. But for some reason the mighty *Shokaku* and *Zuikaku*, nemeses of Pearl Harbor, had been sent on an aircraft ferrying mission to Rabaul, carrying a grand total of nine aircraft there. And so they missed the much larger opportunity to hit *Yorktown* as she withdrew. By the time they were back on the scene, *Yorktown* was much farther away and harder to find.

On May 5 and 6 the two carrier forces groped their way around each other, hoping to engage but wary of being hit. Carrier warfare was still in its infancy, and with no historical experience to draw on, tactics were still being written. The two fleets were less than a hundred miles apart, but still they didn't make contact.

Background noise for the Americans on May 6

included the grim news from 2,000 miles northwest that the U.S. had surrendered Corregidor Island, meaning that it had surrendered all of the Philippines. Would the next loss be New Guinea and then Australia? The news increased the pressure on the Americans even more, if that was possible.

A day later, things would look a little more hopeful for the U.S. But to reach that point, both sides would have to blunder around a bit more. On May 7 the Japanese made an error that greatly helped the Americans. They mistook an American fueling group that included Pearl Harbor survivors *Neosho* and *Sims* for a carrier and a cruiser, and so committed major forces to attacking them. They pounded and eventually sank these two fairly unimportant ships with excessive force, but lost many planes in the battle as the Americans counterattacked. And the real American carriers remained elsewhere, untouched. As for the crews of the two sinking American ships, their personal saga had only just begun.

Also on May 7 the Americans made a similar error, mistaking Japanese heavy cruisers and destroyers for carriers, and sent out an attack force of dive bombers and torpedo bombers from *Lexington* to destroy them. This, however, led to some good luck for the U.S.: The fliers from *Lexington* stumbled upon the Japanese light carrier *Shoho*, and, with all those bombers at the ready, sank her in only ten minutes. Although *Shoho* was not nearly the size of the big carriers that had bombed Pearl Harbor, the sinking of any kind of Japanese carrier gave the Americans a psychological lift. Later that day, fighter groups from *Yorktown* and *Lexington* intercepted bombers and torpedo planes from *Shokaku* and *Zuikaku* and shot down nearly ten of them.

Now in the great scheme of things, losing a light carrier is not a national disaster, although it was certainly a disaster for the crew of *Shoho*. But Japan wasn't used to losing or to being attacked by surprise. Japan's conquests until now had been accomplished cleanly and relatively cheaply. The loss of *Shoho* apparently so unnerved Japanese Admiral Inouye that he held back the Port Moresby invasion force, missing an opportunity that would never come again. When Admiral Yamamoto heard about the pullback, he was livid with anger.

As author Edwin P. Hoyt points out, Admiral Fletcher on the American side also came in for some anger from superiors for his own missed opportunities. A sailor schooled in traditional tactics, he still didn't understand that the aircraft carrier was a different creature. In the opinion of some critics, he thought of it as just another form of battleship that happened to carry airplanes on top. Lesson number one in his schooling had been to keep his fuel tanks full. So Fletcher spent much of the Battle of the Coral Sea—fiddling around, in the eyes of one superior—religiously refueling while losing forward speed and, more importantly, losing the opportunity to hit the Japanese when he had the chance.

Fletcher also erred on May 7 by dividing his force and sending the *Chicago*, the two Australian cruisers, and some destroyers to try to find the stalled Port Moresby invasion force. They never found it, but they came in for a ferocious pounding from the Japanese nonetheless. Yet despite attacks by Japanese bombers based at Rabaul, the Allied force somehow went untouched, even when U.S. B-17s based in Australia mistook them for Japanese and tried to bomb them. There was such confusion that Japanese fighters even attempted to land on *Yorktown*.

After dancing and blundering around each other like this for three days, the two major carrier groups finally engaged on May 8. On this day, as Samuel Eliot Morison notes, their forces were almost equal: The Japanese carrier group had 121 planes, the Americans had 122. But Mother Nature dealt the Japanese an advantage by shielding them from above by clouds and a fog bank while the Americans sat exposed in bright sunshine. Because of the cloud cover, *Zuikaku* was well protected from American pilots, who concentrated on *Shokaku*. While they never scored a fatal hit, one bomb damaged the flight deck enough that *Shokaku* couldn't loft her planes, and *Zuikaku* ended up losing so large a contingent of her aircraft in the fighting that she was temporarily neutralized.

On the other hand, the American carriers were totally exposed to Japanese air attack. *Yorktown* took a bad bomb hit that killed 66 men, but she never lost power. Aviation Machinist Mate 3rd Class William Surgi watched unscathed as shrapnel from a near-miss killed the man standing next to him. It gave him a battle-scarred maturity that he carried into *Yorktown's* next fight, at Midway.

"On *Yorktown* at Coral Sea," Surgi recalls, "I was an ordnance man like my friend P. C. Myers. We were at the ammo locker forward of the bridge watching Japanese planes dive in. One of them got bigger and bigger, and

the closer it got I thought we'd better take cover. A bomb that it dropped just touched the catwalk and exploded in the water. While it missed the ship, it killed Myers, who was right next to me." The other bomb—the one that penetrated four decks—was more serious. Surgi thinks it so damaged the watertight integrity of *Yorktown* that even after the hurry-up repair job at Pearl Harbor a few days later, it made her more vulnerable to damage from the Japanese attack at Midway.

"That other bomb went down four decks," he says. "Before it actually exploded, our guys were spraying it with water, because it was hot. They didn't know if the fuse was active or not." But it was live, and few who were nearby lived through that detonation.

Lexington did not fare so well as *Yorktown*. Don Yeamans, a quartermaster onboard *Astoria*, which was escorting *Lexington* as it had at Wake Island on December 7, saw the Japanese bombing and torpedoing of Lady Lex and the fatal explosion that afternoon that took her down. He and his ship would later go on to escort *Yorktown* at Midway, watching that great ship also sink, and then would meet a similar fate off Savo Island in the first Guadalcanal fight the night of August 8.

Lexington survivor Vince Anderson was 20 years old on May 8, 1942, and a corporal in the 94-man Marine detachment on board Lady Lex. He's hardly objective about this great ship. "She was quite simply known as the Queen of the flattops," he says, 59 years later. "She had set the world speed record from San Pedro, California, to Honolulu. She had undertaken the search for Amelia Earhart in 1937. She had single-handedly supplied power from her generators for the city of Tacoma, Washington, in the winter of 1929–1930, when the municipal power system failed. She was always known as the happy ship of the Navy, and she fielded championship sports teams, too."

As was standard practice from 1775 to 1998, Marines were on board Navy ships for gunnery duty, as well as to guard officers and handle other tasks. Anderson's battle station during the Battle of the Coral Sea was on No. 10 gun, one of the antiaircraft guns on the port side. No. 10 was aft, and like the others was about ten feet lower than the flight deck. Until February of 1942, he had been loader on No. 6 gun, but then his promotion to corporal moved him to No. 10. "I like to say that promotion saved my life," he says. Why? Because around

Continued on page 84

Smoke billows from the exploding *Lexington*. The ship's agony lasted several hours. Around midday, three bombs and two torpedoes struck, causing her to list and starting several fires. Severed gas lines leaked gasoline and fumes that collected below deck. When these exploded, *Lexington* was doomed. About 5:00 p.m. on May 8, her captain ordered the ship abandoned. A legendary vessel, *Lexington* had helped search for Amelia Earhart in 1935 and had once supplied power to the city of Tacoma, Washington, when municipal sources failed.

Dead in the water, *Lexington* loses her crew. Warm water and tranquil seas contributed to the calm and orderly evacuation; once in the water, the men were almost immediately picked up by nearby cruisers and destroyers. Two torpedoes from the U.S.S. *Phelps* put her out of her misery. The *Lexington* lies now under at least 10,000 feet of water and has never been found.

From a small launch, hopeful faces from the *Lexington* peer upward to rescuers aboard the destroyer *Hammann*. The *Lexington* was one of the first aircraft carriers built. The idea had been around for years, but the first carrier, the *Langley,* did not float until the development of the technology of the arresting gear in the early 1920s. The *Lexington* and the *Saratoga,* both converted from incomplete battle cruisers, were next.

Continued from page 77

11:15 in the morning of May 8 a furious 15-minute Japanese air attack hit No. 6 gun, among other targets, and killed everyone at that station.

A total of 137 men were killed on Lady Lex that day, and another 85 were wounded.

Before it happened, Anderson and everyone else on board knew that a big battle was coming. And he recalls feeling pretty confident about the outcome. "Remember, we had already engaged the Japanese several times. We'd been bombed off Bougainville on February 20, 1942, while taking part in the hit-and-run missions. On that day we were attacked by 18 Japanese aircraft, and we ended up shooting down all but two of them. Butch O'Hare was one of our top pilots, and he ended up later with the Congressional Medal of Honor for his actions that day. He became the first Navy ace before he died in 1943, and Chicago named O'Hare Airport after him."

The men of *Lexington* were also feeling pretty confident following the events of the day before, May 7, when fliers from *Lexington* had sunk the *Shoho*. "Our skipper, Capt. Frederick Carl Sherman, was listening to the pilots on the radio as they found *Shoho* and went after her. As a gesture to us, he put the radio communication on the loudspeaker, so we all could hear. Around noon our guys attacked. There was a short pause, and then a voice came on that said, 'Scratch one flattop.' You can't imagine the cheer that went up on deck when we heard that. Lt. Commander Dixon was in charge of that squadron, and they made it back later that afternoon."

Anderson recalls Sherman as a superb captain and a man of "great dignity." He had been a submarine skipper in World War I, winning the Navy Cross. After Coral Sea, he later went on to become a rear admiral.

Anderson remembers how May 7 also had its strange, almost comic elements. After dark, nine wandering Japanese planes tried to land on *Yorktown*, perhaps thinking it was *Shokaku* or *Zuikaku*. "I don't think they were looking for *Shoho*, because she had gone down so many hours before, and they couldn't have stayed aloft that long. When the *Minneapolis* opened fire on them, they peeled off. But then we saw them again on the horizon, trying to land on what must have been a Japanese carrier. We were that close to each other at that point."

May 8 was a much more bittersweet day. Anderson remembers everyone up at dawn and to general quarters. Even as the fliers were preparing for another foray against the Japanese and their two big carriers, the men on *Lexington* knew they were in great danger as well. The sky was clear, so they had no cover above. In due course, after 11:00 in the morning, the Japanese attack did come, and Anderson remembers it as "15 minutes of hell," as more than a hundred aircraft did their best to sink Lady Lex.

"We took three bombs and two torpedoes in that time, and don't think we were just sitting there waiting. The captain had us doing 30 knots, full speed ahead, and we were maneuvering violently from side to side to avoid the bombs and torpedoes. I remember being thrown back and forth as the ship made its turns." Anderson was fuse-setter on No. 10 gun, and with the gun firing about every four seconds, he didn't have much time to think, just to do his job.

Anderson does remember the explosion as his former station at gun No. 6 went up in the first Japanese bomb blast, killing all those who were there. A second bomb hit a boat pocket. A third hit the stack and exploded forward of the stack. "Though all those bombs missed me," he says, "one that missed the ship almost got me anyway. A bomb hit the water next to us and exploded there, sending a plume of water 50 feet up that washed us all off gun 10." He considers himself lucky that he didn't go overboard.

"By that point we were listing seven degrees, but damage control got us on an even keel, and we were soon able to make 25 knots. With the Japanese gone and us thinking the worst was over, we were starting to feel pretty good. The word was we would head for Brisbane, Australia, 1,000 miles southwest, for repairs. That sounded good to everybody."

Then, in the afternoon, hell returned to *Lexington*. But not in the form of Japanese bombers. "Apparently during the attack," says Anderson, "some of the high-octane gas lines that carried fuel from below up to the aircraft had been ruptured. So gasoline and vapor were collecting way below deck. At some point, we theorize that a spark from an electric motor detonated that gas." Whatever the trigger, at 1:00 p.m. the gas went up in a holocaust that would eventually finish Lady Lex. But the crew fought on valiantly to save her, for four more hours.

"During that period I was still assigned to No. 10 gun. Because most of the fires were fore, not aft, I didn't see that much evidence of them from where I was.

But as the afternoon wore on, the heat became unbearable. For my last hour onboard I was throwing ammo overboard, because the heat from below had gotten so bad I was afraid it would explode."

During that interval, Anderson learned that one of his best friends on board, T. D. Germany, had been seriously injured. Germany had a pipe that he had given him from his own collection. Germany now insisted that Anderson take it back, since he thought he was going to die. Anderson argued, trying to reassure Germany that he would recover. But finally Germany prevailed, and Anderson took the pipe. Later Germany was presumed dead and was placed on the flight deck, covered by a tarp, with other bodies that would be left to go down with the ship.

"Finally the order to abandon ship was given, around five in the afternoon, when the ship's navigator put us at latitude 15° 19' S, and longitude 155° 31' E. Captain Sherman personally relieved the Marine detachment because we were the last on board, and we gave him three cheers. He later wrote that the loyalty of the Marines was inspiring.

"Now at this point," says Anderson, "I saw an empty life raft about 400 yards off the ship. I was a pretty good swimmer in those days, and so I started to think about swimming out there. While there were plenty of ships around to take us aboard when we abandoned, as our ship got hotter and the explosions continued, those other ships started pulling back to avoid being hit by flying debris. This was not a good situation, to say the least. I talked to some of my buddies and tried to convince them to jump in with me and swim out to that raft. But they were too uncertain about their swimming ability.

"So I decided to go it alone. I cut the sleeves off my shirt, cut my pants at about thigh length, left my shoes in a row with everybody else's who had already left, and also left my Mae West life jacket for someone who might need it more than I did. Then I slid down a rope and went into the water."

The situation in the water was a lot different from what it had looked like from up on deck. Now Anderson could hardly see the raft at all. The only time he could get a glimpse was when he was on top of a swell. Then he'd go down in the trough and lose it. About halfway to the raft he began to think he'd made a terrible mistake. It seemed as though the raft was moving farther

away. But finally he got to it and pulled himself on board. He rested for a few minutes. Then the reality of his situation began to sink in. He was alone in a small, drifting life raft in a heavy sea, as his ship exploded and burned. He was probably 300 miles from the nearest islands, the Solomons, which were hardly friendly territory. The water was known to be full of sharks. He had no provisions to speak of. In the confusion of the sinking, would he even be noticed? Or would he be swept farther and farther from the rescue ships?

"Over the next half hour I pulled in one pilot and three sailors. A whaleboat from the destroyer *Anderson* came by to check on us. I convinced them to throw us a line to at least tow us behind, so we wouldn't drift off to sea, as seemed to be happening. But the line got fouled in the launch propeller, so both of us sat dead in the water for a while. Then the destroyer *Dewey* came by, and the captain on board shouted through his megaphone that he couldn't stop due to the danger of submarines but that he would circle and throw some cargo nets overboard. Even as all this was going on, the Lex continued to burn and explode, and a couple of pieces as big as a barn door flew past us."

Just before dark, Anderson and the others on the raft climbed onto the *Dewey*. Even as this awful day was ending, the destroyer *Phelps* sank *Lexington* with two torpedoes, and she went down about 8:00 p.m., three hours after she'd been abandoned.

Lexington was gone, but Anderson's adventure wasn't over. He was a young man without a ship. The *Dewey*, jammed with survivors, took two days to travel to the nearest friendly port, Nouméa, New Caledonia, about 500 miles to the southeast. The voyage was so rough, and the destroyer was traveling so fast, that at night Anderson slept under the torpedo tubes on deck and lashed himself down to keep from rolling around as the ship pitched.

Once in New Caledonia, Anderson couldn't actually go ashore, because the Free French and the Vichy French were fighting over control. He transferred to the cruiser *Astoria*, which took him on to Tongatabu in the Tonga Islands, another 1,000 miles to the east, the same port that *Yorktown* had sailed from to enter the battle. While on board, he asked if there were any other *Lexington* survivors. He was told there were two wounded Marines in sick bay. And it was then he found his old friend T. D.

Japanese carrier *Shokaku*, attacked by planes from the *Yorktown*, suffers flames in her bow from a bomb hit on her forecastle. Splashes from dive bombers' near misses crowd her starboard side. Faint tracks at lower left may be erratic torpedoes. *Shokaku* had to spend several months in a Japanese dockyard, undergoing repairs, but later returned to the war. Though both the Japanese and the Americans suffered heavy losses, the Americans are

thought to have won the battle. It protected Port Moresby and Australia and was the first
decisive check to Japan's southward expansion. As the prototype of a series of naval air
battles that would ultimately win the war in the Pacific, it was also the first naval battle in which
the ships never got close enough to fire on one another. This Pacific action made the U.S.
aircraft carrier the king of the fleet. Battleships, from then on, played a secondary role.

Germany, who hadn't died after all, but was in a full body cast. "You son of a bitch, you stole my pipe," Germany said from within his bandages, and Anderson offered to return it to him. Germany declined, because the doctor wouldn't let him smoke. Apparently someone on board *Lexington* had noticed Germany's hand moving from beneath the tarp before he was left to sink with the Lex and the other bodies.

Although *Lexington* was gone forever and the Battle of the Coral Sea was over, the larger military maneuvering wore on. Admiral Fletcher considered pursuing the Japanese in a night attack, but Admiral Nimitz, back in Pearl Harbor, ordered him to withdraw from the Coral Sea. In departing, he nearly stumbled over the survivors of *Neosho*, which was still afloat, and a few refugees from *Sims*, which had long since gone under. But he didn't see them, and their misery wore on for another two days, as they floundered in the waves and heavy seas. Finally on the afternoon of May 11, the destroyer *Henley* found them and rescued the 109 survivors of *Neosho* and 14 from the long-gone *Sims*. Then *Henley* torpedoed and sank *Neosho*.

Now out of this rather confusing haze of battle, how do we determine who won at Coral Sea? The Japanese thought they had. They believed they had sunk two American carriers, not one, and in the tonnage destroyed they were probably the winners. But later estimates claimed Japan had lost a thousand men—nothing to sneeze at—as well as dozens of aircraft, the *Shoho*, and other lesser vessels. On the other hand, even though the American press called the battle a U.S. victory, the *Lexington* was lost, *Yorktown* was badly damaged, and more than 50 planes and more than 500 men were gone. If it could be called a victory, it was not won cheaply.

But what about the larger objective? Despite the fairly equal losses on either side, in retrospect it became increasingly apparent that Admiral Inouye had blinked and pulled back his Port Moresby invasion force. In fact, as would become clear in later months, the Japanese advance to the south had finally stopped. Port Moresby— and Australia and New Zealand—would not fall into Japanese hands. Not that the Japanese wouldn't push and probe, including the horrendous bloodletting six months later at Guadalcanal, which was in the Solomons to the north of Coral Sea. But a line had been drawn,

and in the course of the rest of the war, Japan would not go beyond it ever again. Australia and New Zealand, though on pins and needles, would not be cut off from the other Allies.

To this day, Australia devotes almost as much importance to the Allied victory in the Coral Sea as the U.S. does to the Fourth of July. Vince Anderson has been repeatedly invited to Australia. In 1992 he attended the 50th anniversary of the battle, to be honored as a "savior of the nation," meeting the prime minister of Australia and the then U.S. Secretary of Defense Dick Cheney. That's the very understandable Australian perspective; Coral Sea was obviously life or death for them. For the U.S., I would propose it was also life or death, but one degree removed. Why? Exactly a month later, a much more clear-cut battle took place. Yet the roots of its clarity were to be found in Coral Sea. What were they?

First, the humble oiler *Neosho*, which unwittingly had drawn such vicious Japanese fire because it was thought to be a carrier, may have spared a real carrier from being sought out and hit. At the very least, the Japanese wrongly concluded that they had sunk two or even three American carriers, not just one, which made them more confident about their plans for the big battle at Midway a month later.

Without a doubt, while the U.S. did lose *Lexington* at Coral Sea, if it had also lost *Yorktown*, Midway could not have happened as it did. That's why the Japanese were stunned to see *Yorktown* appear at Midway; they thought it was already on the bottom.

And even more important, *Zuikaku* and *Shokaku*, both veterans of the Pearl Harbor striking force and both carrying the most experienced of Japanese pilots and sailors, were temporarily out of commission. The *Shokaku* needed to repair its flight deck, while *Zuikaku* had lost so many planes that it had to be re-equipped. Because of this, neither was ready for what Japan now had in mind: the Great All-out Battle. This was not unlike Saddam Hussein's "mother of all battles" in the Persian Gulf War, at least in name. But while Saddam never had the power in 1991to hold off the United States, much less the rest of the world, Japan in May and June 1942, with a stroke of luck, could have held off the other most formidable Pacific power.

So Pacific graveyard No. 2 now rolls into graveyard

No. 3: the Battle of Midway. *Yorktown*, limping from its bomb hits, ordinarily would have needed months to be repaired. But there was no time for that. U.S. code breaking and intelligence told Admiral Nimitz that the Great All-out Battle was being set up by the Japanese to draw the American fleet out west of Midway and then to destroy it once and for all.

Admiral Fletcher and *Yorktown* did not have time for months of repairs. They had only days. And so they sailed back to Pearl, even as Admiral Yamamoto and the Combined Fleet were readying themselves for the grand offensive. Never in the war, neither at Pearl nor at Coral Sea, were the stakes so high for the United States. Despite the standoff in the Coral Sea, the momentum was still with Japan. And Japan, even without *Shokaku* and *Zuikaku*, was prepared to commit much more to an attack on Midway than the U.S. could throw back at them. They were prepared to commit more carriers, more tonnage, than the U.S. could muster.

But those were, and are, the concerns of the living. What about the dead—the ones left behind in the Coral Sea so that their compatriots and colleagues might live to fight on another day? Whoever was the victor at Coral Sea, the most concrete evidence of what had been lost those three days lay on the bottom and lies there still. *Shoho*, *Lexington*, *Neosho*, *Sims*, and many other ships and aircraft from both sides had gone down forever. And those were only the mechanical creations of man, not the men who had animated them.

While many of those men on board the dying ships and planes had been rescued, some had not been. Their final moments might have been an instant of pain and shock, as they were torn apart by explosions or gunfire, or a moment of terrible claustrophobia, as the cabin below decks or the cockpit they were trapped in slowly or quickly filled with water, leaving them with no air to breathe. Or perhaps an end less merciful than that— hours or days of drifting alone in the water, injured or not, only to succumb later to a shark or to exhaustion or dehydration.

As for the sunken ships, they are so far down as to have entered another world, a world confined to imagination. According to the lore of her survivors association, *Lexington* may be as deep as 25,000 feet if she went into an abyss that we don't know about. My charts and calculations put her at about 10,000 feet down,

on the bottom of the great Coral Sea Basin that spreads at that same constant depth for hundreds of miles, at the heart of the Sea. Her position when she was abandoned was more or less latitude 15° 19' S, longitude 155° 31' E. And she drifted, without power, for another three hours before she was sunk. How far did she drift, in the wind and swells, in those three hours? Probably not very much; that's a lot of ship for even the ocean to move.

And if we could find her, what would we find? Like *Yorktown*, would she be blistered and gutted by fire, some of her proud symmetry gone? Since her structure was intact up until the last minute of life, and she had to be sunk to be put out of her misery, might her hull, save for the torpedo breaches, still be straight and square?

The answers to those questions likely would be yes if, like *Yorktown*, U.S.S. *Lexington* landed on a bottom fairly flat. What if she came down on an undersea escarpment or precipice? Would that shock have torn her in half, or torn her totally to pieces, in a silent black collapse as devoid of sound and light as the drama of destruction inside a black hole? Would her pieces be scattered a mile down a cliff or a gorge, then buried in sediment, lost to time?

Whatever her condition after her death throes, her remains would not have rusted much at those profound depths. And not much marine life would have changed her color or surfaces. At a constant 35°F, she would be in a kind of suspended animation, almost frozen, the processes of marine and chemical change lowered to their bare minimum. On the other hand, the fierce pressures at her depth would have collapsed anything that was watertight, any bulkheads that were closed, any tubes in her radios, any tires on her aircraft.

More significantly, she would be shrouded in a darkness as deep as any in the universe. No particle of light, save for the strange luminescent creatures that might dart around her hull, would exist there. A fiercely peaceful and almost impregnable underwater crypt; that is graveyard Coral Sea.

May we be lucky enough to one day pierce this veil of time and the depths, to find these long-lost wanderers from our own world. May we someday find, at how many countless fathoms, our fathers and grandfathers who lie forever in the silence of the Coral Sea.

CHAPTER THREE

MIDWAY

Yorktown lost, U.S. wins at Midway, 1942

Graveyard Midway, June 3–4, 1942

MIDWAY ISLAND I KNOW WELL, HAVING SPENT SOME TIME THERE IN my 1998 search for the many ships lost there in 1942. While Hawaii and the islands ringing the Coral Sea are jungled, populated places of some permanence, Midway is really more sea than land. This tiny island is essentially two islets, flat vegetated spits known as Eastern and Sand, and their total area is only about two square miles. They rise just a few feet above sea level, and in a good hurricane or tidal surge could go completely under. In terms of geology, the islands are really the westernmost extension of the Hawaiian chain, part of the Emperor Seamount formation, although they are 1,300 miles northwest of Oahu.

Nobody lived at Midway for any length of time until the 1850s, when the U.S. discovered them and then took possession in 1867. But what they lack in creature comforts and tradition, they make up for in strategic location. Their name says all; they are near the geographic center of the Pacific, and for anyone wanting to cross this ocean, whether for business, pleasure, or more geostrategic purposes, they are well situated.

The U.S. realized their value from the beginning. In 1903 the Americans built a transpacific cable station there, the same year that Teddy Roosevelt designated Midway

A pair of SDB Dauntless dive bombers score a hit on the Japanese cruiser *Mikuma,* trailing smoke, during the Battle of Midway, June 4–7, 1942. Many consider this the decisive battle of the war: Before Midway, the Japanese were successfully on the offensive, taking territory throughout Asia and the Pacific; after Midway, the Allies were on the move.

a naval facility. Growing American air traffic to the Philippines made Midway a refueling stop in 1936, while Navy and Marine facilities grew up on smaller Eastern Island in that same decade. The U.S. Air Force and Navy no longer operate out of Midway. The runway and naval facilities located on Sand Island are now under the control of the U.S. Fish and Wildlife Service, and Eastern is now an unpopulated wildlife refuge.

Flying in from above, you can really sense the almost forlorn remoteness of these islands: No mountain peaks or nearby continents are silhouetted on the horizon, no fishing boats dot the waters, no marks of humanity can be seen other than runways and buildings on Sand Island. Instead, you see nothing so much as the endless enveloping blue of sea and sky, broken only by whitecaps and puffs of cumulus. But you can also sense the military value these spits of land once held. They were nothing more than permanent, unsinkable aircraft carriers. In an era when aircraft had ranges of only 750 miles or so, they were essential to project any lasting military power into such a vast body of water.

Midway had always figured in the Japanese plan for control of the Pacific. Unlikely though it seemed, Midway was the central Pacific anchor of the defense line the Japanese wanted to construct. And Midway would be an ideal place from which to harass the Americans at Pearl.

But as 1942 unfolded, Midway began to acquire even greater strategic value for the Japanese, and also for the Americans. Admiral Yamamoto was reportedly shocked that Jimmy Doolittle had been able to bomb Tokyo from *Hornet* in April, although the American B-25s had had to fly on to landings in China, since they couldn't land back on the carrier. Yamamoto was stunned, even though the damage was light, because all of a sudden, the great seaports at Yokosuka and Yokohama, the steel mills and shipyards, even the exquisite grounds and buildings of the Imperial Palace itself, were potential targets. It seems almost comical that he and his countrymen would be so shocked. After all, they had started a war through surprise attack on unsuspecting American sailors and their ships. Did he not think Japan would draw an equally vicious revenge?

Whatever Yamamoto's errors in reasoning, the Allied harassment of the Japanese in the Solomons and north of New Guinea in winter and spring 1942, and then the stalemated battle at Coral Sea in May, told him the American Navy was somewhere between a nuisance and a threat. The Doolittle raid came too close to home. The Americans had to be drawn into the Great All-Out Battle and eliminated once and for all. And it would be done with Midway as the strategic prize, although the Japanese would feint north, with an attack on the western Aleutians. They hoped to draw the American fleet north and away from Midway, destroy them there, and simultaneously occupy Midway itself, which should have been a reasonable strategy, considering the momentum of the war until then, and the balance of forces. Japan was at the very apex of its power in June 1942, controlling its huge Asian empire and having given none of it back. In equipment, Japan had ten carriers in the Pacific, while the U.S. had only three. Japan had a good six months' lead before U.S. war production would begin to whittle away the materiel disparity.

Even without *Zuikaku* and *Shokaku*, the Japanese armada for the Great All-Out Battle was still huge and seemingly all powerful: almost two dozen submarines, four heavy aircraft carriers, 5,000 men in a Midway Occupation Force, 11 battleships, 3 more light carriers, and more heavy cruisers and transports for the occupation of the Aleutians. Their total was nearly three times what the Americans could muster, although they were divided, perhaps fatally so, into three forces. The core Midway Striking Force, as at Pearl, was commanded by Adm. Chuichi Nagumo.

The Americans could assemble only three carriers, no battleships, eight heavy cruisers, and a little more than a dozen destroyers, with others committed to the North Pacific Force. U.S. carriers assigned to defend Midway included *Yorktown*, *Enterprise*, and *Hornet*. But the Americans had one seasoned commander, Frank Jack Fletcher, veteran of the Coral Sea, and one emerging brilliant carrier tactician, Rear Adm. Raymond Spruance, who in this battle proved both the power of carriers and his own superior vision and strategy. He also had a certain amount of good luck.

The Americans's skill at code breaking was now producing a great deal of information. It's one thing to have a well-mapped strategy based on assumptions of surprise, as the Japanese enjoyed at Pearl. It's another to have an adversary who, without your knowledge, knows much of what you are going to do before you do it. This was the Japanese position going into Midway, thanks to American code breakers. And the Americans enjoyed yet another

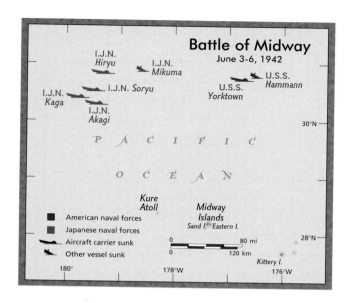

Battle of Midway
June 3-6, 1942

I.J.N. *Hiryu*
I.J.N. *Mikuma*
I.J.N. *Soryu*
I.J.N. *Kaga*
I.J.N. *Akagi*
U.S.S. *Hammann*
U.S.S. *Yorktown*

P A C I F I C

O C E A N

Kure Atoll

Midway Islands
Sand I. Eastern I.

■ American naval forces
■ Japanese naval forces
➤ Aircraft carrier sunk
➤ Other vessel sunk

0 _____ 80 mi
0 _____ 120 km

Kittery I.

30°N
28°N
180° 178°W 176°W

Pacific graveyard gathers a rich harvest at the Battle of Midway. Admiral Yamamoto planned attacks on the Aleutian Islands and an invasion of Midway to cement his hold on the Pacific. Adm. Chester Nimitz countered with a carrier attack that cost the Japanese the four large carriers that had attacked Pearl Harbor; the Americans lost the *Yorktown*.

element of surprise. While they only had three carriers at their disposal, they still had more on the scene than the Japanese expected.

On May 30 *Yorktown*, still aching from a Coral Sea bomb that had killed or wounded 66 men, sortied from Pearl Harbor, parts of her insides shored up by timbers. The Navy had given the ship only three days for repairs that normally would take months, and during that time Bill Surgi was there. "Unless we were directly involved in the repairs," he recalls, "our orders were to stay out of the way. If we left the ship, we weren't to come back on unless we were bringing provisions."

The men of *Yorktown* had been expecting to go to Bremerton, Washington, and off to shore leave after their Coral Sea work. Instead, they were ordered to go to Midway, although mainly to provide rear support to the other two carriers that would be farther forward, to meet the Japanese attack.

Yorktown was the command post for Admiral Fletcher, reportedly still exhausted from Coral Sea and the overnight repairs, as he headed into the most important battle of his career—and perhaps of the entire Pacific War. *Enterprise,* commanded by Admiral Spruance, and *Hornet,* commanded by Capt. Marc A. Mitscher, moved toward the rendezvous point with *Yorktown* at a place they appropriately designated "Point Luck," because without a lot of luck they would fail. All met at the invisible coordinates on the afternoon of June 2.

Admiral Nimitz had given very broad but very important instructions to his commanders before they left. He told them in a letter, "In carrying out the task assigned... you will be governed by the principle of calculated risk, which you shall interpret to mean avoidance of exposure of your force to attack by superior enemy forces without good prospect of inflicting, as a result of such exposure, greater damage on the enemy." Easier said than done.

And yet, what else could Nimitz have told them? What other mission could they have been given?

I've known life-and-death responsibility in my time. During my Navy service I knew what it was to give an order that might result in a mishap, or someone's death, or multiple deaths. I know this kind of responsibility today when I send photographers down in one-man subs into an undersea environment that, when something goes wrong, can turn quite hostile in a millisecond. I know it when I take dozens of people out on the water in the mid-Pacific or the Black Sea, where a storm or fire or explosion could turn an idyllic deepwater excursion into a tragedy.

Although we don't like to think about it, airline pilots and sea captains know this responsibility every day. Air traffic controllers, food and medicine producers, oil and chemical refiners, engineers who build power plants and bridges and dams, those who handle stores of weapons in peacetime, all have that same responsibility, even though the rest of us don't often think about it. Their sloppiness or incompetence can result in lives snuffed out.

Life-or-death responsibility is magnified a hundredfold in war. War is by nature the most hostile environment anyone will ever face. Not only can equipment fail or weather turn bad, add to it the fact that people on the other side are trying to kill you. That is their job. You are trying to do the same to them. Now carry it to the next level of life-and-death responsibility. Imagine the responsibility you hold when someone in essence is trying to kill your entire country, or at least do it great harm, and you are the one charged with defending your country. Those were the stakes that Admirals Nimitz, Fletcher, and Spruance faced at Midway. I doubt there was any Pacific battle that had such clear and enormous consequences.

Not only might the American admirals lose their ships, their men, and their own lives, they also knew that the struggle for Midway wasn't a distant move on an oceanic chessboard that was too remote to have consequences back home. No, they knew, even if the public did not, that U.S. defeat at Midway might have brought the Japanese threat closer to our own continental shores. There were plans on the books for a Japanese invasion of Hawaii. And if Japan got that far, was there any reason to think the Japanese Combined Fleet would have treated the citizens of Los Angeles or San Francisco or Seattle any more decently than they did those sailors and airmen running defenseless at Pearl Harbor, or the unfortunate Chinese at Nanking, or those Marines they beheaded after capturing them at Wake Island in December 1941? Maybe they wouldn't have been so cruel on the eastern side of the Pacific, but in 1942 the U.S. command couldn't take the risk of finding out. If they failed in the defense of Midway, and in neutralizing Japan, they might have lost the war.

So the Americans simply had to win at Midway; at the very least, they had to stop the Japanese advance. And if the Japanese wanted to succeed in their plan to hold and control Asia and the Pacific, they also had to win. If they did not destroy the U.S. Pacific Fleet at Midway, they could not hold onto their Greater East Asia Co-Prosperity Sphere. Ultimately, although not many of them yet admitted it, if they failed at Midway they would not be able to protect their precious homeland from foreign vengeance.

With that awful responsibility, three carriers rendezvoused the afternoon of June 2. They were so close to each other, and the American command was so worried about being detected, that they kept radio communications to a minimum, relying instead on signal lamps. But if those failed, the Americans had another technological card up their sleeve. Just as the Japanese were good at night fighting because of superior vision equipment, the Americans had devised TBS, a low-frequency radio that permitted up-close radio contact between ships, such a low frequency that the Japanese couldn't detect it.

What were those three ships like as they awaited the fateful battle? Did they have their own personalities, even though to the outside observer they seemed so similar?

The U.S.S. *Enterprise* would go on from Midway to serve in battle after battle, to eventually become the most decorated ship in the U.S. Navy. Of the more than 20 major actions of the Pacific War, she would miss only two of them. Nine hundred and eleven Japanese planes eventually would fall to her fliers and her guns, while she would send 71 Japanese ships to the bottom, and another 192 would be damaged or obliterated by her bombers. Perhaps no other ship would go on to so personify the American fighting spirit in the Pacific as *Enterprise*.

Commissioned in the late 1930s, she was the second of three *Yorktown*-class carriers, the others being *Yorktown* and *Hornet*, her sisters at Midway. Her design incorporated variations on the older *Lexington* and *Saratoga*, but she was lighter in the water and more maneuverable. She measured more than 800 feet from stem to stern, had four huge steam turbines that could deliver 120,000 horsepower, but *Enterprise* and her sisters displaced a third less than the older carriers, while carrying the same number of aircraft and a third more aircraft fuel. This meant more bang for the buck, more capacity to deliver one-two punches. She and the other new carriers were also more seaworthy. Still not immune to torpedo damage, but if hit they proved that even after sustaining debilitating damage they could keep afloat.

Hornet was nearly identical. She had taken the Doolittle raiders almost to Tokyo, and would go on from Midway to the next great battleground, Guadalcanal. Eight hundred and nine feet long, she'd been launched in late 1940 by the Newport News Ship Building & Dry Dock Co. Christened by Mrs. Frank M. Knox, wife of the secretary of the Navy, she was commissioned in October 1941. Mitscher was her skipper. In the run up to Pearl Harbor, *Hornet* had trained out of Norfolk. In early 1942 she'd startled some of her crew by launching two Army B-25 medium bombers while at sea, an experiment that certainly helped in preparing for the later Doolittle raid. On March 4 she sailed for the Pacific, via the Panama Canal.

Yorktown was also 809 feet long, carried 25 Wildcat fighters, 33 Dauntless dive bombers, and 13 Devastator torpedo bombers. She had eight five-inch guns, and forty antiaircraft guns. And *Yorktown* had the distinction in 1936 of being christened by Eleanor Roosevelt. This great ship was in part a product of the jobs-creating Works Progress Administration, the Depression-era program to employ the jobless. She was also the first carrier to be named after historic naval ships and battles. *Yorktown* blazed a trail in other ways, too. A so-called "island" on her starboard side contained her command facilities and enclosed her funnel. Two flight-deck catapults helped launch her aircraft. Pearl Harbor day had found her not in the Pacific but in the Atlantic, one of five U.S. carriers there. Incredibly, while at the war's start the U.S. had only eight carriers in both oceans, to Japan's ten in the Pacific, by the end of World War II, the U.S. had more than one hundred carriers.

These three massive ships were the bulwark of the American defense of Midway. Admiral Nimitz, in an intuitive stroke, positioned the ships to the northeast of Midway, where he knew they were beyond the range of search aircraft from the oncoming Japanese fleet, surmising that American planes based on Midway, with their range of 700 miles, would be able to sniff out the Japanese first.

Now just what kind of force was coming toward the Americans? Nimitz knew it was vastly larger. But Japanese naval tacticians had a predilection for dividing their forces to lure the enemy into a pincer, seal off retreat, and then pour in from the sides for the kill. When the plan didn't work, as was sometimes the case, it degenerated into a puzzling naval shell game, a Samurai display of much steaming and maneuvering, but not much else. Whether the tactic worked depended on whether the enemy did what he was supposed to do. Admiral Yamamoto intended to divert the Americans north by attacking Dutch Harbor in the Aleutians on June 3, feinting that way to convince Nimitz that the main Japanese thrust would come there. Once the Americans were drawn north, then the Japanese would cut them off, in the Great All-Out Battle.

But Admiral Nimitz's plan was to make sure he did things the Japanese would not expect him to do. Rather than operate robotically, seeing ahead one move at a time, he would see ahead three moves, and be in a position to surprise and pummel the enemy. He also would not separate his force, because it was already too small. He thought the three carriers fighting together, near Midway, had a better chance for survival and success.

On came the Japanese, nonetheless. Admiral Nagumo's force had two battleships, two heavy cruisers, and 12 destroyers, but at the heart of the force were the four big carriers, *Kaga*, *Akagi*, *Soryu*, and *Hiryu*. Other than the missing *Shokaku* and *Zuikaku*, these were the carriers that had hit Pearl Harbor six months earlier.

Akagi was the biggest, 855 feet long, originally built as a battle cruiser but converted to carrier status in the years 1935–38. She carried 18 Zero fighters, 18 Val dive bombers, and 18 Kate torpedo bombers.

Hiryu was 746 feet long, built at the Yokosuka Naval Yard in the late 1930s. She also carried the 18-18-18 complement of aircraft that was standard on all the carriers save *Kaga*. *Hiryu* possessed the heaviest armor of any of the four Japanese carriers.

Soryu, like *Hiryu*, was 746 feet long, built at the Kure Naval Yard, and finished in 1937. She was fast and maneuverable, with the same aircraft complement, but to gain maneuverability, she had sacrificed heavy armor, so she was more vulnerable to attack.

Kaga stretched 812 feet, had been laid down as a battleship, but in mid-construction was refitted as a carrier. She carried 18 Zeros and 18 Vals, and 27 Kates.

As at Pearl Harbor and Coral Sea, Mother Nature threw Japan and her force several breaks. First, they were sailing into the wind; so to launch their planes they didn't need to wheel around and tread water, but could continue on course and not lose time. They were also shrouded in fog, making them harder for the Americans to see. But these were not vital advantages. And the fog cover could also obscure Nagumo's view of what he was headed into, both metaphorically and physically. The closer Nagumo got to his target, the more he realized that he was truly sailing into the unknown. He had no clear idea of just what kind of American welcome would greet him this time around. Would the heavens be good to him again, and deliver him a Midway as sleepy as the Oahu he had found six months before? His uncertainty was compounded by the fact that Admiral Yamamoto, several hundred miles to his rear, was so strict about radio silence that he didn't report the surge in American naval radio activity, a sure tip-off that they were preparing for the Japanese arrival. Even more incredibly, Yamamoto didn't report to Nagumo that a U.S. Catalina based in Midway had, on the morning of June 3, overflown one part of the advancing fleet, the Midway invasion force headed by Vice Adm. Nobutake

On the aft end of the carrier *Enterprise*'s flight deck, Devastator torpedo bombers wait their turn for action. *Enterprise* entered the war on December 7, 1941, when her scout planes tangled with Japanese planes attacking Pearl Harbor; her war ended on May 14, 1945, when a kamikaze attack near Japan holed her flight deck. She engaged in all but two of the 20 major Pacific actions, downing 911 enemy planes, sinking 71 ships, and damaging or destroying 192 more.

A pilot on *Enterprise* signs his flight log after completing a mission. During 1942 alone, *Enterprise* was struck 5 times by Japanese bombs, killing or wounding nearly 300 of her men. During several months late in that year, with all other U.S. carriers out of action—either sunk or forced to withdraw for repair—*Enterprise* was the only operational U.S. carrier in the Pacific. A sign on her hangar deck read: "*Enterprise* vs. Japan." Her crew, during active duty, comprised nearly 3,000 men.

Kondo. And the night of June 3, the Americans had even bombed that force, but done no damage.

With each mile they drew nearer, the difficulty of Nagumo's task became more obvious. He had a double objective to soften up Midway by bombing and to eliminate whatever the Americans could assemble to oppose him. Which task he undertook first was contingent on whether the Americans had carriers and carrier-based aircraft near enough to oppose him. When the time for decision came, Nagumo asked aloud with almost tragic foreknowledge of what was coming, "But where is the enemy fleet?" No one had an answer, so Nagumo elected to assume there was no fleet until it was proved otherwise. He would undertake the Midway bombing first.

Despite its physical resemblance to the same juggernaut that had hit Pearl, the Midway Striking Force was not its former super-charged, spotless self. Unlike Pearl, which was a year in the planning, Midway had come together in little more than a month. And, like Admiral Fletcher, the Japanese attackers were weary from half a year of fighting in waters near New Guinea and the Solomons.

One Japanese survivor, Yuji Akamatsu, a torpedo bomber pilot, joined us in 1998 for my Midway expedition. He confirmed my own musings about the Japanese cultural rigidity that might have made them more vulnerable to the freewheeling and flexible Americans in post-Pearl battles, despite their Samurai code and ruthless methods. One symbolic example: He told me that even though Midway was a good three or four time zones east of Japan, the clocks on *Kaga* and all the other ships were still set on Tokyo time. And ships' routines followed Tokyo, not physical reality, to the point of having breakfast at noon and dinner late at night.

Another Japanese flyer, Mitsuo Fuchida, wrote, "The storm of battle was about to break...and for the first time in six months, Fate did not seem to be smiling upon us. No change, however, was made in the operations plan. All forces plunged onward through the boundless fog, like stagecoach horses driven blindly forward by a cracking whip."

And a third Japanese, a destroyer officer also named Fuchida, even wondered whether Nagumo was out of his depth altogether. "I began to feel dissatisfied with his apparent conservatism and passiveness," Commander Fuchida wrote. "His once vigorous fighting spirit seemed to be gone, and with it his stature as an outstanding naval leader. Instead he seemed rather average, and I was suddenly aware of his increased age."

Night fell on June 3 as these two huge fleets were drawing closer. Thousands of American men were bivouacked on Eastern and Sand Islands, either to defend Midway or support the ships or aircraft positioned there. Admirals Fletcher and Spruance were preparing for the greatest test of their naval careers, and their lives. Not only did Midway hang in the balance, but so did the security of Hawaii and perhaps the continental U.S. They knew that once their forces engaged, life-and-death decisions would need to be made in a matter of minutes or even seconds, reflexively, instinctively, intuitively.

In the haze of battle, there would be no time for reflection, and incoming information could be confused or garbled or nonexistent if communications should get knocked out. And yet the wrong decision could have consequences that could take thousands of lives and reverberate for decades. For example, General MacArthur's decision to hesitate when the Philippines were attacked, December 8, 1941, would take years and thousands of lives to rectify.

Hours before dawn on June 4, and still under a protective cover of overcast, 108 Japanese planes were launched from their four carriers and charged with the bombing of Midway Island. Wind at their faces, the carriers had had no need to turn or to lose speed to launch. Despite the private doubts of a few, the overall feeling of the Japanese was still total confidence. After all, they were the conquerors of Asia. And the Americans were poor warriors, undisciplined and on the retreat. To provide for his protection, Nagumo held back 93 aircraft to deal with enemy ships, if he could ever find any. But the last thing he was expecting was enemy carriers. And so he sent out only a skeleton search force. By 7:00 in the morning the planes had found nothing. Nagumo felt reassured.

Survivors of Midway's fury rekindle their friendship after 58 years. As teenage trainees in Florida, Jack Iskin (above, at left, and opposite, at right) and Harry Ferrier had a photo taken while on leave. Each assumed the other was killed during the battle. But Jack spotted Harry, alive and well, in a 1999 NATIONAL GEOGRAPHIC story about Midway—and the two old friends are together again.

Several hundred miles east, and almost simultaneously, came the call to general quarters on *Yorktown*. Because of the heat below decks, and because of the mission coming up the next morning, Aviation Machinist Mate 3rd Class Bill Surgi had slept on deck all night. "Our scout planes were about to take off. As an aviation mechanic, I had the responsibility to take care of any mechanical problems that came up. Once the planes were away, I went to my mess for breakfast. Then I went back to my battle station, which was the fire station in the catwalk amidships, opposite the island. There were about five of us there. Anticipating that if we got hit we would certainly have fire, we uncoiled the fire hose—these were three-inch linen hoses—so that we would be ready when the moment came."

On Midway at 6:00 a.m., a Marine brought the news that enemy forces had been sighted 150 miles northeast. Minutes later, Midway radar picked up the advancing

Japanese air unit. It was about half an hour away.

The time for engagement had come.

First, the Americans scrambled from Midway every fighter they had, even though they sensed it would not be enough. Then, with the confirmed reports of two Japanese carriers moving toward Midway, Admiral Fletcher from *Yorktown* ordered Spruance and *Enterprise* and *Hornet* to head toward Nagumo's main Japanese striking force. Fletcher very cogently understood that if he could injure or neutralize the main carrier force, then his chance for other successes would rise accordingly. Nagumo's force was the beating heart of the Japanese beast, and he would try to take it out.

At 6:30, and only minutes after Fletcher's order, the 108 Japanese planes hit Midway, to begin a 20-minute bombing run. While the American fliers were outnumbered, they did score hits, and island antiaircraft fire also scored. It wasn't enough to stop the bombs, but miraculously the

Continued on page 108

A geyser arises from the port side, amidships, of *Yorktown* at the moment of impact, mid-afternoon on June 4. This is the second of two Japanese type-91 aerial torpedoes that struck the ship, under attack by planes from the carrier *Hiryu*. Heavy antiaircraft fire has

Yorktown crewmen navigate a burning, listing deck to tend their injured ship and their wounded shipmates. Here, at gunmount four, the area of the deck most heavily damaged by one of the bomb hits, able-bodied men replace casualties. The chief petty officer at right has tucked his trousers into his socks to reduce the risk of skin burns.

An American destroyer, either the *Hughes* or the *Balch,* stands by as the abandoned *Yorktown,* seen here from the stern, lists badly to port. Dangling lines were used by crewmen to leave the ship. Mortally wounded on the first day of the battle, *Yorktown* stayed afloat another two days before torpedoes from a Japanese submarine sank her.

Struck by two torpedoes from Japanese sub *I-168*, Yahachi Tanabe in command, *Yorktown* lists as crewmen prepare to abandon ship. Despite a furious attack by American destroyers, the Japanese sub escaped and Tanabe survived the war. A little before 5:00 a.m., crewmen on the six American ships solicitously encircling *Yorktown* lowered their flags to half mast, removed their hats and helmets, and came to attention. At 7:01 a.m. *Yorktown* rolled onto her port side and sank.

Continued from page 101

airfield was not put out of action, and about 30 percent of the Japanese planes went down or were damaged enough to flee the scene. With smoke billowing in the tropical sky, the remaining Japanese turned around just before 7:00 a.m. and headed back for the four big carriers.

Simultaneous to that, Midway-based American Avenger torpedo bombers were just now sighting Japanese ships, after encountering and dodging Japanese bombers, headed for Midway. Japanese Zeros instantly surrounded the planes. In a blizzard of Japanese machine-gun fire, the Avengers started going down. Only one was still in the air as the smoke cleared, piloted by Bert Earnest, who was bleeding from his neck and feared he couldn't control his Avenger's elevation. But miraculously, Earnest was able to turn the battered bomber around and head back to Midway. Not that it was the same island he'd left behind two hours ago. Home base was still smoking from the Japanese bombing. He made his desperate approach with only one wheel down. No other Avengers made it back, and none of their torpedoes seemed to hit home. A later attack by Devastator torpedo bombers would prove just as fruitless.

With Midway reeling from the bombing, American planes going down right and left, and three big American fuel depots burning, Nagumo at this point probably felt he was winning. But he still didn't know about those three American carriers, lurking to his east.

Perhaps aware that the runway was still in operation, the returning Japanese aircraft radioed that Midway needed another pounding. So Nagumo had 93 aircraft refueled and rearmed to go back for a second strike, a move that took a critical 15 minutes. In a predictable world, this would have been the right thing to do. In the Japanese plan, the second wave would go out, the airfield and American antiaircraft guns would be neutralized, and the overall plan would advance on schedule.

But just before they launched, the first reports of American ships came in. And now the battle really began. Not only was it a battle of men and ships and weapons, but now the battle of the minds began, expressed in a series of decisions on both sides that would turn the course of war.

Admiral Nagumo, totally thrown off plan, had to make the most important call of his career. Should he go back and continue softening up Midway, or should he scrap that plan to protect his carriers? What to do, what to do? The beloved admiral had met his match. With full battle pouring down on him, he took another 15 minutes to decide what to do. Then, with a vital half hour lost, he realized he had no choice. He had to let one mission go, the Midway second wave, and he had to rearm his planes to hit ships. Eleven American ships was the report. Eleven! Where had they come from? What kind of ships were they? They weren't supposed to be there.

And then, another piece of hard reality crashed in on him. Even though his planes were rearming to go bomb these 11 enemy ships, they couldn't take off yet. Why? Because his fliers were still coming back from Midway, low on fuel, some damaged, and they had to land. Knowing that there was no time to wait, still he would be forced to wait, even as the enemy was surely moving against him. A terrible dismay and dread must have begun to settle in on him, and onto those few on board who knew the full situation. To see the minutes ticking away, minutes leading toward what might be disaster, but not to be able to do anything about it.

Nagumo wasn't just the victim of an unfortunate turn of events. He had been mentally outmaneuvered by Admiral Spruance, who in perhaps one of the luckiest and most prescient pieces of guesswork in the Pacific War had anticipated just the box Nagumo would find himself in, and had helped squeeze it even tighter. From *Hornet* and *Enterprise*, Spruance had already dispatched an all-out attack force of 20 Wildcat fighters, 67 Dauntless dive bombers, and 29 Devastator torpedo bombers. The objective was to catch Nagumo in that terrible dead time of confusion, refueling and rearming. *Yorktown*, meanwhile, got off six fighters, 17 SBDs, and 12 TBDs to help with the effort, though a bit later than the main force.

The planes from *Hornet* and *Enterprise* flew for an hour, an hour when Nagumo steamed relentlessly east, trapped in the box Spruance had built. He even arranged his four carriers in a boxlike formation. Then just after 9:00, he undertook a change in course that unwittingly threw off the first American wave, and earned him a brief respite. Nagumo turned east-northeast to look for the mysterious American ships. In having done so, he caused the first wave of dive bombers and fighters from *Hornet* to miss him. They never saw him. But the slower *Hornet*-based Devastator torpedo bombers somehow did not miss Nagumo, and found themselves gallantly flying in to attack a very formidable enemy with no additional air support at all. Just like the Avengers a few hours before, the hapless *Hornet* Devastators flew into a buzz saw; all 15 were shot down. Ten out of 14 Devastators from *Enterprise* were also shot down, and nearly all the Devastators from *Yorktown* met the same fate. Worse for the Americans, none of these planes scored a single hit. While the Devastators had flown without air cover, a terrible handicap, they were also handicapped by their poor speed, and soon after Midway, this useless aircraft was taken off the rolls.

By 10:20 a.m. or so, depending on your source, this final American torpedo attack was over. Not a bomb or torpedo had hit the Japanese. So utter was the American failure that for an instant—an eternity in the course of a battle—the Japanese had their overweening confidence affirmed once again. Not only were the Americans incompetent idiots, Japan was also invincible. Avengers couldn't stop her, Devastators were a joke. Midway would be the next Japanese base for the control of the Pacific.

But then, Dauntless dive bombers from *Enterprise* and *Yorktown*, having taken off separately and arrived together by coincidence, appeared at about 10:22 a.m., and in one of the greatest reversals of fortune in military history bombed the Japanese carriers *Kaga*, *Akagi*, and *Soryu*. While the Devastators were the butt of jokes, the Dauntlesses were held in great esteem by those who knew them. And for good reason: One could argue that the Dauntlesses and their pilots, guided by Spruance's brilliance, saved the day at Midway, and perhaps turned the course of war.

The *Akagi* was the first to suffer. A bomb hit and exploded in her hangar, where Japanese torpedoes in turn began to explode, then another hit the Japanese planes on deck that were still rearming to go after the just-discovered American fleet. As *Akagi* was becoming a fireball, Admiral Nagumo was faced with the humiliation of having to abandon his flagship. He moved to a nearby cruiser, where he suffered the further ignominy of having to order the sinking of his own gutted flagship to keep it out of enemy hands.

Kaga was next, hit squarely by four bombs that set the whole ship afire. A small crew stayed on in the event she could be saved, but she burned all day and into the night, finally exploding and sinking.

Now dive bombers from *Yorktown* found *Soryu* scrambling to launch her planes. *Yorktown* fliers hit *Soryu* so hard

with three bombs that she too had to be abandoned. For the coup de grace, U.S. submarine *Nautilus* torpedoed her such that she broke in half and sank.

It was all over in six minutes. From the apex of imperial power and arrogance, Japan's Combined Fleet had slid into stunned silence. While a few minutes earlier Japan had had four heavy carriers to America's three, now America had three and she had only one. We must try to imagine the incredulity that Nagumo and his surviving men must have felt that in that instant, when their pride and confidence turned into something else, something they had never known or planned for. Was it utter disbelief? Was it real anger at having been defied? Was it fear of retribution from the unforgiving commanders back home? Or was it sorrow at seeing proud ships and men that were the core of the striking force gone forever into oblivion?

The only big Japanese carrier left was *Hiryu*. As the horrible morning wore into afternoon, Nagumo, while licking his wounds, still looked for revenge. The opportunity came. Early that afternoon *Hiryu* got her planes off and headed them for *Yorktown*, and the 18 dive bombers, 10 torpedo bombers, and 12 fighters did their job. At 2:45 p.m. two torpedoes crashed into the port side of *Yorktown*, broke her hull and sent water flooding in belowdecks. They also jammed the rudder, knocked out power, and ruptured fuel tanks. She listed nearly 30°, so severely that her skipper, Capt. Elliott Buckmaster, feared she might collapse from gravity strain at that angle, since she had not been fully repaired from the Coral Sea bomb. So he gave the order to abandon ship.

Bill Surgi and *Yorktown* were now living through their second major military action in 30 days. "I remember we were hit by dive bombers before lunch, and then the torpedoes got us after lunch," he says. "I watched the torpedo planes come in, paying close attention. There was a certain beauty to them, because I'm a model maker, and I was thinking about building models of those planes. When the first torpedo struck, it threw me upward, and I hit my head, though wearing my tin hat. When I came to, I had to tear away a fire hose to get away. My buddy Patterson was impaled on a catwalk, and I called for help."

Surgi had broken an arm, although in the thick of battle and evacuation it was more of a nuisance than a source of pain. First he climbed into a lifeboat full of other wounded. But because the ship's power was gone,

Continued on page 114

Precarious trip to safety takes a wounded *Yorktown* survivor from the *Portland* to the *Fulton*, which transported the men to Pearl Harbor. Most survivors of the *Yorktown* either slid down ropes to the water or jumped. Many recall rows of shoes lined up along the starboard rail. One remembers gingerly touching the water with a toe before dropping in, to see how cold it was.

In the battle's aftermath, time is available to care for wounded. By 5:30 p.m., all of *Yorktown's* survivors had been taken aboard American destroyers in the vicinity. Surprisingly few men were lost. The destroyers reported taking aboard some 2,270 men, and the Navy's final report claimed "about twenty-three hundred" survivors were picked up.

Woebegone and miserable, Japanese survivors huddle on the deck of an American ship. On June 19, well after the battle, they were spotted by an American PBY plane hundreds of miles from Midway. The seaplane tender U.S.S. *Ballard* picked them up—35 Japanese sailors, members of the carrier *Hiryu*'s engineering force. Left behind when the ship was abandoned on June 5, they had made their way topside and found a small boat as their ship sank under them. They had been sailing for nearly two weeks trying to reach friendly territory. The sailors finished the war as prisoners of war in Pearl Harbor.

the boat couldn't be lowered. They all were told to swim, so in Surgi went, still carrying his faithful tin hat. "I went in the water wearing an aviator's life jacket," he said, "and I had the bottom part loosely cinched, so it was loose and floated up in front of me. It turned out to be a nice place to rest my broken arm. I was in the water for about four hours total. One destroyer came over to pick us up, but then when I heard general quarters sounded, I figured the attack was still going on, and I would be less of a target if I got away. So I swam in the other direction."

The next ship to come by was the destroyer *Benham*, eventually refuge for more than 700 survivors, so many that it put the ship at risk of capsizing. "Three cargo nets were hanging over the side, and the *Benham* crew told us to climb up," he says. "I tried to climb the forward net, but my arm hurt too much and I didn't have the strength. There was another one at midships. I couldn't climb that one either, and I let myself drift aft, near the prop guards. Now I realized the danger I was in. Those props had razor edges on them, so I got one arm in that last cargo net, and held on. Some guys above told me to climb up. I said I was too hurt and tired. So two of them climbed down and actually lifted me up onto the ship.

"Fifty years later, I was at the Australian Coral Sea anniversary [the same that *Lexington*'s Vince Anderson went to], and the young U.S. Navy guy next to me at dinner struck up a conversation. We got to the subject of the *Yorktown*. It turned out his grandfather had been one of those guys hauling us up onto the *Benham* fantail. He had told his grandson this story. I got goose bumps when I realized our connection."

Because he was injured, Surgi went for treatment to a temporary aid station in the wardroom. There the stewards served him tomato soup. He sat under the wardroom table and tried to sip the soup. "It looked good, it smelled good, it tasted good," he recalls. "I sipped some. But I'd swallowed too much salt water and oil while I was swimming, and they didn't mix. I upchucked, and they sent me out of there." Surgi eventually made it back to the fleet. He would later serve on the new *Yorktown*, the new *Lexington*, and even had a stint on the original *Enterprise*, before the end of the war.

Despite the severe list of *Yorktown*, the evacuation on June 4 was fairly orderly. Although many sailors went into the water like Surgi, 2,270 men of about 2,300 on board

were rescued by the carrier's escorts, including the destroyers *Benham* and *Hammann*. Amazingly, though, the big carrier did not go down. She floated on that afternoon, and through the night, and another day and night.

The final American blow was yet to be delivered. That afternoon, just as the last of *Hiryu*'s bombers were coming back from their attack on *Yorktown*, bombers from *Enterprise* arrived over *Hiryu*. Despite some midair confusion on the part of the Americans, and averted collisions due to a course change, at least one and maybe four bombs hit *Hiryu*, exploding belowdecks. And for a fourth time that day, American fliers turned a proud Japanese ship into an inferno. *Hiryu* burned on through the afternoon, damage so total that all but Rear Adm. Tamon Yamaguchi abandoned her. He committed hara-kiri sometime that night when he concluded there was not a shred of hope that his ship could be saved.

And now, with four carriers gone, the beating heart of Japan's Midway Strike Force had been cut out, leaving it a Japanese carrier escort force with no carriers. The sorrowful situation was apparent to anyone who understood naval strategy. Commander Fuchida, already disillusioned with Admiral Nagumo before the battle, now thought Nagumo had taken leave of his senses. "The grim situation was painfully clear," he wrote. "Our air strength was wiped out. The enemy still had at least one carrier intact, we had failed to render the Midway airfields ineffective, and some of our ships were still within striking range of the planes based there. With command of the air firmly in enemy hands, the outcome of the battle was a foregone conclusion."

Others in the Japanese fleet were not so realistic. Desperate plans were made for a late-night attack on Midway, then discarded when it was understood that while the Japanese might dominate the night theater, postponing their retreat until the next morning would still put them within striking range of the American planes. Yamamoto had visions even yet of luring the Americans into the Great All-Out Battle. Nagumo did not give up the ghost until a fortuitously mistaken intelligence report came in late the afternoon of June 4. Japanese scouts claimed that they had "sighted 4 enemy carriers, 6 cruisers, and 15 destroyers at a point 30 miles east of the burning carrier. The enemy force is proceeding westward." Though wrong, the U.S. had only two operative carriers, it was enough to dissuade Nagumo.

Other Japanese had already intuited the implication of their day of horror, even if they didn't understand high strategy. Eight hundred men had died on *Kaga* alone. The *Soryu* was underwater, *Hiryu* and *Akagi* were abandoned hulks. The heart of the force was cut out; how could the body keep on going without a heart?

The sorrow of that afternoon was expressed by Haruo Yoshino, who looked on the remnants of *Kaga* from a nearby ship. "About sundown, everyone was ordered up on deck. It was miserable, shameful. The splendid *Kaga* had looked so dignified just that morning. There is no way to express it with words. It gave me a taste of the bitterness of war, the bitterness of defeat. Our destroyer moved in and fired a single torpedo. With the setting sun behind us and the sinking ship to the east, it was almost like shadow painting. I felt nothing but misery."

Spirits were much higher on the American side. The bold gambles by Nimitz, Fletcher, and Spruance had paid off handsomely. With four heavy Japanese carriers knocked out, the tide of war had been turned, at least in the eastern Pacific. Midway was still American, and Hawaii and the U.S. West Coast were out of danger. Spruance, who had been given tactical command of the carriers in mid-battle by Fletcher, had done particularly well. His ability to see around corners and two or three moves ahead made him the champion of the naval chessboard.

But there was tragedy on both sides, too. Japan had lost as many as 3,500 men, four major carriers, and about 300 aircraft. The U.S. had lost about 300 men, *Yorktown*, and more than 100 planes. Behind those numbers were individual tales of terror, suffering, and wretched death. Men were dismembered by torpedo hits, disemboweled by flying shrapnel, impaled on equipment, choked and burned in spilled fuel, sealed in sinking cockpits and in doomed compartments belowdecks, even crushed by the shock waves of depth charges exploding as they swam in water just above.

While the Japanese had done most of their mourning on the afternoon of June 4, with the loss of four big carriers, the final American loss didn't come until early on the morning of June 7. Proud *Yorktown* had floated on for two nights and a day, her condition not worsening. In fact, preliminary salvage operations had begun, and to many of her loyal crew who were clamoring to go back aboard and help out, it seemed like she might bounce back, just like many of the ships at Pearl Harbor had and just like

she had done after the Battle of Coral Sea. A lone tug, *Vireo*, was even laboring to pull her east on the afternoon of June 6, but without much success. A skeleton crew was on board, assessing damage, pumping out water, correcting her list, clearing out classified documents, even finding a few more survivors.

And several destroyers were supposedly providing escort, but judging from what happened later, they were not vigilant enough. On the afternoon of June 6, in living proof that a dead rattlesnake can still bite, Japanese submarine *I-168*, only recently informed that her own carrier fleet had gone down, doggedly stalked the wounded American carrier. The Japanese captain was incredulous that *Yorktown*'s alleged escorts seemed unaware of his presence, as he crept closer and closer. Finally, he fired his torpedoes, jolting the Americans from their reveries. He hit *Yorktown* as well as the destroyer *Hammann*. *Hammann* sank quickly, while *Yorktown* hung on through most of another night, and then finally rolled over and went down early on the morning of June 7. *I-168* dodged more than 60 depth charges and maneuvered so brilliantly, and with such luck and determination, that she escaped American revenge.

When *Hammann* was torpedoed while it was alongside *Yorktown*, it sank instantly, and then many of its depth charges went off as it descended, killing even more sailors who had survived the sinking. When the violence was over, the captain of *Hammann* was found in the water holding onto two sailors who, in fact, were dead. One of the sailors was a Robert Ballard, more than likely a distant cousin of mine. I didn't know that until I was at sea during my 1998 search effort and was reading one of the many historical works brought aboard by naval historian Chuck Haberlein.

The ones that didn't get away, who weren't fast enough or clever enough or experienced enough or well-designed enough, or who were just in the wrong place at the wrong time, populate Midway to this day. Because Midway was such a critical battle for both adversaries, and because there was such heavy symbolism in the five big carriers and other ships and aircraft that went down on those days, June 4–7, 1942, I decided to mount an expedition there in 1998. I was determined to find the *Yorktown*, one of three carrier heroes of Midway for the United States. And if I could, I would also find one or more of the Japanese carriers *Kaga*, *Akagi*, *Soryu*, and *Hiryu*. After 56 years, many Japanese wanted some closure, almost as if the loss of those great ships, and the abrupt naval reversal that they heralded, were such that they wanted to come to terms with this in a more direct way.

Seeing a graveyard up close can do that. Even if the men who animated those ships are long gone. The ships, particularly at the depths I expected to find *Yorktown*, would be amazingly well preserved, as long as the bottom topography they encountered is not overwhelmingly hostile. The water at 17,000 feet is bitter cold, which inhibits corrosion and organic growth. There's no wind or wave action. It's almost like our sunken ships are frozen in time.

But to get closure with *Yorktown* and the others, I had to find them. No small task. As at Pearl and everywhere else, I had to ask the two questions: What am I looking for? And where is it? In the case of *Yorktown*, the target was a good 800 feet long—unless like *Titanic* it had broken up on the way down or on impact. And in the case of *Yorktown*, it should be sitting out in the middle of what I had hoped would be an underwater version of the Great Plains. In other words, nice and flat.

Size of the target, and the depth, and the undersea terrain all tell me how to configure my search. Working 17,000 feet down on a flat plain, I know I need to use sonar. And there are two factors, range and resolution, that you need to deal with. If you want to be able to see the maximum distance underwater, you must use sonar at low frequency, but to do that you also must sacrifice resolution. If you want your underwater sonar image to be a clear silhouette of your target, then you use high-frequency sonar, but that's at the sacrifice of distance.

At *Yorktown*, I would be working with a search area that was more than 200 square miles. That's a lot of ground to cover. And I had two locations to consider. One was a site to the north, established by historian Samuel Eliot Morison and the Naval War College. The other was farther south, based on logs from the destroyers on that final salvage attempt on June 6--7, 1942. I favored the latter site, maybe because the log records from the salvage attempt, even if recorded in the confusion and heat of battle, were as close as I could get to being there for the sinking myself.

In the case of *Yorktown*, I also knew the target was big, I knew it was deep, and I hoped it was in the flats that are fairly common northeast of Midway Island. If it wasn't in the flats, then the *Yorktown* sonar signature would be competing with signatures from rock outcrops, cliffs,

boulders, you name it. Save for another telltale clue, which I'll talk about in a minute, I would never be able to distinguish it on sonar.

I pondered gambling, by restricting my search to the flatlands, which tracked with the destroyer escort logs. After all, I only had so much time, a month, and only so much money with which to do this search. I would "mow the lawn" of these 200 square miles in the most efficient way I could, yet not miss *Yorktown*. With our dynamic positioning system keeping me right on the mark, I would mow in swaths that might not touch exactly, but there would be no gaps wider than the width of *Yorktown* itself. We call these gaps in sonar swaths "holidays," and some explorers try to overlap their swaths so there is no holiday; in other words, they ensonify 150 percent. But that means they spend much more time mowing the lawn, burning fuel, burning time, burning money. I could be more realistic and strive to ensonify 100 to 120 percent, knowing that just like swinging a flashlight beam across an irregular surface, I still might miss *Yorktown* if there was a hole in that bottom where she just happened to land.

I decided to gamble. The search area was larger than normal; it was very deep; it was a remote location; and I had a limited amount of money to spend. I gambled by changing tactics and using the MR-1 sonar from the University of Hawaii. This sonar wasn't designed to find sunken ships. It was designed to find underwater mountains. Many people thought it would be very difficult to see an object even as large as *Yorktown* in the sonar trace, and impossible to see if it had broken up. If we ran a line perpendicular to the ship's long axis, we wouldn't see it at all. We had to run parallel to the long axis to have a better chance of seeing it. That's why I ran two sets of lines perpendicular to one another (east to west and north to south).

To increase my chances of seeing the ship, I slowed the towing speed as much as I could, to about five knots. Any slower and the tow fish would become unstable and start fishtailing, which would make it impossible to see *Yorktown*. Once I found *Yorktown* I would be looking at an object about the size of a grain of rice. But small hills would also look like rice grains, and I saw a lot of them. The way I eliminated this clutter was to look at the target from all sides. If it was a hill, the sonar would "jump" each time I looked at it from a different angle. But because *Yorktown* was so narrow, it wouldn't "jump."

On the trail of the sunken *Yorktown*, the author watches a sonar image of the Pacific seafloor.
U.S. Navy crewmen maneuver their ATV—an advanced tethered vehicle. The submersible
descends from the ship and transmits back sonar and photographic images of what it finds.

The only other problem I had was with what is called the "nadir," the area directly below the tow fish. Obviously, side-scan sonar looks to the side, not down. When you are towing the fish near the bottom, this unseen area, or nadir, is small, but as the depth increases, the nadir increases, like a spreading shadow. Because we were searching in 17,000 feet of water with the sonar towed near the surface, the nadir was very large, more than one kilometer. As a result, I needed to overlap my coverage to insure I included the area of the nadir from previous lines. This pattern increases search time, but one advantage of towing the *MR-1* near the surface is that I could tow much faster, about five knots, compared to only one knot when towing conventional sonar near the bottom. To shoot my signal that far down, I would use low-frequency sonar, about 12 kilohertz. I would make

sure my holidays were no greater than the footprint of *Yorktown*. As it turned out, I passed over *Yorktown* on my very first MR-1 line, and it was in the nadir. If I hadn't run a later line to cover that area, I never would have found the ship.

We started our search in early May 1998, using a flat-bottomed vessel called *Laney Chouest*, once used to tend oil rigs. As at Pearl, I had with me my usual crew from the Institute for Exploration in Mystic, along with a somewhat different cast of folks from National Geographic, some fine Japanese and American survivors, including Bill Surgi from *Yorktown* and Harry Ferrier, who had been the radioman from the single surviving Avenger, and a film crew headed up by long-time friend Peter Schnall. I also had Bruce Applegate on board, leader of the University of Hawaii team that operated the *MR-1*.

Among the bones in the Midway graveyard: A Japanese heavy cruiser, bombed and sunk by U.S. carrier-based planes; and the *Hammann*, a destroyer assisting in the salvage of the *Yorktown* before it sank. Fatally wounded by the same torpedoes that finished off the *Yorktown*, *Hammann* went down fast, head first (photo sequence above). As it sank, its depth charges exploded, killing or badly injuring many who survived the sinking.

In Midway lagoon, the relics of war attract fishes and divers. This plane, probably an American, was likely downed while defending the island on June 4. On the island, little remains to remind visitors of war: gun emplacements, bunkers, a hangar. Laysan albatrosses soar across now quiet beaches.

As always, we worked our way through the inevitable series of technical and mechanical problems. And I decided to hedge my bets, not gambling on finding *Yorktown* in the flat terrain. Instead, by May 5, we had mowed the lawn in a huge, 500-square-mile area. We even ended up doing the mountains in the northern sector after all. Why did I do the mountains, when it was such confusing terrain for the sonar? Well, while there's no way we could have picked up *Yorktown* by itself in that terrain, I thought we might see some geological evidence of a big ship impact, like an underwater landslide if she'd come down on sloping terrain. Remember, even though I work underwater, I'm really a geologist by training, and I know how to read the bottom. A big landslide had led me to *Bismarck*, which had come slamming into the bottom and triggered a landslide that carried the ship more than a mile

down slope. A massive ship falling to the bottom, thousands of tons of steel traveling at even 20-30 miles an hour, would hit very hard. It would have some sort of geological footprint, whether an impact crater or a landslide.

Not only did we mow north to south; then we mowed the same area east to west. This gave us a pretty good sonar mosaic to work from. No targets stood out waving American flags or with antiaircraft guns pointing at us, but the ones we'd found were few enough in number that by May 5 I felt ready to try for a visual examination, using the Navy's advanced tethered vehicle, or ATV.

Desire is one thing, but ability is another. Unfortunately it took us several days to get the ATV working; she finally went under on May 7. On the eve of the launch, my sonar guru Karen Sender convinced me to go after one particular target that she just felt good about. It was the right size when shot from several angles, and even the right height, assuming *Yorktown* was about half buried in mud.

In rereading my logs, I'm reminded that the early days of the search brought more disappointment than discoveries:

"On May 5, our ATV is lowered over the side and began its 17,000-foot vertical journey to the bottom of the sea. One hour later and 5,000 feet down the brightly lit TV monitors inside the ATV's control van suddenly went black. A massive ground was detected in the vehicle's electrical tether and all the power to the vehicle was turned off. One hour later, the ATV was back on deck and a search of the electrical system quickly located a ground where the tether attaches to the vehicle, a problem which would take a full day and a half to fix.

"While the vehicle was undergoing its repairs, we used the available time to install a series of three transponders around the sonar target that we suspected was the *Yorktown*. This network of bottom beacons will be used to actually determine the location of the *Laney Chouest* and the ATV while working on the ocean floor.

"On May 7 at 4 p.m. local time, the ATV began its second descent. As it drew closer to the bottom, more and more people began to fill the control van and the main lab, where separate TV monitors had been placed for the overflow crowd.

"The ATV sank lower and lower until its altitude was less than 500 feet and its range to the target was 500 yards. The search sonars were running and everyone's eyes were glued to the TV screens—when suddenly something went terribly wrong. A cloud of unknown origin rolled past the cameras, before they went dead. At first we thought we might be able to continue the lowering at least to a few feet above the bottom, in an attempt to scan the target with the vehicle's sonar to determine if in fact it was the *Yorktown*. But the damage was so severe that the decision was made to bring the ATV back to the surface.

"Three hours later, the ATV was lifted out of the water. Its instrument cluster looked as if a bomb had gone off. In fact that is exactly what had happened. Two 16-inch diameter glass pressure housings holding light ballast to drive our powerful underwater lights had imploded. It was as if five sticks of TNT had exploded amid our instrument package. Two television cameras were destroyed, the tracking transponder was blown free of the vehicle, and the pressure gauge destroyed. The shock wave from the explosion had done additional damage as it moved through the surrounding pressure housings full of other instruments.

"Clearly, the ATV was out of action and would remain so for many hours."

Even now I recall how I felt that day, how the meter was really running on this expedition and I had nothing to show for it. Because I only had my crews and equipment for a limited time, and we still had a hell of a lot to do, I had to execute some fancy footwork. I made one of those midcourse corrections that are inevitable in my business, just as in the heat of battle. Since we couldn't visually identify the *Yorktown* target until the ATV was repaired, then we would mow the lawn nearly 200 miles to the northwest. We would look for three of the four lost Japanese carriers—*Kaga*, *Akagi*, and *Soryu*—that had gone down fairly close to one another. *Hiryu* was farther away, and as I considered it, our odds of success were three times greater if we looked in one area that probably held three ships than in another that might hold only one. While it rankled me to not be able to look for *Yorktown* and be done with it, we'd at least make some good use of our down time.

Not that looking for the Japanese carriers was any easier. This time around we were mowing an area 25 by 10 nautical miles, 250 square miles in all. Another huge chunk of ocean and ocean bottom. On the spur of the moment, we managed to get hold of what proved to be an excellent satellite topographic map that showed terrain much like the *Yorktown* area, abyssal plain in the south, seamounts in the north.

We found two promising targets, one each for *Kaga* and *Akagi*. I chose to go after *Kaga* first, if for no other reason than both of our Japanese survivors were from *Kaga*. Our ATV, while partly operative by this point, took forever to get to the bottom. And once there, the sonar pings from the ATV were only the soft images of undersea slopes and hills. Later, it turned out that our prospective "*Kaga*" was nothing more than a volcanic rock outcrop.

With that inauspicious audition, I turned us back to the *Yorktown* search area, like Nimitz and Spruance now forced to go for broke. I had no more cushion, no time, no money, no sure thing. What had seemed like such a promising target there now ate at my confidence. Kathy

Sender had felt good about the sonar profile, better than she had about the Japanese blips. Was she going to be proved right? It wasn't until May 19—the month now two thirds gone—that we were back at the *Yorktown* site with the ATV going down.

Looking back at my log now, I see how depressed I was. Those Japanese signatures had looked damn good, but they were only mud and rock. I was running through in my mind how to break the news to National Geographic and everybody that we'd failed—our time was up and the money was gone. I would have to send all those survivors home with no closure, the film crew with nothing in the can but endless shots of the ATV being repaired. Not a good feeling. Bill Surgi told me he was pretty down at that point, too. He'd brought along the tin hat he'd worn on *Yorktown*. But those failed Japanese targets had spooked him, and he was on pins and needles.

The ATV was 16,000 feet down and cruising across the bottom when I got into the control room that fateful morning. My log tells it all:

"As I walked through the lab, I looked at the remote sonar display and didn't like what I saw. The strong targets were soft and round looking, clearly a sloping bottom surface.

"I went into the ATV control van as the pilot was having difficulty driving. After a few minutes, it became clear he couldn't control the vehicle. Then a discussion developed as to why. Was there too much cable out and he was anchored to the bottom? Or was there not enough cable out and he was fighting the ship with a short leash? The chief decided the cable was on the bottom and began pulling it in. Shortly thereafter the vehicle started moving backward but that didn't initially resolve the situation, since taking in cable would pull the vehicle backward in either case.

"While moving backward, we picked up a small target, perhaps a piece of wreckage but certainly not geologic. The bottom in this area is covered with manganese nodules and has an apparent slope.

"Slowly the pilot began to gain control of the vehicle as we began driving east in the direction of the *MR-1* sonar target, moving the ship as we went."

I guess I hit my lowest moment of despair just before the dawn of discovery. The ATV's onboard sonar began to slide from the monotonous sound of flat ambient sea bottom to a rising ring, as more and more changes in the profile registered. The strange sonar ringing was like music to my ears. I knew this sound, from other expeditions, and from my Navy work. This was most likely splatter from the impact on the bottom. We know that when a big ship like *Titanic* or *Yorktown* goes down, it can make quite a mark on the seafloor.

As we got closer, I saw our first mud ball. Instantly visions of the *Titanic* came to mind. Clearly, this was splatter from a tremendous impact. As we continued forward, splatter gave way to a bulldozed bottom with sharp clumps. Like the edge of an impact crater. Then came the telltale outline of a long sharp image. As we drew even closer the outline of the flight deck appeared. It had to be the *Yorktown*, although it might be the U.S. destroyer *Hammann* that sank alongside the *Yorktown* that day. Then a piece of shining metal almost like aluminum passed by. Then the clear image of massive wreckage. We slowly rose up the wreck trying to determine where we were, either bow or stern. It looked like the stern to me for some reason, but the amount of damage was too great to make out any clear landmarks. As we settled back down, we could see the edge of a hole with flat decking around it. It was an elevator opening. The monitor then revealed the ship's island and we knew where we were. We were on the port side of the ship. We drove along the port edge of the flight deck and then traversed the deck toward the island. When we reached the other side we could see the base of the crane at the aft end of the island. We then spent the rest of the dive driving along the island on the inboard side and finished by rising up past the bridge.

It was indeed *Yorktown*, although I couldn't officially say so until we'd found her name and ID number up on the hull. Bill Surgi said he wasn't sure it was his ship until he saw the crane. Some of us may have been wondering if we had found *Hammann* instead, because she had gone down so close by. But the crane and flight deck clinched it for us.

Thanks to the tireless work of my crew, and some damned good luck, we had found *Yorktown*, at the 11th hour. What shape did we find her in? Considering all those torpedoes and bombs she had taken at Coral Sea and Midway, and 56 years resting at 17,000 feet, she looked pretty good. She was in one piece, still listing much as she had in those final two days of her life. But this time she was listing to starboard, not port, and she was sitting in mud, not on the ocean's surface.

Bill Surgi now suggested we have the ATV look into an elevator opening on the flight deck. But that was too dangerous. Instead, we looked in from the side. Sure enough, there in the big belowdecks space that served as an auditorium for the crew, we got a tough angle shot of the remarkably well-preserved mural that depicted all the voyages of *Yorktown*. We could make out the detail of the mural, and a hint of color. We could even see the painted outline of the globe and the painting of a searchlight beam, which we later compared to a photo from 1942 that showed a jazz combo performing right in front of that same illustration.

Just minutes after we had made these discoveries, hydraulics problems on the ATV cut the mission short, and while we were all hungering for more, up came the ATV. But the next day we went back down, and had more time to explore. Bill also had us look for that fateful port catwalk just aft of the midships elevator where his friend—who eventually survived—had been impaled on the railing. It was gone, although we found a big torpedo hole below that area on the port side, caused by the air-launched torpedoes that Surgi had watched come in and that had thrown him and his buddy so hard they were injured. The holes from the final torpedo blasts shot from sub *I-168* hid below the mudline on the starboard side. Other things were missing that had still been on board when Surgi abandoned ship, like the tripod. He guessed it had come off from the crash impact on the bottom.

But despite the missing parts of a once grand ship, in those video excursions we were able to see through to *Yorktown*'s true self, to her essence, to her sheer graceful bulk. If through some miracle of technology you were one day able to go down to her resting place and had enough ambient light in that surprisingly crystal-clear water, you would see what looks like a huge craft dropped down from space, shorn of many of the antenna and cables and protrusions that had once made her serviceable, but now reduced to her core, which is still massive and formidable. She would look gray-blue to you, dappled by the effects of fires and explosions, spills and ruptures, or by the slight changes wrought by undersea chemical reactions. You would see a huge sunken sea-beast from another time, a steel dinosaur out of another era, when deluded men still thought they could conquer the world, and others needed to oppose them.

You would see the surprisingly light layer of silt on the flight deck, and the mounts of 1.1-inch antiaircraft guns. You would scan the bridge and the antiaircraft gun tub below. You would see two 20mm guns on her bow, and her identification numeral 5 on the port bow. You would see fire hoses still dangling from fighting those final flames on June 4, and the battered pilothouse, and the armored battle lookout just below the bridge that gave some protection during combat. You would see the same crane that Bill Surgi instantly recognized, although the mighty arm that once lifted heavy loads like aircraft, would have fallen down. You would see heavy machine guns pointing at all angles, the searchlight platform, and the open mouths of all three elevators that once lifted aircraft from belowdecks. You would see the degaussing cable running around the top edge of the hull, put there to neutralize the ship's magnetic charge.

You would see forlorn portholes and doorways opening into a sepulchral interior, like gazing into the empty eyes of a dead man. Although most sources agree that everyone made it off *Yorktown* by June 7, either dead or alive, Surgi has heard otherwise. He heard that a small damage-control crew was trapped below at some point in those final hours, were told they would be rescued, but then in the haste of the surprise sinking went down with the ship. Was it true? If so, who were they? Whose fathers, sons, brothers? Do they still haunt this ship today, awaiting the shouts and the rescue that never came? Is this deep and silent place their home now?

There are no answers. In those few hours that we were able to send a video camera down to *Yorktown*, we saw nothing along those lines. But what would we have found? Short of seeing a ghost, it has been too long. The ocean erases all evidence of the dead, swiftly and forever.

Then we went exploring anew, this time intending to look for *Hammann*, the destroyer that had been escorting *Yorktown* during that futile salvage attempt on June 6 and 7. *Hammann* had gone down in only five minutes after *I-168* had got it, and we theorized it wasn't too far away. But first, we looked for *Yorktown*'s debris trail, hoping among other things to find some of the planes that were pushed overboard during the salvage attempt. Without sonar, I used the same search strategy I'd used to find *Titanic* and *Bismarck*, towing a deep camera vehicle running at right angles to where I calculated the trail lay.

Three miles down, *Yorktown* (right) sits upright, amazingly intact. The author's team found her on May 19, 1998. Her "island," the command center, rises on the starboard side; an aircraft elevator shaft gapes open on the wooden flight deck. Detailed photographs (above) document her wounds.

While we did find three unexploded depth charges from *Hammann* that had gone down with her, we had to cut the May 20 mission short to get back to port. Problems with the ATV, and deteriorating weather over the next few days, only allowed one more dive, even as our mission time was running out.

During all those explorations, Bill Surgi was never far from the action, as the ATV moved over and around the ship. This silent wreck had been his home through two bloody battles, Coral Sea and Midway. To finally see it, both dead and yet alive with so many memories buried until now, when for so many weeks we had been afraid we might find nothing at all, deeply affected him. It affected me.

In my years working with survivors, I've noticed two commonalities among these men. First, how hard it is for many of them to talk about what happened in the war. And how for many of them, it was the most dramatic and powerful experience they ever lived through. The caricature of the veteran who talks on and on about what he did in the war is really not typical, at least among the survivors I've known. I wonder if the big talkers lived through the near-death experiences that the quiet ones did. To be around horror and carnage, day after day, for three-and-a-half years, to see your buddies burned alive or dismembered or drowned, does not lend itself to storytelling.

It may well be that there is an unspoken agreement among those who saw the worst, that the rest of us should be spared that experience. After all, that's part of why they went to war: To spare their families and their countrymen and their descendants the pain of being attacked or enslaved. I appreciate and respect that.

On the other hand, I, who have one degree of separation from this titanic war, want to keep the memory alive. I think our very fortunate younger generations, for whom even Vietnam is just a distant echo, need to know how the driving forces of our modern world—the democracy and freedom and mass prosperity we so take for granted—didn't just happen on their own, but were bought with the most terrible sacrifice, the sacrifice of hundreds of thousands of lives. And how, but for some very brave men and some very clever commanders, many of us on the scene today might never have been born. Or if born, would have had very different lives, in a world perhaps unrecognizable.

A darker world would have been ours. A world where, even if we had been able to protect our American continental fortress, we might today have been hemmed in on east and west by hostile powers. Surrounded by oceans that were not open for transit and commerce, except at the indulgence of those who controlled them. A world less rich by half. A world where American technology might never have reached its full flower, and global wealth creation was driven by diktat, not by free enterprise. Imagine just for a moment, given the arrogance of the Axis, if the warlords had won, or had achieved a mid-Pacific truce with the U.S., or had held continental Europe and half of Russia.

In retrospect, the outcome of World War II may seem to have been inevitable now. Japan, as Samuel Eliot Morison said, was "idiotic" to take on the U.S.

And yet...

If *Yorktown* had sunk in the Coral Sea or had gone on to Bremerton on May 30 instead of to Midway, American firepower at Midway would have been diminished by a third. Would those dive bombers from *Enterprise* and *Hornet* have done as well?

If Japanese intelligence had been just a little bit better in May and early June 1942, and had known of the three U.S. carriers, or even two of them, lurking near Midway, would Japan have attacked as she did? Would she have suffered such losses?

Even more plausible, if Admiral Nagumo's scout planes had turned up the U.S. ships just an hour earlier than they actually did, wouldn't he have been able to refuel and turn his fighters and bombers around in time to, maybe, do to us what we did to him?

We will never know. All we know is how things turned out. And as the survivors grow older and their memories dim, at Midway we have found only one huge iron remnant of those who paid the total price, with their lives. I wish we had found at least one of the Japanese carriers, and some aircraft, memorials to all those American and Japanese fighter and bomber crews who went down in dogfights or antiaircraft fire near Midway or adjacent to the five carriers that went to the bottom. Or those doomed fliers based on the sunken carriers who, when returning from missions, had nowhere to land but the drink.

In memory of all of them, the survivors from both countries who came along with us in 1998 mounted a fine ceremony of remembrance.

As Bill Surgi said on that Memorial Day, May 25, 1998, "Here lies my home for ten months. In peace and war. Now that we have seen where she lies, let her lie still.

Another ghostly relic of the battle lies at the bottom of Midway lagoon. An obscure coral atoll,
Midway achieved fame only by the happenstance of its strategic location: Lying near the geographic
center of the Pacific Ocean—midway—it became an important stop in transpacific travel.

My shipmates and I were here when a glorious page in our history was played out. We were doing our best. This helmet I wore at my battle station on June 4, 1942. Oh, yes, I do remember that day. And now I cast these petals on the water in memory of those who have gone before us."

That is how it is today. We remember the dead, and we live in peace. But it was different on June 7, 1942. Then we ached at the recent loss of the dead. And we staggered under the burdens of war. For the Americans, although the Midway victory was great, it was only the first step in a coming journey of many thousands of miles—across bloody ocean and island jungle, pushing Japan back across the Pacific. For the Japanese, while Midway was a terrible defeat, it was only their first, and so it was more easily erased from their minds. Their propaganda machine did not mention the awful debacle at Midway,

and Japanese officers, even in the privacy of corridor or cabin, hardly spoke of it. They could pretend it never happened. And if in their private thoughts they now knew growing uncertainty, they could still comfort themselves by pointing to the Asian empire they still held.

But the huge empire would now be contested. The next Pacific battlefield and graveyard is far, far to the southwest of Midway. Back to the wild regions of New Guinea and the Solomons. In particular, back to the northern rim of the greater Coral Sea, to a wet and somehow sinister jungle island with an Arab-Spanish name that would set new records for killing and carnage. While mighty *Yorktown* was on the bottom, *Hornet* and *Enterprise* would go on to this next fight, around and about a steaming island hardly into the fifth century, much less the twentieth. An island and a battleground, called Guadalcanal.

UNDER THE WINGS OF AN AMERICAN FIGHTER, JAPANESE TRANSPORTS SMOLDER OFF GUADALCANAL, NOVEMBER 1942

CHAPTER FOUR

GUADALCANAL

Marines land on Guadalcanal Aug. 7, 1942

August 1942–February 1943

WHAT IS GUADALCANAL, THE PLACE? AT 2,000 SQUARE MILES and with jungled volcanic peaks reaching 8,000 feet above sea level, it's the largest of the Solomon chain, which stretches 900 miles from northeast New Guinea toward the New Hebrides, across the northern rim of the Coral Sea. The inhabitants, then as now, are largely Melanesians, speaking more than 100 languages and dialects. This tribal, village-centered society with only marginal contacts with the outside world was a most unlikely place for a duel to the death between global powers for control of Asia and the Pacific. But as 1942 wore on, that is what Guadalcanal came to be. Why?

"Guadalcanal," a Spanish name with Arabic roots, dates from the 700-year Moorish reign over Iberia and the Spanish colonial exploration of the Solomons. "Guad" is a corruption of the Arabic word *wadi*, meaning river, and together with the Spanish word meaning channel or canal, roughly translates into river channel. It seems odd to call a jungled island with volcanic sand beaches a river channel. But in fact the island of Guadalcanal does stand at the edge of an invisible channel in the ocean, a stretch of water running 500 miles from Rabaul, New Britain, in the Bismarck

American battleship *South Dakota* fires a salvo from her forward turrets during the long struggle for Guadalcanal. The Japanese had occupied the small island, one of the Solomons, in July 1942, and built an airfield there; for months the Allies and Japanese fought furious land and sea battles for possession of the island and the waters around it.

Archipelago, down "the slot" through the Solomons. This intangible channel, much like the Mississippi or the Danube, would serve during World War II as a flowing conveyor belt of ships, men, and materiel to further the control of that part of the world. Japan relied on this channel to run its resupply operations known as the Tokyo Express, feeding men and weaponry ever southeastward, building air bases and ports along the way, fortifying its control over that unlikely slice of earth and ocean. The Tokyo Express would run day and night, striving to create a critical mass of men and naval and air cover that would finally allow the overland invasion of Port Moresby, New Guinea, just to the south. Once the Japanese consolidated their power down through the Solomons, they could threaten the South Pacific outposts of the Allies at Noumea and elsewhere. They could control New Guinea—and the entry to Australia.

The Allies, led by the Americans, had other ideas about this threat. The question was, could they come to agreement on what to do and, if so, would they have the power to pull off their plans? The first priority for the Allies in 1942 was to defeat Hitler, and the U.S. and Britain were in a constant discussion over how to allocate forces in the two theaters. The British, with their island home under Nazi blitz and separated by only a few dozen miles from Hitler's Wehrmacht, understandably thought that Japan, though a mortal enemy, should be held at bay until Germany was beaten. The Americans on the other hand, and certainly the Australians and Kiwis in New Zealand, felt the hot breath of the Japanese enemy more intensely.

But even with that issue of priority out of the way, what to do? Where should the most effective Western resistance be directed? Even as Japan rolled on to victory after victory, and as the Philippines finally collapsed, American strategists were looking hard at how the tide could be turned, Japan could be rolled back, and Asia liberated.

Some thought the U.S. should strike out straight across the central Pacific, from Midway on to the Marshalls, Carolines, and then the Marianas, coming up what amounted to a "central highway" to Tokyo. But others, championed by MacArthur, wanted to take the southern route, up the Solomons, safeguarding Australia, destroying the base at Rabaul, then moving on to the promised liberation of the Philippines, and north to Japan. The U.S. was still a long way away from being able to pursue either strategy. But when the time came, it would be nice to know which way to go.

As strategists pondered the map in the first half of 1942, increasingly the initial priority seemed to be to hold off the Japanese push toward Port Moresby. While it was too early to challenge any other part of the empire, at least the southeastward advance should be stopped.

Then, even as the embers of Midway were still hot, the U.S. in June ascertained that the Japanese had decided to go all out to fortify their position in the Solomons. Adm. Ernest King, a proponent of the more aggressive strategy against Japan focused in the Solomons, now feared that unless the U.S. acted quickly, the Japanese might actually consolidate their positions adjacent to New Guinea and the Coral Sea. Japan had already established its seaplane base at Tulaghi prior to the Battle of the Coral Sea. But as that stalemated battle proved, Tulaghi wasn't enough to support an invasion of Port Moresby; the Japanese needed stronger air support if they were going to take all New Guinea and hold it. They needed more air bases in the Solomons, and the first one they elected to build would be on Guadalcanal.

In early July 1942, the Americans began planning to capture Tulaghi and Guadalcanal in what they called Operation Watchtower; only a few days later, they learned of an airfield under construction at Guadalcanal. The Americans threw their offensive into high gear.

There is no single Battle of Guadalcanal; Guadalcanal was really a series of vicious naval encounters and bloody land battles that went on from August 1942 until February 1943. Nearly 50 ships from both sides went to the bottom of what came to be called Iron Bottom Sound, and thousands died on land and sea. Guadalcanal also set a pattern for many of the engagements that would follow, as the U.S. doggedly pursued its strategy to roll Japan back. Fierce naval and air combat would be combined with amphibious action, as thousands of men were landed to take island redoubts that were defended to the death by the Japanese.

The first U.S. amphibious assault in the South Pacific went disarmingly well. On August 7, in a daring surprise attack, U.S. forces swept ashore at Guadalcanal and took the airfield. By the next day, they had also taken Tulaghi. Three U.S. carriers, *Enterprise*, *Wasp*, and *Saratoga*, supported the invasions. Adm. Frank Jack Fletcher commanded the invasion fleet.

If only the rest of the war had been that easy. But it was not to be. The taking of the two airfields was followed on August 9 by a U.S. naval debacle that is known as the Battle of Savo Island. It should have been a fair fight, with forces about evenly matched, but in fact, it made the U.S. look like the Laurel and Hardy caricatures the Japanese were using to psych up their troops. Savo Island was so disastrous for the U.S., and American errors so numerous, that later investigations pointed the finger of blame at just about everyone—so no one was penalized.

Once the Japanese commander, Vice Adm. Gunichi Mikawa, heard about the surprise American invasions on August 7, he assembled an impromptu naval force that would prove very effective. It included the flagship *Chokai* and four other heavy cruisers, two light cruisers, and one destroyer. They set off at full speed for Guadalcanal, and because they were steaming along in broad daylight down the slot in the Solomons, they should have been seen. And they were—on August 8, by an Australian air patrol, but for some reason the report didn't make it to the American command for another eight hours.

The second error seems to have been Admiral Fletcher's decision to withdraw his carriers a full day early, on August 8, leaving all the other ships in the area at the mercy of whatever Japanese air attack materialized. Aside from the fairly green Marines onshore at Tulaghi and the new Guadalcanal airfield, which would be renamed Henderson Field, the victorious American force was now exposed.

A third mistake: The ships that remained on the scene were divided into three ineffective groups. H.M.A.S. *Australia* and her sister ship *Canberra*, plus *Chicago* and two destroyers guarded the southern entrance into Guadalcanal Sound; *Vincennes*, *Astoria*, *Quincy*, and two destroyers guarded the northern approach; and a third group was positioned between Guadalcanal and Tulaghi, where it missed the battle completely. But worse, these three groups had no battle plan and only poor contact with one another.

Named after the battle, Iron Bottom Sound holds the remains of some 50 American, Australian, and Japanese ships that went down here or in adjacent waters, as well as numerous planes and small craft. A pattern for island warfare was also set at Guadalcanal: intense naval and air action coupled with amphibious landings.

The fourth error went to Rear Adm. Richmond Kelly Turner, commander of the South Pacific Amphibious Force. He decided on his own that the Japanese would not attack the night of August 8, and compounded that by sailing off to have a late-night conference with his Australian counterparts. As a result, when the attack did come, he and his ship were off the scene, and he had left interim command to a very unfortunate subordinate, Capt. Howard D. Bode of *Chicago*.

Finally, when Japan sent scout planes flying over the sound at about 11:00 p.m. that night to see what awaited them, the Americans concluded they were friendly aircraft and let them circle the area for a good 90 minutes. Thus the Japanese pilots were able to send back detailed information on ship positions to their own ships, which were actually just out of sight.

Confident of their night-fighting capabilities and the bizarre response of the Americans, the Japanese charged ahead full speed. Coming into what would later be known as Iron Bottom Sound, between Guadalcanal and Savo Island, at around midnight, the Japanese lit up the scene with flares so as to better see their prey, and in a furious bombardment and torpedo attack destroyed *Canberra* in a few minutes. Then *Astoria* was turned into a fireball and *Quincy* was sunk, followed to the bottom a short time later by *Vincennes*.

During this crisis, interim commander Captain Bode in the *Chicago* was in position to fire away at the Japanese cruisers that were pulverizing the Americans, but instead he sailed off after an enemy destroyer. Bode was so disgraced that he later killed himself.

What was it like for the sailors on deck during this hellish time? Early in the morning of August 9, around 1:40 a.m., as he recalls, *Astoria* quartermaster Don Yeamans finally learned what it was like to take a full Japanese air attack head on. Not that he, a veteran of Coral Sea and Midway, had been just a spectator thus far. At Guadalcanal, *Astoria*'s mission was to support the amphibious landing of Marines. *Astoria* and the other destroyers had shelled the islands, working in four-hour shifts around the clock, so by August 8, everyone was tired. Then, on that fateful day leading up to the night attack, Japanese horizontal bombers had hounded the U.S. ships for hours, although in Yeamans's recollection they only scored one solid hit, the transport ship *Coolidge*.

That night, he was on the bridge. "We knew the Japanese were coming," he says. "We'd known they were on the way since sometime in the afternoon. But what we didn't know was how they had speeded up, and would get to us that night. They'd accelerated from 17 knots to 24. Not knowing that, our captain decided that general quarters wouldn't be sounded until 4:00 a.m. He wanted everybody to get a good night's sleep.

"The first thing I remember of the Battle of Savo Island was after one in the morning," he says. "I heard a tremendous explosion in the far distance, and then I could see fire on the horizon. It was the *Canberra* being hit, about eight miles out. Then the shells started hitting us, around 1:40 a.m.—just a few minutes after *Canberra*. I saw the explosions as they hit, and everybody started yelling. The other quartermaster, Roy Radke, was a good buddy of mine. Without getting authorization from the captain, he sounded general quarters right then and there. All hell broke loose. For a few minutes he was in danger of being court-martialed, as

everybody argued about what to do with him. When it was clear we were under attack, the mood changed. I calculate that Roy's action probably doubled the number of survivors."

When the first shells hit, Yeamans was standing on the port side. Then he heard a huge explosion at starboard and ran to see what had happened. Crew member Larry Armbrust had had his eye blown out, and others were attending to him. Just before Yeamans left to return to his original position, another shell hit where he was headed, killing navigator Guy Eaton and chief quartermaster Brom. Then, as though destiny were homing in on him, a shell hit right where Yeamans was standing.

"The blast knocked me ten feet," he says. "I was deaf for a month. To this day I have no eardrum on my right side. But after I came to, what got me was how everyone was doing his job, following orders, helping out. I didn't see any panic like you see in the movies. No, everybody was calm, even though terrible things were going on all around us.

"At this point the captain ordered everybody off the bridge. We had a hard time getting out of there under fire, but we got to the forecastle. Once there, we found nobody could get aft, to where the fires had broken out.

"I ended up in a raft," Yeamans says. "First the destroyer *Bagley* picked me up. Around daybreak we went back to the *Astoria* to pick up wounded. At this point the captain ordered all able-bodied sailors back onto the *Astoria*, to try and save her. So I went back on. We organized bucket brigades and fire brigades. That day we also had the heaviest rain I'd ever seen in my life, and it put out the fires on deck. But that didn't help the ones below.

"There was also an attempt to tow *Astoria* with a tug. The tug tied us up and pulled us stern first. But a huge hole had been blown in our stern, and as we started to move, huge amounts of water flooded into her hull. When it was clear this was going to sink the ship, the tug stopped. Maybe it was too late for us by then. Around noon, we were ordered to abandon ship. This was the second time I abandoned *Astoria*. And for the first time I was afraid."

Yeamans was afraid because all morning, sharks had been circling the wounded ship. While he was ready to deal with incoming Japanese fire, he wasn't eager to tangle with a shark. And this time around, he didn't have a raft. He would have to go into the drink.

"Aside from my own concerns," he says, "I was also trying to get Roy Radke to jump ship. Roy couldn't swim, so I kept coaching him: 'One, two, three,' I'd say, and then he wouldn't jump. After about three such attempts, I told him he was on his own. The ship was just about to roll over, and if he didn't get off, he was gone. So he finally jumped."

For life preservers, the two men used the watertight cylindrical containers for five-inch shells. As they moved away, the *Astoria*, protector of *Lexington* and *Yorktown*, rolled over and sank stern first. The men were picked up by the destroyer *Buchanan*. "From there," he says, "I went to the transport *Jackson*, which took me as far as the New Hebrides. Then I rode the *Wharton* to Pearl, and finally on to San Francisco. You don't know how glad I was to see that bridge. Later I was reassigned to a converted British yacht that was doing duty as a sounding craft in the North Atlantic. The other guys would complain about how cold it was up there. I said, 'At least we aren't being shot at.'"

By the end of this slaughter, the U.S. had lost four heavy cruisers, a destroyer, and nearly 1,300 men, including many officers; half as many were wounded. Japan also had been given an opportunity to take back her airfields. The American transports and Marines on shore were now totally at the mercy of the attackers. This was Japan's opportunity for total victory. But what did the Japanese do? In a twist of irony, the side that had been almost error-free in the first naval battle for Guadalcanal now made the biggest mistake of all. Just as Admiral Inouye had hesitated in his moment of relative victory after Coral Sea, pulling back his Port Moresby invasion when he probably could have charged ahead, Admiral Mikawa also held back, and then withdrew. He thought that Fletcher and his carriers were still in the area, and on that mistaken premise he swiftly pulled back to the safety of Rabaul.

So after having been walloped, the Americans were given an accidental reprieve. Despite Allied naval ineptitude, the new Solomon airfields still remained in American hands. But just barely, because without air cover, the remnants of the American fleet that had brought the Marines and survived the Battle of Savo Island now had to withdraw.

In the coming weeks, the action at Guadalcanal shifted to land. The U.S. now had 16,000 Marines on shore. Japanese intelligence had failed to ascertain so large a presence, and thought it was only a few thousand. Misinformed and still hampered by overconfidence, the Japanese in the third week of August now mounted a relatively small counter-invasion to the east of the U.S. presence at Henderson Field. One group of more than 800 Japanese, who had been trained to occupy Midway and never got the chance, planned to redeem themselves on Guadalcanal. They charged into battle against a superior adversary, and in one hellish night were totally exterminated by the Marines, who lost only several dozen men.

This pattern of combat—more akin to slaughter—would become an unfortunate characteristic of the way the two countries would meet in battle, as the U.S. fought its way up the various Pacific island chains toward Japan. Japan would increasingly entrench its men on those islands it still held, in caves and bunkers, under orders to fight to the death and never surrender. The only way to end their threat to Americans was to kill them.

That first overwhelming American jungle victory, at the Tenaru River, began to boost morale among the Marines and the Army, who had watched the Japanese sweep so efficiently across similar jungle terrain in the Philippines and elsewhere in the Greater East Asia Co-Prosperity Sphere. Maybe there was hope for the Americans after all, when it came time to go toe-to-toe on land.

As the days ticked by, and the Americans became ever more dug in at Henderson Field, it would become increasingly difficult for the Japanese to dislodge them. Yet, for the moment, the Americans had lost control of the naval arena, and had no air strength to speak of. The Japanese had a huge base at Rabaul and other forces arrayed to the north, in the Carolines. Why didn't they throw all their firepower at Guadalcanal and retake what had been theirs? Perhaps they just didn't think this American foothold was significant enough. Perhaps they were still fixated on holding their forces back for what they thought would be a more important engagement. Whatever the answer, their hesitation would come back to haunt them.

Late in August Admiral Yamamoto did decide to hit back harder. He sent a more sizable force from the anchorage at Truk Lagoon, including Pearl Harbor

Terror of night battle lights the skies over Tassafaronga as a force of American warships surprises a much smaller group of Japanese destroyers. With Japanese forces on Guadalcanal in dire need of resupply, Rear Adm. Raizo Tanaka had developed the technique of loading supplies into barrels and throwing them overboard from destroyers speeding close to shore.

He was engaged in this action on November 30 when Rear Adm. Carleton Wright attacked with four destroyers and a line of cruisers. But at this point in the war, American torpedoes were short-range and inefficient. Not so those of the Japanese: Tanaka ordered his ships to turn and fire, sinking one American cruiser and putting three others out of commission for a year.

carrier veterans *Shokaku* and *Zuikaku*, fresh from their post-Coral Sea repairs and re-equipping, and the smaller *Ryujo*, plus three battleships, nine cruisers, thirteen destroyers, and a swarm of submarines. But strangely, in light of the onshore massacre his men had suffered a few days before, he sent a small landing force of only 1,500 men to reinforce his beleaguered garrison on the western tip of Guadalcanal.

The Americans would face him with *Enterprise*, *Saratoga*, and *Wasp*, and they were in position by August 23. But once in place, Admiral Fletcher now began to worry about fuel again. Thinking he had several days before the Japanese would arrive, he sent *Wasp* off the scene to fill up with fuel. With his carrier force now reduced to two, he had miscalculated badly.

On the morning of August 24, American scout planes first found the carrier *Ryujo*, about 280 miles from the American carrier position. Shortly thereafter, another group of Japanese ships was discovered 245 miles away. Planes were immediately dispatched from *Enterprise*, and on the way out they passed Japanese attack planes inbound for Guadalcanal. While these Japanese planes reached the island, they failed to inflict much damage on Henderson Field. At this point Admiral Fletcher ordered planes to be launched from *Saratoga*, bound for *Ryujo*.

Early in the afternoon, radio reports clarified the nature of the second group of Japanese ships. Apparently much bigger game was within range: *Shokaku* and *Zuikaku*. Fletcher attempted to divert his fliers from *Ryujo* to the larger carriers, but due to radio failure was unable to get his orders through. Some of them did stumble on *Shokaku*, which was about 60 miles in front of *Ryujo*, and managed to score one hit. But the bulk of the American fliers headed on to *Ryujo*, and began to pummel her with bombs and torpedoes. She took a punishing collection of hard hits and, at 8:00 that night, sank to the bottom.

But American elation was short-lived. Even as American planes were en route to *Ryujo*, Admiral Nagumo was sending fighters, dive bombers, and torpedo bombers from *Shokaku* and *Zuikaku* to hunt for their counterparts. By midafternoon, *Enterprise* was under fire and had suffered three serious hits. A bomb near the aft elevator killed several dozen sailors and started a fire. Watertight integrity was broken; the ship

listed three degrees. Two other bombs caused damage and fatalities, one at a five-inch gun gallery and one on the flight deck. In all, about 74 men died and another 90 or so were wounded.

As *Enterprise* cleaned up the damage, the crew found she was still able to make nearly full speed. But at about 5:00 in the afternoon, rudder control was lost just as another wave of attackers from the Japanese carriers was hunting for her. In a major run of good luck for the U.S. forces, the attackers couldn't find their target, *Enterprise*'s rudder control was regained, and the Americans averted a disaster.

Later that night, Admiral Kondo, head of the battleship force, tried to find the American carriers, but failed and withdrew. Other Japanese ships shelled the Marines on shore, failing to dislodge them but making their lives perilous in the process. The Battle of the Eastern Solomons was over. It was judged an American victory because the Japanese airfields were still in American hands. But the victory was a narrow one, since two Japanese carriers remained untouched.

August 1942 closed with a bizarre mishap and a major personnel change in the U.S. command. Admiral Fletcher's flagship *Saratoga*, operating southeast of Guadalcanal, was torpedoed by a lone Japanese sub. Again his worst fear had come true. He already had lost *Lexington* at Coral Sea and had lost *Yorktown* at Midway. Would he lose "Sara" too?

In effect, he did. While *Saratoga* didn't sink, she took months to repair, and so was out of action at a time she was sorely needed. Samuel Eliot Morison suggests that this was why Fletcher was reassigned to the North Pacific, never to return to the critical theaters where the Pacific war would be won.

Tactical mistakes at Guadalcanal show the brutal verdicts on quality of leadership that real combat can render. Just as we never know who will be a hero until men come under fire, we also don't know who has the ability to win a war until war breaks out. Fletcher had had a proud career, and he was a loyal and prudent man. But in the eyes of some of his critics, his innate caution and formative years in the old school of battleship tactics put the mind-boggling new world of carrier strategy beyond him. Just as the Pacific War made Spruance a winner, it told Fletcher he would need to serve in some other way.

September and early October planted the seeds of the next major naval encounter, the battle of Cape Esperance on October 11–12. During the interim period, it's not as though the two sides were just resting, awaiting their next date with destiny. No, in fact both sides were engaged in a mirror-image effort to fortify their respective holdings on the big island. The Japanese still held the western end of Guadalcanal, while the Americans controlled strategically critical Henderson Field.

A curious pattern evolved during this time. Just as the U.S. and Japanese divided the island, they also divided the day and night. During daylight hours, U.S. sea power was fairly dominant, so escorted transports brought in troops and supplies on a daily basis. But night went to the enemy, and the Americans hunkered down during the darkness while Japan ran its Tokyo Express resupply effort down the slot from Rabaul.

Tokyo Express was becoming a formidable operation. Despite some initial hesitation in early August, by the end of the month Admiral Yamamoto and the Japanese High Command had realized that primitive little Guadalcanal was now the fulcrum of the shifting balance of power in the region. If the island could not be retaken and the airfields recaptured, the perimeter of the empire would be in danger in a second important region. The Japanese had been trounced in the mid-Pacific; would they now start to concede the south?

The on-again, off-again invasion of Port Moresby over the mountains from Japanese enclaves in northern New Guinea was on indefinite hold. While Japan had thousands of men and several bases in the north, they were now left to bide their time while the focus shifted to Guadalcanal. And they had another obstacle in their path: Port Moresby now had more than 50,000 Allied men there under Gen. Douglas MacArthur.

Back onshore at Guadalcanal, while neither side dared try to eliminate the other party, they clashed constantly during those weeks between naval battles. A mid-September Japanese offensive called the Battle of Bloody Ridge saw 1,000 Japanese slaughtered, while only a few dozen Marines died.

Almost to the day of that battle, the carriers *Wasp* and *Hornet* were ordered to act as escorts for a huge resupply and transport convoy headed for the American encampment at Henderson Field. The scene was fairly tranquil until Japanese subs appeared out of nowhere and in a stunning blow destroyed *Wasp*, while also hitting the battleship *North Carolina* and destroyer *O'Brien*. The loss of *Wasp* was not good for the Americans, although most accounts tend to give it short shrift. For Vice Adm. Robert L. Ghormley, Fletcher's replacement, it must have felt at the time like two steps forward and three back. In reality, it was not so bleak, for eventually the United States prevailed. But on a day-to-day basis, or even month-to-month, any movement toward victory was hard to discern. The best that could be said was that the U.S. was not retreating anymore.

At 741 feet long, *Wasp* was smaller than *Hornet*. She'd been built at Quincy, Massachusetts, by the Bethlehem Shipbuilding Company and was launched in April 1939, christened by Mrs. Charles Edison, wife of the assistant secretary of the Navy. After shakedown cruises off the East Coast, *Wasp* had done duty in the North Atlantic in support of convoys bound for Europe, and in late 1941 and early 1942 had ferried British aircraft from Scotland to the embattled British forces on Malta.

Jack Martin was a seaman 2nd class on *Wasp* on September 15, 1942, the day she went down. Only 18, he had joined the Navy just before his birthday. He'd joined because he was only earning $10 a week in his home state of Missouri. He had two brothers in the military, both of whom happened to be at Pearl on December 7, 1941. Both survived that attack, although his brother Leon, a Marine, would later die in the bloody 1943 invasion of Tarawa in the Gilbert Islands.

Compared to the action that some other sailors had seen, Martin considered that he and his *Wasp* crewmates had had a pretty easy time of the war, even up to the day when she was sunk.

"A lot of us had what we called 'free day' that day," he said, recalling how ordinary September 15 had seemed. "While my usual duties were on the deck force—painting, scrubbing, cleaning—that day I was on the 20mm gun watch, forward of the bridge. I was sent below decks to get a Thermos of water. At about 3:30 in the afternoon, while I was down below, the first torpedo hit and exploded, and knocked me down. I got up and picked up the Thermos. Then the second torpedo hit, and it may have gone right through the ship, because it didn't explode, but it knocked me down a second time. Then the third torpedo exploded,

Continued on page 146

Braving a blizzard of flak, four Japanese bombers come in low at Guadalcanal seeking vulnerable U.S. transports, at left. In August, in the Allies' first major offensive in the Pacific, Americans successfully landed some 6,000 Marines on Guadalcanal, seizing the island's airfield from the 2,000 Japanese defenders. Over the next few weeks, both sides brought in more and more forces, and frightful fighting took place. By October, the Japanese had 36,000 troops ashore. Supply transports for both navies were fat, slow-moving targets, under nearly constant attack.

Blossoming like a fiery chrysanthemum, a Japanese bomb explodes on the deck of the U.S.S. *Enterprise*. Other bombs put holes in the carrier's flight deck, damaged one of her airplane elevators, and temporarily disrupted her steering control. But she was able to withdraw to fight another day. The most decorated American ship of World War II, *Enterprise* would be home to some 30,000 men over the course of the war.

Oily waters burn just beyond *Enterprise's* rail, minutes after two Japanese dive bombers narrowly missed the ship and crashed in flames. American carriers, vulnerable to attack by bombers as well as torpedoes, were later fitted with a torpedo blister along three-quarters of their hulls, both above and below waterline. To protect against attack from the air, they soon bristled with 20mm and 40mm antiaircraft guns and radar-controlled fire directors.

Continued from page 139

and I and the Thermos went down again. At this point, I dropped the water and decided to get the hell out of there." Never having been under attack like that, Martin had no idea what was going on. But once he got back up on deck, the whole forward part of the ship was in flames. The torpedoes had hit right under the gun mounts where he had been on duty, and if not for the order to go get the Thermos, he might not have survived. "One of our officers from the Third Division who did stay behind was blown 60 feet from the gun mount, and he landed up on the bridge. He was badly injured, but survived.

"We'd sent 18 of our aircraft over to *Hornet*," he adds, but planes were still on board, and some of the crew started pushing them over. The ammo magazines were exploding, we'd lost all power, and all communications were done. The word was passed to abandon ship, and so like all the other crew, I headed for the fantail of the ship." Among those abandoning were the injured, mostly from severe burns. Only some of them would survive. Of the roughly 2,700 men on the ship when she was hit, 185 died.

Although the ship was mortally wounded, her screws were still turning for the first part of the evacuation, Martin recalls. "Some of the guys panicked and jumped in too soon, or too close to the screws. I bet 85 of the 185 we lost were their own fault, for jumping too close to the screws. They just got sucked under. People were doing crazy things. I saw one guy jump over fully dressed and with a big field telephone strapped on his back. I'll bet the weight of it broke his back when he hit the water."

Once in the water, the trick was to survive. There were no lifeboats, but Martin made it to a raft. On board that raft, the wounded had been placed on a wooden pallet in the middle, while able-bodied sailors floated in the water, hanging on the side.

"I was in the water for about four-and-a-half hours, as night fell. It was a long time. And I thought I'd been through a lot, until I found out that some of us were in the water all night long. Finally the destroyer *Lansdowne* picked us up. The *Wasp* was sunk by torpedoes from *Lansdowne* and went down around 9:00 that night."

While on *Lansdowne*, Martin saw four burials at sea, burn victims now wrapped in canvas bags and put overboard. From *Lansdowne* he went to *Salt Lake City*, which took him to the New Hebrides, and then on to the mainland U.S., where he was reassigned.

After the sinking of *Wasp* in mid-September, the stalemated land forces continued to reinforce themselves, and Guadalcanal became a microcosm for the whole war. After Japan's dazzling sweep across Asia, she was now truly stalled by an enemy gradually becoming her equal. Still, the Americans could not yet muster enough punch to roll the enemy back decisively. As evidence, the Tokyo Express seemed to be growing in intensity. On the night of October 11, a huge enemy convoy arrived, including seaplane carriers and destroyers loaded with soldiers, supplies, and ammunition. American forces were determined to slow down this flow, and just before midnight opened fire on the Japanese, surprising them.

But both sides failed to distinguish properly between friend and foe; both sides held their fire when they should have let loose with everything they had; both sides mistakenly shot at their own countrymen. On October 11–12 Japan lost the cruiser *Furutaka* and the destroyers *Fubuki*, *Natsugumo*, and *Murakumo*, while the U.S. destroyer *Duncan* was eliminated. This engagement could best be called a stalemate, and despite the muddle of the naval battle, both sides were able to keep landing materiel and reinforcements for their respective land garrisons.

Skirmishes continued through October 15, and on the night of October 13 the Japanese mounted a ferocious bombardment of the American airfield from their cruisers, blowing holes in the Henderson runway, destroying nearly 50 aircraft, and killing Marines and GIs. In some analysts' eyes, October 15 was the low point of the American campaign on Guadalcanal. The growing American forces onshore were still suffering from supply disruptions. Fuel was a critical problem, especially for aircraft.

On occasion, Henderson-based fliers had to forego attack opportunities because of insufficient fuel, or had to scrounge fuel from damaged planes so they could fly short missions. Although resupply was attempted by aircraft, they couldn't carry enough fuel as cargo to be worth the trouble. Submarines also were used. Even the humble *Vireo*, the tug that had tried to save *Yorktown* at Midway, played a part at Guadalcanal, towing a barge loaded with gasoline.

Laney Chouest, the author's research ship, is a former Louisiana mudboat meant for operating around drill rigs in the Gulf of Mexico. Here off Guadalcanal, it carries *Sea Cliff*, a three-man submarine, and *Scorpio*, a remotely operated unmanned craft, both for searching the seafloor.

On October 18, Admiral Ghormley was replaced as Commander, South Pacific, by Vice Adm. William F. "Bull" Halsey. Like Fletcher before him, Ghormley was a solid skipper. But Admiral Nimitz believed that naval victory in the South Pacific required a more charismatic and inspiring leader, and Halsey was seen to be that man.

As America puzzled her way through these situations, Japan now sensed the balance of war shifting in its favor once again and designated October 22 as the day it would retake Henderson Field. Aggressive bombardment of the U.S. camp began, and Japanese land forces surged forward, trying to break through the American perimeter. But despite heavy American losses, the Japanese were held back. Meanwhile the Japanese fleet steamed offshore, awaiting word that Henderson Field was theirs. By October 25, the Japanese thought they were about to win. Knowing that *Wasp* was gone, they believed their four carriers—

Zuikaku, Shokaku, and two light ones—would give them the edge. But what they didn't know was that *Enterprise* was back in action after bandaging injuries sustained a few weeks before.

The last carrier battle of Guadalcanal began to take shape in the Santa Cruz Islands, several hundred miles east of the Solomons. Early on the morning of October 26, after reading several reports of Japanese carriers being sighted, Admiral Halsey ordered an all-out attack on the enemy flattops. Only an hour earlier, the Japanese had sighted *Hornet* and dispatched their own aerial attack. As in other carrier battles, the two opposing air forces passed each other on the way to their respective targets. Several American bombers went after light carrier *Zuiho* and put her out of action for the time being. The Japanese force meanwhile arrived over *Hornet*, missing *Enterprise* for the moment, which was still under cloud cover. *Hornet* took a punishing attack from more than two dozen Japanese planes.

Dangling from its mother ship, *Sea Cliff* heads off to work. The craft belongs to the U.S. Navy, which participated in this expedition to help commemorate the 50th anniversary of the Guadalcanal battles. Navy submariners pilot the submersible.

Even as *Hornet* was on the ropes, her own fliers arrived at *Shokaku* at about 9:30 in the morning. While they didn't sink her, they hurt her so badly she was out of commission until mid-1943. The light cruiser *Chikuma* was also injured badly enough to go to the sidelines. But by midmorning, it looked like another standoff. The Japanese now went after *Enterprise*, trying to tip the balance their way. While they hit her several times and killed nearly 50 of her crew, none of the damage was serious. But wounded *Hornet*, being towed by a destroyer to a safe haven and repair, was bombed again. She was abandoned at about 3:30 in the afternoon.

Hornet coxswain Clarence Logsdon, age 23 and in command of the lookout division, lived through that perilous day on his duty station above the bridge, forward of the signal bridge.

"*Hornet* was a happy ship," he says. "We had two good skippers. Everybody liked it. But everybody also understood that we were in war. Life was tough while we were at sea. Most of the time in the South Pacific we were four hours on duty, four hours off, around the clock. That meant everybody was sleepy all the time. During your off period you didn't have much time to do more than sleep, eat, do your laundry, or clean up. I think we'd been at sea for 101 days straight by the time we were sunk. We were running short of food, although we had plenty of fuel. The food wasn't bad, considering the circumstances. The only shore leave we got during the Guadalcanal period was at Noumea, New Caledonia.

"Some time that morning of October 26," Logsdon continues, "the first wave of Japanese planes came in, and they let us have it. One crashed into the signal bridge just 20 feet from me and killed everybody on it. Not from the crash itself, but from the aviation fuel. They were all on fire, and they died right in front of us, before we could do anything to help. A good friend of mine was among them, a signaler 1st class named Nations. After they were dead, because of the efforts to save the ship, we had to move them out of the way.

"I think the Japanese had put a death warrant on *Hornet*," says Logsdon, "because of our role in Jimmy Doolittle's raid on Tokyo. When those enemy planes would fly in that day, they ignored every other ship on the scene and just pounded *Hornet*. It was a revenge thing." Logsdon thought his own number was up when a Japanese dive bomber headed straight for the ship and didn't pull out of his dive.

"I remember him coming right at me," he says. "I thought, this one has Logsdon written all over it. He released his bomb, but kept coming down. I couldn't take my eyes off him. But why hasn't he opened fire or pulled out, I kept thinking. I wondered if maybe he had been hit by a shell and was dead. He and the bomb finally crossed the ship from the port side, and crashed into the water 50 yards from *Hornet*. To this day, every time a I hear a plane in a dive, it reminds me of that experience.

"After that first wave," he says, "I told somebody that if anyone was to ask how long that first attack had lasted, I would have answered, 'an hour.' In fact, it was only six minutes long. But it sure seemed like an hour."

While *Hornet* was badly hurt, she wasn't considered finished yet. While much of the surviving crew fought fires or tried to deal with the list that Logsdon guesses went to 30 degrees, he remained at his duty station, heading the lookout division. "I don't remember much about that time," he says. "I don't remember eating or anything else during that whole attack."

As the day wore on, the crew made determined efforts to save the huge carrier. They even got her under tow by a destroyer. But every time they thought the battle was over, Japanese planes would reappear. Finally around 3:30, the order to abandon ship was given, and the crew had to go over the side.

"The distance from the flight deck to the water is pretty high," says Logsdon. "I ended up climbing down a rope to the water. For some reason the guy behind me was really pushing me, saying I wasn't going fast enough. When I got to the end of the rope, there was a bucket attached, and because I was trying to get out

of this fellow's way, I got my foot caught in the bucket. I finally had to let him go around me before I could get my foot out. Later on, while we were swimming, this same guy found an officer's cap floating in the ocean and put it on. He said it was the quickest promotion he'd ever gotten."

Logsdon and the others were in the water for only about half an hour while the destroyer escorts circled, picking up survivors. He was picked up by *Anderson*. Once *Hornet* was considered lost, *Anderson* and others fired torpedoes into the dying vessel. Among survivors like Logsdon and others, there is some dispute about whether it was American or Japanese torpedoes that sent her down. Whoever delivered the coup de grace, *Hornet* went under early on the morning of October 27.

Encouraged by the sinking of *Hornet*, Yamamoto wished to continue the battle in hopes of taking down *Enterprise*. But Big E and her escorts withdrew from range, thus ending the engagement.

Tactically (though not strategically), the Battle of Santa Cruz Islands looked like a narrow Japanese win. The U.S. now had only *Enterprise* and *Saratoga* left of her Pacific carrier fleet. In nine months, *Lexington, Yorktown, Wasp,* and *Hornet* had all gone to the bottom, In effect, Japan's Midway losses of *Kaga, Akagi, Hiryu,* and *Soryu* had been avenged, albeit slowly. How would the U.S. bounce back?

As October rolled into November, the U.S. position on Guadalcanal began to look even more precarious. By mid-month, the uninterrupted Tokyo Express had brought Japanese troop strength up to the level of the U.S. force at Henderson Field for the first time since the Americans had seized the airfield. Admiral Yamamoto was now throwing everything he could at Guadalcanal. To balance this effort, the U.S. also needed to keep bringing in men and materiel. But how to do it without carrier support?

Never a shy and retiring fellow, and with no other choice than to let Japan dominate the theater and perhaps evict the Americans, Admiral Halsey elected to fight without the carriers, letting the battleships and cruisers show their stuff. The cruisers *Atlanta, San Francisco,* and others escorted a convoy of freighters and transports to Lunga Point off Henderson Field on November 11 and 12. Two dozen American submarines were also patrolling the waters off the Solomons, as insurance.

Continued on page 154

In one of the war's earliest amphibious landings, U.S. troops wade ashore on Guadalcanal. Most of the men were Marines barely out of boot camp, who had been slated for several more months of training before seeing any action. Their one rehearsal for an amphibious landing, on Fiji, had been a disaster; and they were carrying the same model rifles used by the Marines of World War I.

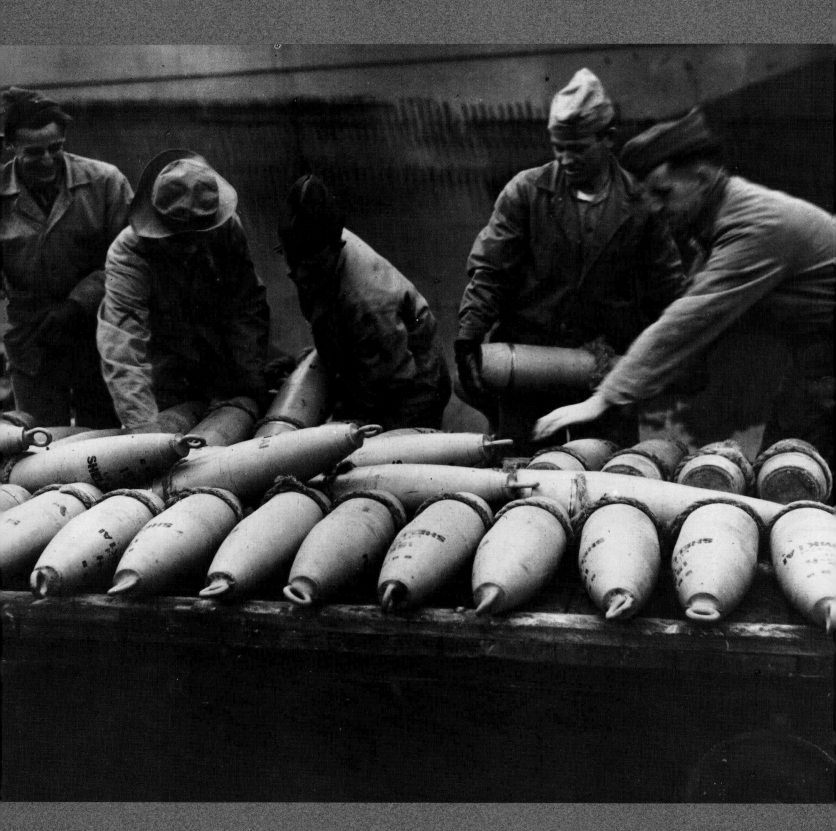

On Guadalcanal, unloading munitions—and reinforcements—became a never-ending chore. Historian Richard B. Frank calls the battle for this island "a literal turning point," because once victory was secured here, the Allies could turn directly toward Japan. "After almost exactly six months of struggle, sweat, and blood," Frank adds, "the 2,500 square miles of fevered jungle and sunbaked plain called Guadalcanal was in American hands."

Taking care of their own, Marines tend to the wounded. In addition to Japanese gunfire, thousands of Americans on Guadalcanal were felled by malaria. Nonetheless, according to historian Harry Gailey, the Marines "performed what appears to have been superhuman feats" here and throughout the Pacific. To their families back home, remote Guadalcanal moved in just a few months from total obscurity to the legendary status it still retains.

On November 12, what is called the Naval Battle of Guadalcanal began, not far from the coordinates of the first American-Japanese fight off Savo Island. As American transports were unloading that day, Japanese bombers hit them. While they were fought off with only slight damage to the Americans, Japan came back that night with a huge Tokyo Express made up of ten destroyers, four cruisers, and two battleships, outnumbering what the Americans could muster. The two forces didn't meet until after midnight on November 13, but once under way the encounter was furious. The first American ship to go down was the destroyer *Cushing,* followed by the destroyer *Laffey* and the brand new destroyer *Barton,* with most of her crew, while the destroyer *Monssen* was burned into oblivion. Later that morning the light cruiser *Juneau* sank with her crew of 700. Among them were the five Sullivan brothers, whose tragic loss prompted the Navy Department to end the practice of assigning family members to the same ship. The cruiser *Atlanta* was later scuttled.

Joe Baker was a 17-year-old seaman 2nd class on *Cushing* on November 13, 1942. Originally from Colorado, he'd joined the Navy after Pearl Harbor. He'd gone aboard *Cushing* as an apprentice seaman, but his commander promoted all apprentices to seamen 2nd class their first day on the ship. Baker's initial combat experiences were at Santa Cruz on October 26, when *Cushing* was escorting *Enterprise.* "I saw the air battle over my head," he says. "We were shooting at Japanese planes all day. Afterward we picked up about 20 of our downed pilots, either from *Enterprise* or *Hornet.*"

He recalls how on November 12, the ship was bombarding the Japanese encampment on the west end of Guadalcanal. "While we were doing that, we got reports of about 20 Japanese planes coming in. We and the other ships knocked almost all of them down and rescued more of our downed pilots afterward. By that point, we'd been shooting for several days, and we were tired. But the officers warned us we'd have another long night. Half could sleep for four hours, the other half would be on duty."

American intelligence had said that this night's Tokyo Express would be unusually large. While the Americans might be outnumbered and outgunned on the water, the decision was made to block the enemy convoy and prevent it from unloading. In effect, this would mean a nighttime naval battle, a surprise to the Japanese, who had grown accustomed to moving their ships about after dark without serious threat.

After midnight, Baker was at his general quarters station, gun 3. He remembers the crew of that gun clearly and says that the gun captain was John Vilyou, a "good hard-nosed gun captain." Baker is still superstitious about the omens surrounding him when he and *Cushing* went into battle that night. "As we went toward the approaching Japanese, we were the lead ship going in, of 13 ships in all. We were in destroyer squadron 13, and here it was just barely Friday the 13th.

"Everyone was following us, and just as we started in, two Jap destroyers crossed in front of us. To keep from ramming them, we made a hard right. Unfortunately, all the ships behind us misunderstood what we'd done, and they all took the hard right as well."

The result, in his opinion, led to a fatal disorder that put everyone at high risk. "At this point," according to Baker, "we all started shooting at each other. The Japanese battleship *Hiei* hit us at least 13 times. That was one mean battleship. All those hits stopped us in the water. She came down our starboard side firing away. We had no power by that point and had to do everything manually. Every time one of those Japanese searchlights came on, we tried to fire back at it. *Hiei* was so close we could see her men running around on deck. She was that close."

Death was also that close, on a night that would see two rear admirals and hundreds of sailors die. Although Baker won't dwell on it, of the approximately 200 on board *Cushing,* a third died in the attack and a third were wounded. In his words, "Bodies were flying all over the place." One friend apparently found a body on deck that had been blown in half by the Japanese shells. He was certain the dead man was Joe Baker, and was surprised and glad to see Baker alive later.

Fire and explosions wracked the ship from all those direct hits. With the ship dead in the water, *Cushing*'s skipper ordered everyone to leave. "I was getting ready to abandon ship with everyone else," Baker says, "but my gun captain said, 'Not yet.' With the *Hiei* so close on our starboard side, he wanted us to get off as many shots as we could. So we manually pulled our gun around to point it at the *Hiei.* Three or four of us had to sit up on the gun barrel to get it down to the right angle for firing.

The only ammo we had was night shells, but we loaded them and got off two rounds at the enemy ship. One of them hit the bridge. Once we'd done that, our gun commander said we could jump ship."

Baker went in with a life jacket but fell into an oil slick so bad that the jacket was quickly ruined. Somehow he survived in the water for another 16 hours, well into the next day. "Finally our rescuers pulled alongside," he says. "The first thing I noticed was a .45 pointed at the bridge of my nose. Before they would let us on board they wiped off all of our faces to make sure we weren't Japs."

Cushing, wallowing in her death throes, floated until an explosion took her down on the afternoon of November 13. The carnage continued throughout the day. The Japanese battleship *Hiei* was sunk by a combined force of fliers from *Enterprise* and others from Henderson Field. It was the first Japanese battleship the Americans had ever sunk. On November 14, the U.S. destroyers *Preston* and *Walker* went down, and early on the 15th, Japan's battleship *Kirishima* was hurt so severely she needed to be scuttled.

What to make of this melee? While the tonnage of American and Japanese iron sent to the bottom looked about equal and seemed so mutually debilitating that neither side could ever muster a naval action again, historians judge the rolling three-day Naval Battle of Guadalcanal to have been a narrow American victory, because Japan's all-out efforts to recapture Henderson Field and push back the fledgling American offensive in the Solomons failed. Specialists conclude that just as Midway drew the line in the mid-Pacific, Guadalcanal drew the line in the South Pacific. And then, despite furious resistance, both the lines started to roll back in the direction of Tokyo.

But movement toward Tokyo was still measured in inches rather than miles. On November 30 the Japanese inflicted a painful naval defeat as the Americans tried to interrupt another Tokyo Express by night. The cruiser *Minneapolis* was immobilized, *New Orleans* and *Pensacola* suffered explosions but were later repaired, and the cruiser *Northampton* was sunk outright. But despite this and other Japanese successes and the formidable efforts of the Tokyo Express, it seems that Tokyo's forces on the island were not getting what they needed to survive, much less to take back the island. In fact, they were starving.

By early January, Prime Minister Tojo, architect of the lightning occupation of a huge chunk of Asia, had to make a very painful decision. His strategy—built on advance, conquest, and occupation—now harvested the bitter fruits of defeat and withdrawal. His grand plans were starting to unravel, and strategists in Tokyo were being forced to do what Americans had done since Pearl Harbor day: improvise. Were they up to the task?

As Japanese troops on Guadalcanal foraged for food, Japanese resources were now being diverted to the central Solomons island of Munda, another 200 miles back up the slot, another 200 miles closer to the base at Rabaul, and another 200 miles closer to Tokyo, which was still 4,700 miles away. At Munda, the Japanese would build a new airfield, to replace the one they had lost at Guadalcanal. The question was, would it serve the same purpose? Was it there to support the postponed invasion of Port Moresby? Or was it defensive in nature?

On January 4, 1943, Prime Minister Tojo decided to quietly remove his forces from Guadalcanal, conceding it to the Americans. So gradually and discreetly did he do this that the Americans didn't know they had won the island for another month. They even mistook the evacuation as a resupply, because it looked just like the old Tokyo Express. And the Japanese didn't just turn tail. No, they fought bitterly to cover their retreat. On the water they were still able to score a few points, such as sinking the cruiser *Chicago*, which had survived the August debacle at Savo Island only because her skipper, Captain Bode, had mistakenly taken her out of the fight. Fulfilling the date with destiny she'd missed in late summer, *Chicago* was sunk on January 30, 1943.

On February 7, U.S. forces finally learned that Guadalcanal was theirs. They swept through the Japanese camp to discover that nobody was home. Oddly, the duel to the death that had been building since August ended in a whimper.

What sort of a tally sheet had the U.S. and Japan run up, after all that death and destruction? The U.S. Marines and U.S. Army had won the land battles with many fewer casualties than the Japanese. About 24,000 Japanese had died on or around the jungled island with the Arab-Spanish name, versus 1,600 Americans dead, 4,200 wounded in combat, and several thousand more felled by tropical disease. Naval losses, however, were another matter. According to Samuel Eliot Morison, the losses at sea have never been calculated, although he says that each side lost two dozen combatant ships, totaling nearly 50. And that doesn't count the transports or support craft like PT boats.

What an agonizing victory for the United States, and at what a price in blood and iron. What an orgy of ship sinkings. Unlike the later one-sided shooting gallery at Truk Lagoon, most of the Guadalcanal ships went down in fiercely contested battles.

I was drawn to search for graveyard Guadalcanal in 1992 for a variety of reasons. First, because there are so many ships permanently at rest in Iron Bottom Sound and adjacent waters. And because Guadalcanal marked the beginning of the U.S. advance on the Japanese homeland. And finally, because the name of that once-obscure island has become metaphorical for all the courage, the folly, and the tragedy of the Pacific War.

In the summer of 1991, I conducted a preliminary sonar survey of Iron Bottom Sound and adjacent waters. The bottom there is about 2,000 feet down, not nearly as deep as at Coral Sea or Midway. Unlike the vast search area of featureless ocean at Midway, at Guadalcanal the search area was fairly well defined by Lunga Point and Savo Island. And unlike Midway, my targets didn't number five. I knew that nearly 50 combatant ships were on the bottom, plus countless other transports, aircraft, tugs, PT boats, tenders, and so on.

Looking back on it, that preliminary expedition was handicapped not only by the usual technical glitches, but also by a lack of equipment and money. We were operating on a shoestring, and during the month that I spent out there, it seemed as if everything was falling apart at increasing speed: the ships, electrical systems, tether cables, and switches. Still we plowed along, "mowing the lawn" with sonar. While we did pick up a number of targets that I was pretty sure included the H.M.A.S. *Canberra* and some of the destroyers and perhaps one or two of the Japanese ships that had gone down near Savo Island, sonar reports weren't good enough for National Geographic, the potential sponsor of further exploration. I needed visual confirmation.

With only 24 hours left before I had to get on the plane and leave, I resorted to a risky solution. We towed a video camera suspended just above the bottom across

the sound, attached to the sonar we'd been using to map possible targets, knowing that the sonar and camera might hit a ship's stack or volcanic protrusion and be lost forever. We first tried this over a target I thought was a Japanese destroyer. We used sonar to give us a feel for the bottom before switching on the camera. Suddenly the bottom came into view. We were clearly above the ship. Quickly the sonar operator lowered the camera sled toward the ship, then leveled it off, easing it to about 15–20 feet from the wreck. It nearly gave me heart failure to work this way, but it made for great pictures. After about four passes over the ship our nerves once again gave out, and we hauled the sled back to the surface to see how we had done.

The results were fantastic. We had great images on the video and could only assume the stills were just as good. Was it a Japanese destroyer? Time would tell. We could make out torpedo tubes on the deck of the ship, but both American and Japanese destroyers carried such tubes. With what we thought was the destroyer *Yudachi*, or something like it, under our belt, our confidence grew. Without thinking further, I gave the order to head for what I thought was the *Canberra*. The weather was great. We were in the groove. Now was the time.

Before we knew it, we were drifting in the current above what I thought was the Australian heavy cruiser *Canberra*. It had become the focus of our trip because it was one of the largest ships to go down in Iron Bottom Sound, the first to be destroyed in the Battle of Savo Island, and the only Aussie ship lost there. The Australian High Commissioner had greatly helped us in getting our permits, and the crew of our search vessel, *Restless M*, was from Australia, so *Canberra* was a constant subject around the dinner table. As we made a camera pass over what we thought might be that ship, word started to circulate—and our Aussie crew began to migrate into the control room to see the action unfold.

We entered maybe-*Canberra*'s location into the navigation computer. Once on site, we lowered the camera sled until it was 150 feet above the bottom, and the first camera run began. Soon, a large target passed beneath the camera sled as it was lowered farther and the camera systems were turned on. The sonar trace revealed a very complex superstructure having numerous deck levels. We didn't have to see visually to know we were on top of a large ship.

One of countless skeletons in the Guadalcanal graveyard, this U.S. Navy Hellcat carrier-fighter didn't enter the war until early 1943—after most of the big carrier battles had already been fought. But it was a powerful plane and a match for any Japanese aircraft of its day.

To get really good images, we had to bring our ship to a stall position, an exercise that proved to be utterly hair-raising at Guadalcanal. Normally, risky operations such as camera runs are carried out in the comfort of a control van, where we sit at the terminal of a computer, punching in commands that drive a sophisticated dynamic positioning system. The computer instantaneously converts our positioning requests into digital commands to the ship's complex thrust system, which includes bow and stern thrusters. Regardless of the winds and currents at the site, the thrusters hold the ship on station, hovering directly over the target while the camera lowerings are made.

But *Restless M* had no such system. Like *American Islander* at Pearl Harbor, it was just a simple ship with a simple engine, a single screw, and a rudder. It had no bow or stern thrusters to spin it on its axis or to move it sideways. For me, overcoming this lack was a real challenge. Standing at the wheel on the bridge, I used

nearby islands to sense my location. Savo was due north, Cape Esperance lay to the west, and the Florida Islands were to the east. I had a rudder indicator, a gyroscope, and a navigational display that showed the movement of the ship and the speed we were making over the bottom. The wind, currently blowing out of the southeast at about 10–12 knots, would have to serve as my bow and stern thrusters.

Our method was to head into the wind and then throttle back on the controls until the ship stalled out over the wreck—and then let the crew below in the control room make runs or thrusts toward the bottom.

Again and again we circled the sunken ship, stalling out over its decks below. Again and again the camera sled darted downward, fired off its cameras, and escaped without becoming entrapped in any wreckage. We repeated these familiar steps over and over, until I felt that we really were starting to push our luck. If the camera sled happened to get tangled on a gun barrel

Continued on page 165

"Those have got us," said Ensign Durr to Rear Adm. Leigh Noyes, as they saw torpedoes approach their ship, the carrier *Wasp*. Two, fired by Comdr. Takaichi Kinashi from a submarine only 1,000 yards away, struck *Wasp*'s starboard side a moment later. The explosions threw airplanes on deck into the air, while high-octane fuel from tanks and the pumping system burst into flames. Here, a distant *Wasp*, her fire-fighting water system knocked out, burns helplessly and begins to list.

Wasp survivors take their ease aboard the crowded destroyer *Laffey* after their ship went down. *Laffey* would later suffer attack from three Japanese ships. Her stern blown away, her steering and propulsion systems destroyed, she burned out of control and exploded as she sank, killing many still aboard or in the water, including her captain.

AN AMERICAN LEGEND

After several attempts, John F. Kennedy, second son of the U.S. ambassador to Great Britain, was finally accepted for Navy enlistment in 1941, when he was 24. His bad back had been the obstacle. Ensign Kennedy first held a desk job at the Office of Naval Intelligence in Washington, D.C., then a brief assignment in South Carolina, as well as officers' training in Chicago. But in 1942, he saw what he really wanted to do. He wanted to captain a patrol torpedo boat, a PT.

PT boats appeared in 1940, and they were built of plywood. Most took shape in Bayonne, New Jersey, at the Elco Navy Division of the Electric Boat Company, later acquired by General Dynamics. PTs ended up serving in all naval theaters of World War II. Aside from John Kennedy's sinking, other PTs have their place in history. One captained by John Bulkeley bore General MacArthur and his family just before the Philippines fell to Japanese invaders. More than 300 PT boat crewmen died in action, out of more than 60,000 who served on the craft. More than 500 PT boats were launched in World War II, of which about 70 were lost. Roughly 30 of those went down in combat, while 40 succumbed to Mother Nature, accident, or friendly fire.

The PTs were about 80 feet long and, with three engines of between 1,200 and 1,500 horsepower each, they could make 40–45 knots. They weighed between 40 and 60 tons. But because they were built for speed, not endurance or safety, they were constantly breaking down, and their torpedoes weren't terribly reliable.

PT service attracted Kennedy, as it did other young New Englanders with sailing backgrounds, because the small boats were fast, their missions were exciting, and they offered a certain freedom and independence that not many in the military could enjoy. Jack Kennedy did his PT training in Rhode Island, but his back problems kept him from getting an immediate assignment. Yet by July 1943, he found himself in the Solomons, part of the naval support for the New Georgia campaign to wrest the Japanese air base at Munda from its builders. He lived in a thatched hut while he and his crew refurbished the dirty and battered boat they were given: *PT-109*.

They began to go on night training patrols, and in mid-July Kennedy was ordered into combat. His mission: to disrupt the Tokyo Express coming down the slot.

On the night of August 2, 1943, fifteen PTs sought to prevent Japanese convoys from moving through Blackett Strait, the body of water that separates the volcanic island of Kolombangara from New Georgia. Not afraid of these small attackers, Japanese destroyers powered straight through them. The young PT warriors fired torpedoes but scored no hits. And worse: Lieutenant Kennedy found himself directly in front of destroyer *Amagiri*, which plowed right into *PT-109* and cut it in two. Two members of the crew of 13 died, but the other 11 went into the water. Nine of them climbed onto a makeshift raft while Kennedy stayed in the water, towing a wounded crewman.

Five hours later they made it to a tiny island, where they found enough coconut milk and fresh water to stay alive. But Kennedy wanted his men rescued, and he swam back out into the strait the next night, carrying a pistol for protection and a

Youthful skipper of *PT-109*, John F. Kennedy barely escaped Guadalcanal with his life. On
the night of August 2, 1943, his boat was split in half by Japanese destroyer *Amagiri*, killing
two crew members and wounding others. Kennedy and 11 surviving men made their way to
a nearby island, where they spent several days hiding from the Japanese while a rescue was
arranged. Kennedy's heroism in the war would help fuel his political career decades later.

Built for speed rather than safety or durability, PT boats housed three large engines within a plywood hull that ran about 80 feet long and could race along at 40–45 knots. Not surprisingly, they attracted young sailors with a taste for excitement.

---

lantern for light, hoping to find a U.S. ship. Luck wasn't with him. The next morning he wrote a message on a coconut shell and dispatched an islander to take it to an Australian coastwatcher, one of the scattered Allied covert surveillance teams that radioed reports of Japanese ship and troop movements. A large group of islanders came back to rescue Kennedy and his men, taking them to safety in a camouflaged dugout.

The Japanese base at Munda finally fell to the Americans on August 5. With *PT-109* gone, Kennedy was assigned to a gunboat, but saw little combat. After nine months in the South Pacific, and plagued with intensifying back pains, Jack Kennedy returned to the U.S. for surgery. He was

awarded the Purple Heart and the Navy and Marine Corps medal for Gallantry in Action.

As for *PT-109,* she's probably lying in about 1,000–2,000 feet of water in two pieces, and no one knows how much of her plywood hull has survived. Says author Ballard, "Someday, I'd like to look for her, this sunken reminder of how a slightly different position or speed for *Amagiri* or *PT-109* might have changed the outcome of history. If Jack Kennedy had died in Blackett Strait just as his elder brother, Joe, died in super-secret Project Anvil in England in 1944, the President who succeeded Dwight D. Eisenhower in 1961 might have been Richard Nixon, Lyndon Johnson, or Hubert Humphrey. Or someone else."

Continued from page 157

or a torn railing on the bridge, that would mean one camera sled—and visual confirmation—lost forever.

Time seemed to melt away. We had started our first camera runs in the debris field about 7:00 in the morning. By the time we finished our final run on what I thought was *Canberra* it was midnight. It was hard to believe we had gone nonstop, but we were now sensing fatigue.

As the camera sled came back aboard for the last time, everyone gathered in the control van for the replay. Once again, the cheers went up as images of anti-aircraft guns passed beneath our camera. We had done it. We had great images. We had pulled it out of the fire with only hours to go.

But that was just my preliminary expedition to Guadalcanal. The following summer we came back to the scene, this time with the support of the U.S. Navy. We had enlisted the *Laney Chouest*, which we would use later at Midway, replete with her dynamic positioning system and two state-of-the-art Navy submersibles, the unmanned *Scorpio* and the manned minisub *Sea Cliff*. We came back to finish the work we'd done the year before, to find and photograph as many ships as we could, including Japanese vessels. And this time around we came back with a film crew, assorted Navy underwater specialists, as well as battle survivors from the U.S., Australia, and Japan.

All in all, we found 13 ships in our two-year effort—*Atlanta, Ayanami, Barton, Canberra, Cushing, DeHaven, Kirishima, Laffey, Monssen, Northampton, Quincy, Yudachi,* and an unidentified wreck we think was either *Little* or *Gregory,* one of two destroyers lost in minor actions in September 1942. We found the first ship that Japan fired on in the Battle of Savo Island—the doomed *Canberra*—although it was not the wreck that we had photographed in that high-risk attempt the previous year; that turned out to be the cruiser *Northampton*. And we found the last big ship sunk during the Naval Battle of Guadalcanal, the Japanese battleship *Kirishima*. Not bad, though I wish we could have found every ship and plane that went down during that hellish time.

Looking back over my logs from the expedition, I remember several days in particular. One was July 26, 1992, when we did a dive on what I thought was *Akatsuki* but what turned out to be U.S.S. *Monssen*. As soon as I, the pilot, and our cameraman Mark Shelly got inside the *Sea Cliff* minisub and sealed the hatch, the temperature and humidity became unbelievable. It had to be in excess of 100°F and 100 percent humidity, an underwater sauna if that's possible. The heat was intensified for me because I'd put on sweatpants under my jumpsuit, thinking it was going to be cold. After all, the ocean temperature at 2,000 feet down runs in the mid-30s, and I expected that would chill the minisub. No such luck. Diving this way was such a physical ordeal that I later decided not to take a battle survivor in his 70s down with us. I had wanted to do it, but if something went wrong we'd have a hell of a time getting him out of the minisub. And the medical facilities at Guadalcanal were just about what one would expect on an island in the developing world. I wanted this mission to be a success untinged by tragedy.

Water depth was around 2,200 feet, and about halfway down we dropped weights and came to a halt. After trimming out the sub, we dove the rest of the way, landing on an undulating, coarse-grained, white-sediment bottom with a current of about five knots coming from the east. We picked up the sunken ship on our sonar at a range of about 500 yards. We were heading west when we landed, so the ship was directly behind us. Turning around, we began heading the sub toward the sonar target. Visibility was good but not excellent; we could see out about 30 feet. As we continued to close on our target, driving along at about six feet above the bottom, the pilot suddenly saw a hull in the distance and came to an immediate halt. Our sediment cloud caught up with us, covering us and dropping the visibility to zero. The sunken ship was acting like a windbreak, keeping the sediment hanging over us. The cloud seemed to take forever to clear—actually, about 30 minutes—before we could barely make out the hull in front of us, at a range of about 35 feet. We could see white sea fans and sea anemones attached to the vertical rising hull.

I wanted to move forward and use the vertical steel hull to calibrate my cameras, so we went about 12 feet from the ship and stopped again. Once more we were covered by our sediment cloud and had to wait another 20–30 minutes for it to clear. As the dust finally dissipated, the pilot expressed concern that if we advanced any closer we'd have the ship's hull hanging out over us. Clearly not a good idea for our minisub, so

0.35

7.29

104.

Her starboard plating replaced by marine growths, the Australian heavy cruiser *Canberra* lies on the bottom. Attacked by five Japanese ships during the night of August 9, *Canberra* suffered 24 hits in just four minutes. Hopelessly damaged, she was scuttled the next morning.

we decided not to push our luck and go closer without knowing anything about the ship and its structural condition or how precariously it might be seated in its resting place. I requested that we pump variable ballast so the sub could rise and then continue to power up and over the ship, to do a series of camera runs along the axis of the ship.

At first the pilot was a little nervous about hovering over the ship. Additionally, as soon as we rose clear of the hull, the current hit us in the face and wanted to push us back off the wreck. This was clearly the case when the pilot turned to drive along the axis of the ship and increased his sail surface to the current. Despite a first run that was a little ragged, we finally reached the bow of the ship, where we were reassured to find that the vessel was sitting upright, not heeling over as we'd initially thought. Its bow was pointing northeast

on a bearing of 30–35 degrees. We executed excellent second and third video runs as the pilot gained confidence in the directions we gave him.

We had great visibility from our vantage point 30–40 feet above the wreck. We could see the main guns and the two sets of torpedo launchers, each consisting of five tubes side by side. The smokestacks had fallen over so that we could see the holes they'd left in the deck. After our third run we felt we knew the ship. We then moved out over the bow into mid-water, spinning around, and descended to face the bow and begin collecting high-quality color video.

As the sub landed, the copilot reported a hard ground in the port-side battery pod. That shook the pilot so much he wanted to return to the surface immediately. It was hard to argue with him because the dive had gone so well. Trying to salvage as much as I could from the moment, I asked him to close in on the bow as he rose, so I could get some good color stills. As we rose, we saw that the bow was beautifully ornamented with sea anemones and long, gooseneck barnacles, a magnificent sight.

We had another great dive on July 29, when we conducted a joint operation with *Sea Cliff* and our ROV *Scorpio*, over the wreck of *Canberra*. We landed approximately 500 yards from the ship, and when we started driving toward it we began to see debris scattered across the ocean floor. As we came up on *Canberra's* bow, it reminded me of my second dive on *Titanic*. The ocean bottom here was covered with anchor chains, and I could make out a deep hole next to the port bow of the ship. While waiting for *Scorpio*, we tried to rise, but the pilot had blown the fuse on the lift props, so we couldn't power up. We then began to pump ballast, but still we didn't ascend. Next we began to drop weights, with no result. We dropped all of the auxiliary weights but still we didn't rise more than a few feet.

Being 2,000 feet down in a very hot minisub with limited oxygen and life support, I began to feel a bit nervous, to say the least. The thought of entanglement came to my mind. I remember how, when I dived on *Ben Franklin*, we unknowingly were dragging a long tube full of lead, which controlled our altitude above the bottom. We would rise until we'd lifted enough lead off the bottom to equal our buoyancy, and then we would stop. I began to imagine that the chain we'd seen on the bottom near *Canberra* was now attached to our stern. As we dropped weights, we would rise until we lifted enough chain to equal what we'd dropped, and then we would stop rising. The same thought clearly was on the pilot's mind. He requested that *Scorpio* come look at our stern to see if anything was attached. *Scorpio* saw nothing.

While we couldn't maneuver, a strong running current enabled us to ascend far enough to land on the bow of the *Canberra,* just in front of the forward gun. Our stern came to rest on an anchor windlass, which caused the sub to go bow down, making it difficult to see *Scorpio*. To fix that, we rested the forward portion of the sub on the splash guard, just in front of the forward gun. This gave the sub a better angle for viewing. We then directed *Scorpio* in front of us, to backlight the gun.

After the first run, the unmanned *Scorpio's* crew on the surface wanted to inspect the ship by heading aft along the starboard side. The plan was to go around the ship and come up on the port side, but the currents were so strong they couldn't pull it off. As if things weren't difficult enough already, surface winds had increased to 40 knots, making it hard for *Laney Chouest* to move *Scorpio* back toward the bow where we were waiting. As a result, what we thought would take 30 minutes turned into three hours. Finally *Scorpio* returned to do some additional backlighting.

We then requested that *Scorpio* move back to the bridge and wait for us. We began to pump ballast again, but the sub wouldn't budge. We pumped all but five pounds of variable ballast before, miracle of miracles, the sub finally began to move up, albeit slowly. But instead of moving ahead past the two forward guns to the bridge, we were blown off the starboard side of the ship by the current, and ended up beneath *Scorpio*. We began to back away from the ship and drop down to the bottom. After what seemed like an eternity, we got the situation under control and headed out away from the wreck, while the crew above recovered the ROV *Scorpio*.

What the hell was wrong with the sub? I was determined to find out once we got back on our mother ship. It turned out that *Sea Cliff* was carrying a massive load of mud, which the pilot had plowed up while transiting toward the ship in the early part of the dive. Better mud than anchor chains or cargo nets or lead pipes.

And so it went. We had good days and bad at Guadalcanal. Just like in the thick of battle, sometimes the bad days are so bad and so numerous you begin to wonder why you are out there at all. You begin to question if you are getting what you want. You wonder if entropy and inertia and the god of technical glitches aren't winning. But then you see the faces of the surviving veterans when you roll those videos or develop your color stills. You see the wrecks themselves, so little changed from the day they went through their death agonies and sank into that watery resting place. You get a priceless glimpse into a past, into a war, into a world that is gone forever.

We found 13 wrecks at Guadalcanal, but could only identify 12. I wanted to find 50 if I could. I wanted to fill in that incomplete mosaic that is our history of the Pacific War, to find all the ships that survivors and veterans write and call and e-mail me about. Joe Baker, the superstitious young sailor who, in the naval Battle of Guadalcanal, rode *Cushing* into the maw of death on Friday the 13th of November, might say I was smart to stop at 12. But that's not the way I am. I want to find them all. If I have the time and the money, I'll try.

But there are so many other battlefields and graveyards yet to find and explore. After Guadalcanal, the great Pacific War ground on and on, taking the fight ever closer to Japan. The Allies continued to push the empire backward, fighting a culture that didn't accept the idea of retreat or surrender, that would rather die in battle or commit hara kiri than acknowledge the error of its ways.

Even though the U.S. was on the offensive, and Japan was inching backward after Guadalcanal, in late 1942 and early 1943 we were still fighting the war on Japan's terms. We saw that we would have to assault and win island fortress after island fortress, spending blood and treasure in the process. It would be nice to say that we would win because of the innate justice of our cause. But as I pore over the story of the Pacific War, I'm forced to conclude that we won, just as Yamamoto feared from the start, because we were bigger and stronger and had more men and metal to throw at them. Since the Japanese grand strategy of building the mid-Pacific defense line was now a lost dream, their hard reality became an inevitable collapse of that which had once expanded with such ease. Just as a supernova falls back into the swallowing pit of a black hole, so the Greater East Asia Co-Prosperity Sphere was beginning to implode.

In 1943, however, that implosion was still tentative. By spring, huge numbers of Marines and GIs had been assembled in rear-area bases such as Nouméa. General MacArthur was eager to move up the slot and make it an American slot. But not until July did the real advance begin, because only then did MacArthur feel that air, land, and sea control were sufficient.

One good omen for the Allies, in April 1943, was their brilliant interception of Admiral Yamamoto when he flew to Bougainville in the Solomons to inspect the Japanese naval base there. U.S. codebreaking told of his flight plans, and American P-38s from Henderson Field met him in the air that morning. They shot down the bomber that carried him, killing all aboard. The archi-

tect of the daring plan to defeat America was now dead, one more casualty of the great Pacific graveyard.

When the time came to move forward, the U.S. went for the new Japanese base at Munda, on New Georgia Island in the central Solomons, built just as Guadalcanal was being abandoned. Believe it or not, it took 34,000 Marines weeks to dislodge one fourth that many Japanese from Munda. On their island bastions, the Japanese had the advantage of holding the high ground, while the U.S. had the disadvantage of attacking from the sea. Up the Solomons the U.S. inched in July 1943. *PT-109* (*see sidebar, pages 162-164*) went down as part of the campaign to take Munda, which finally fell on August 5. Progress, to be sure, but not fast enough. The Allies had another 4,700 miles to go to get to Tokyo.

Then someone realized that perhaps it wasn't necessary to let the Japanese set the agenda; the Allied forces didn't have to crawl along the island pathway stone by stone. Instead, they might leapfrog some locations, and not expend time and treasure to clean out every enemy nest. They would pass on to the next stone or two, take that one, and in the process, weaken and cut off those left behind.

That was certainly the case with the big base at Rabaul on New Britain. MacArthur wanted to take it, but Gen. George Marshall ordered him to leapfrog it and deal with it later. After all, Rabaul had 100,000 Japanese troops and tons of equipment and supplies earmarked for the invasion of Port Moresby that never happened. Taking Rabaul head-on would make the Guadalcanal bloodbath look like a tea party. Instead the U.S. would push its way up the slot, fighting the Battle of Bougainville, hitting the Japanese bases on the north coast of New Guinea, piercing the Bismarck Archipelago toward the lost Philippines that MacArthur had vowed to return to—with or without taking Rabaul.

By February 1944, MacArthur was landing troops in the Admiralty Islands, and by April the U.S. had taken Manus, the largest of that island chain, also seizing the first-class anchorage at Seeadler Harbor, which would become a major U.S. staging area in the push toward Tokyo. So by early 1944, Japan's withdrawal up the "southern highway" to Tokyo was well established. MacArthur was happy as a clam, moving ever closer to the Philippines. But was that enough to win the war?

At rest for the past six decades, this propeller marks the Japanese battleship *Kirishima*, scuttled by her crew after participating in what would be one of the last battleship-to-battleship fights of the war. The last big ship sunk during the battle for Guadalcanal, she was one of 13 wrecks found by the author and his team.

Not at all, in the minds of the U.S. high command. The "central highway" to Japan, the one that led through the mid-Pacific islands—the Marshalls, the Gilberts, the Carolines—also had to be secured. Japan's Combined Fleet still had huge stores of men and ships based in places like Truk in the Carolines. These forces could still wreak havoc, even if they couldn't lure the Americans into the Great All-Out Battle.

And so with the approach toward the Philippines well under way in early 1944, our story moves to the more northern battlefields and graveyards—places like Truk and Tarawa and Enewetak—where thousands died and where dozens of great ships went to the bottom.

But before we do, let's quietly remember those from all nations and of all ranks who went down in Iron Bottom Sound, or up and down the slot through the Solomons, including Isoroku Yamamoto himself. They made our history; they made our world. While standing on the volcanic sand beaches of Guadalcanal and Munda and the Santa Cruz Islands, I think of them. I think of all the lost carriers, of *Wasp* and *Hornet* and *Ryujo*, of all the fine battleships, cruisers, and destroyers like *Hiei*, *Kirishima*, and *Canberra*, and the submarines, the doomed transports, and PT boats. I think of the thousands who died. They went down for republic and for empire. They mingled their blood with these tropical waters, and they mixed their steel and their bones with these coral reefs and sandy shores, with these sweltering swamps and winding rivers. These almost prehistoric lands so far from the center of things are forever touched by the memories of our terrible history, our brave legacy.

CHAPTER FIVE

TRUK LAGOON

Marines assault Tarawa, November 1943

Tarawa, Truk Lagoon, Enewetak, 1941-1942

WHILE BOTH FIGHTING FOR AND LEAPFROGGING ISLANDS UP THE "slot" to reach the Philippines was essential to evicting Japan from the South Pacific, the central Pacific "highway" through the Gilberts, Marshalls, and Carolines also had to be secured. Not only did Japan have considerable quantities of ships, men, and materiel based in the area but also it could draw on these resources to impede the Allies' southern campaign. These islands would be the necessary stepping-stones and staging areas to support the final American hammering of Japan itself. A militarist nation that would fight to the death, and commit suicide before surrendering, would most likely have to be conquered on its own soil, and occupied, before it could be subdued. That would be no small task for the Americans, crossing 4,500 miles of water between Pearl Harbor and Tokyo. The central islands would provide a pathway.

But the amphibious island campaign through the central Pacific, based on lessons learned in the Solomons, would be very complicated. Huge numbers of men, ships, and aircraft had to be coordinated, often without ever coming together until D-Day—operations that in their own way were as complicated to pull off as the effort to build the atomic bomb.

A TBF Avenger, by 1944 the most common bomber on carriers, flies over a Japanese *Asashio*-class destroyer already under torpedo attack. To pressure the Japanese elsewhere, the Allies in February 1944 began attacking their base at Truk in the Caroline Islands, destroying some 300 aircraft and 200,000 tons of merchant shipping there.

Advance planning and a mind-boggling logistical train were critical, as was the ability to see around corners and to think three steps ahead. Leaping into battle without adequate forces and adequate planning, when intelligence about enemy strength was not always adequate, could turn a seeming advantage into sudden disaster. The best example of how not to fight this island war was that arrogant and suicidal Japanese ground assault early in the Guadalcanal campaign, the Battle of Alligator Creek. More than 800 of 900 Japanese troops had died or been wounded, versus only a few dozen American defenders. The only way the American attackers could overcome the entrenched Japanese defenders was through a combination of superior force, superior planning, and superior strategy.

It took months for the U.S. to assemble all the pieces to attempt this with reasonable confidence. And in the process, much of the massive operation would pass through Pearl Harbor, where this gigantic war had started two years before.

But by the fall of 1943, the critical mass of American men, ships, and materiel had reached a level sufficient to win high-command approval for an offensive campaign in the central Pacific, the equal of which was already under way down south. The first thrust was in the Gilbert Islands, called Operation Galvanic.

The first part of the Gilberts campaign was a softening up by carrier-based planes. Bombers were sent over on a daily basis beginning in mid-November, while surveillance aircraft swept again and again over the area, trying to ascertain the strength of the Japanese forces there. Meanwhile, the huge amphibious and support force was being built up with components from Pearl, as well as from American bases in French Polynesia.

The naval component of the Galvanic striking force was the new Fifth Fleet, under the command of Vice Adm. Raymond Spruance, which included the new carriers *Yorktown* and *Lexington,* replacing their namesakes that had gone down at Midway and Coral Sea. Plus three smaller carriers and almost two dozen new destroyers.

The massive amphibious arm was led by Rear Adm. Richmond Kelly Turner, with a ground force of predominantly Marines commanded by Maj. Gen. Holland M. "Howlin' Mad" Smith. The Americans in

Operation Galvanic numbered more than 100,000.

The easiest ground assault came on the Gilbert Islands atoll of Makin, and even it provided a foretaste of difficulties to come. Defended by only about 800 Japanese, Makin still required four days to be subdued by an American force two dozen times that size. The ground attack went like molasses, permitting Japanese submarines to pump torpedoes into the idling American support fleet.

Japan also showed off its still superior night-attack prowess, which included dazzling flares that lit up American targets like deer in the headlights. The American "baby flattop" carrier *Liscome Bay* went down on November 24, taking more than 600 men with her, including Rear Adm. H. M. Mullinnix. Navy Seaman Leonard Bohm was 19 years old at the time, and he believes that the nearly 650 men who went down with his ship constituted the greatest loss of life in a U.S. carrier sinking. U.S.S. *Hamilton* lost more men, but it didn't sink.

"Our ship had a brief life," Bohm says. "She was commissioned on August 6, 1943, and she went down on the morning of November 24, so we on the crew hardly got to know each other. She was built at Vancouver, Washington, and was less than 500 feet long. She was that new class of baby flattop. They built 75 of them, and five were sunk. We were the first to go down." After the debilitating losses of the four large and very expensive carriers in the Pacific, the smaller class was designed to be expendable. Each one carried about two dozen planes.

At predawn on November 24, 1943, Seaman Bohm had just returned to his bunk from general quarters. His normal duty in the event of a hit was helping build wooden racks to shore up watertight doors and partitions. As he lay in his bunk, suddenly there was an impact and all the lights went out. Bohm and the other survivors would have only 20 minutes to get off the boat.

"I don't know who led me," Bohm says. "But I and some of my bunkmates made our way up above. We came out on the catwalk. My chief was above me, and he ordered me to back out of there and get on a knotted rope, to lower myself into the water. Just beyond him, the ship was engulfed in flames. He ordered me onto the rope because of the fire, and because there was too much risk in jumping. Big pieces of flight deck had been blown into the water. So I went in with an inflatable life-belt. Once in the ocean I gave it four puffs and it inflated."

There, in the rising light of dawn, he could see the damage done to *Liscome Bay*. One or two torpedoes had hit fuel and ammo and blown away the mid-section of the ship forward of the bridge. The engine room was gone. A major piece of the flight deck was gone. The remainder of the ship was engulfed in what looked like the flames of a volcano. There was no hope of saving *Liscome Bay*, nothing to be done but to try to save yourself. After all, the baby flattops were built to be expendable, and their sheer numbers offset the loss of a few.

"I saw her go down," Bohm says. "She went down stern first with her bow up in the air. There was no suction. Most of the men who died never knew what hit them. We lost a rear admiral, and our skipper, plus all those men." He spent two or three hours hanging onto a piece of floating flight deck and trying to swim on his back. He'd been taught at boot camp that staying on his back was easier to do for long periods. Finally a destroyer, U.S.S. *Neville*, and a transport, U.S.S. *Leonard Wood*, picked up the 285 survivors. Of the wounded who came onboard, two died on the *Neville* and were given burials at sea. Bohm wasn't aware of any more deaths after those. *Neville* took him back to Pearl Harbor.

Surpassing the loss of life on Makin Island and *Liscome Bay*, the bloodiest Gilbert ground assault had already taken place on the coral atoll of Tarawa. It had begun on November 20 and wore on for four days. The main action was on Betio Beach, really a two-mile-long separate island adjacent to Tarawa that held a Japanese airfield, and a lot of Japanese fortifications. More than 4,000 Japanese troops awaited the attackers, while the U.S. Marines and others coming at them numbered more than 18,000.

The U.S. challenge was to get close enough to the island to unload all those men and supplies fast enough to minimize exposure on the beach and in the surf to withering defensive fire. Weather and tides were also a factor. The decision was made to come ashore on the morning of November 20 at Betio, the most accessible of several very forbidding landing spots. While it was the best that could be found on that little atoll, Betio was hardly an ideal spot.

Surprised in their snug harbor—11 major islands and scores of islets within a 40-mile-wide lagoon—the Japanese lost a few dozen ships and thousands of men on February 17,1944. With waters in the lagoon not much more than 200 feet deep, sport divers come from around the world to explore Truk.

As it turned out, Mother Nature, unfamiliar territory, and the enormity of holding such a disparate force of ships, planes, landing craft, and men to the same schedule worked against the U.S. The first landing force, using quasi-experimental LVT small transports, ultimately got its men on shore, but almost all of the LVTs were lost. Then the tide fell so dangerously low that tank-bearing, second-wave transports got stuck on the outer sandbar, and the tanks had to plow onshore through water that was waist deep or higher, stalling out engines. And troops had to flounder hundreds of yards through the same water, wading across a no-man's-land where they were totally exposed to enemy gunfire.

By midafternoon, the Americans were unable to move beyond a tiny beachhead and were still at risk of being turned back. By the evening of November 20, 5,000 men had landed, but only 3,500 of them remained alive and unhurt. The carnage happened the next morning, as reinforcements were again handicapped by a low tide that resulted in more than

Continued on page 181

With a furious patter, shells and shrapnel raise plumes of ocean spray. Here a Japanese torpedo bomber flies through intense antiaircraft fire to attack a U.S. carrier. Despite such attempts by the Japanese to strike back, American forces had their way at Truk: In two days they flew 1,250 sorties there, dropping 400 tons of bombs on ships and 94 tons on airfields and shore installations.

Trailing smoke screens, three Japanese ships futilely attempt to evade attack. Among the ships sunk at Truk were half a dozen tankers, probably the most serious loss to Japan. From several of them, even after half a century, oil continues to seep, worrying environmentalists. Scientist and diver Sylvia A. Earle, who has dived here, advises doing nothing. "Nature is achieving the goals men seek. May we have the patience not to interfere," she wrote. After the heavy losses at Truk, Radio Tokyo began for the first time hinting at the possibility of defeat: "The attacking force is already pressing upon our mainland," it broadcast.

Continued from page 175

300 deaths. Finally, the returning tide allowed the tide of battle to turn as well, so that by November 22 the Japanese began to lose ground. On November 23, the U.S. finally took Betio and Tarawa, with only a handful of Japanese of the original 4,500 still alive. But the victory was not easy. The U.S. had lost about 1,000 men, and more than 2,000 had been wounded.

One player in this vicious battle, as well as throughout the remainder of the central Pacific campaign, was the cruiser *Indianapolis,* which we'll look at in more detail in Chapter 7. In fall of 1943 she became the flagship of Admiral Spruance, commanding the Fifth Fleet. She sortied from Pearl Harbor on November 10 with the main body of the Operation Galvanic force, and by November 19 was one of the cruisers shelling Tarawa to soften up the Japanese positions. The next day she acted as a fire-support ship for the landings, and even shot down at least one enemy plane. She continued shelling Japanese positions until the U.S. took the island on November 23.

Graveyard Tarawa turned into a laboratory for later amphibious assaults. The only good thing one can say about that horrendous loss of life is that it compelled American planners to look hard at what worked and what didn't. Islands like Kwajalein were taken with much lower losses, thanks to Tarawa. And of course, painful as it was, Tarawa was a victory, and put the airfield in the hands of the U.S., and the U.S. that much closer to Japan.

But these are the only consolations for those who rest in graveyard Tarawa, whether in the shallows or on the beach or deeper into the island. More than 5,000 men from both sides died at Tarawa in those bloody days. I haven't been able to explore the waters of the Gilberts or the Marshalls, but my friend Jim Delgado has done work there.

"You can still see American helmets and rifles in the shallows at Tarawa," says Delgado, although underwater human remains are long gone. "This is because

"Another Spot Where Old Glory Flies," newspapers captioned this photo. A palm tree serves as a flagpole for Marines on Tarawa in the Gilbert Islands. The Japanese commander thought defenses here would last a thousand years, but Marines took the island in just three days.

soldiers were jumping into the surf in full gear, and when they were shot in the crossfire or drowned, the equipment stayed on the spot. You can still see American amphibious craft all over the reef."

Delgado has also explored underwater at Makin, where Japanese ships rest. "The whole idea of the amphibious war really comes across on these island graveyards," he says. "At Kwajalein, you can see a very well-preserved Japanese Zero in the shallows. During the battle, it tried to land, hit the water, flipped. It has broken wings."

Delgado says the Marshallese refuse to touch the wrecked Zero to this day, so there it remains. Apparently there's some reverence for the wreckage akin to a cargo cult like that which arose in the South Pacific. "That Zero at Kwajalein still has paint on it," says Delgado. "It's like time stood still."

Once the Gilberts were secure, the key to continued U.S. success was to maintain momentum. Just as forward momentum feeds on itself and plays to the advantage of the attacker, it works against the defender, who must pull forces back and create new defensive perimeters where none might have existed. It's such a confusing and demoralizing process that the trick in warfare is to keep pressing so that the enemy stays off balance. The risk to the attacker, of course, is in outrunning critical supply lines, or being cut off within enemy territory, which can be just as disastrous. But neither happened in this campaign.

The next step was the Marshalls to the northeast, as the U.S. pressed along the central highway, eventually aiming for the Marianas, where bombing raids against the Japanese home islands could be staged. Kwajalein, the first target in the Marshalls, is a sea-lion-shaped ring of coral islets, surrounding an inner lagoon, measuring more than 60 miles from nose to tip; in fact, it is the largest coral atoll on the globe.

The American assault would focus on the three islands deemed most important, where Japan had the heaviest presence—a pair of islands in the northeast ring called Roi and Namur, and Kwajalein Island in the south.

The assault presented particular problems, since there was no outer beach on which to land. In the open sea, men and materiel had to be transferred from larger craft to smaller boats called "alligators" and "ducks."

The invasion of these three islands was set for January 31, 1944. But landings would also have to be undertaken on nearly 30 other islands, using more than 40,000 American troops, to totally secure the atoll. Fifth Fleet flagship *Indianapolis* was again a key player in the cruiser group that bombarded the islands of the atoll. Her shelling on January 31 knocked out enemy shore batteries, and the following day she blew up a blockhouse and other shore installations, also providing advancing American troops with a creeping barrage of shellfire. She entered the huge lagoon on February 4, and remained there until the atoll was secured.

Motor Mechanics Mate 1st Class Eugene Beck, on LST 226, was also part of this massive amphibious operation at Kwajalein. Twenty-year-old Beck had left his job as a lab technician at a Mutual Citrus Company in California; he was responsible for tending to all the engines, motors, and mechanisms that kept the ship operating. "We were a flagship," Beck says. "We had a full captain on board who commanded 15 LSTs. We carried about 20 tanks and up to 600 troops from the Army and Marine Corps, and our crew numbered around 57.

The LST was about 228 feet long, and as we traveled through the open sea, you could see the ship bend from stem to stern. That flat bottom made it particularly rough in the water, and the bending was something to see. If you weren't used to it, to see the ship bending like that could be disturbing. One night before the landing we had a force of Marines on board. A couple of my crewmates and I were kidding around up on deck with several of the Marines who were still awake. As the ship bent, we started talking about how we didn't think she would make it through the night. That really scared the Marines, who went below and woke up all the rest of their mates. The whole crew spent the rest of the night up on deck with their Mae West life jackets on, ready to sink."

As a swimmer from California who wasn't afraid of water, Beck took the occasional duty of swimming underneath the flat-bottomed LST to cut free hawser lines that periodically got wound around the propellers. "I'd put 15-pound weights on my waist, and wore a mask with an air hose to the ship," he says. "Sometimes I was under the ship for an hour, while I cut off the twisted rope with a knife. Being under that long didn't bother me, although I was always on the lookout for sharks or barracudas. I never saw one in all the times I did that." The hawsers were part of the process of the offshore loading of the LSTs. Often Beck's ship was tied up to a larger vessel, taking on tanks and jeeps and ammo and other supplies, and the usual fenders weren't enough to cushion the LST as the seas slammed it up against a bigger ship. "Each time we did this, we got a little more bent out of shape," he says. "I'll bet every steel beam on our ship was bent from that loading and unloading, and the main deck was rippled from it."

Sleeping on that flat-bottomed LST was no treat, although Beck says the food was okay. Once, in the galley, he was pleased to find a can of powdered lemonade that he had personally inspected in his previous civilian job at the citrus company. Sleeping was another matter. "That flat bottom made traveling so rough, that I actually had to strap myself in the bunk to keep from rolling out while I was asleep. And as we would go over a wave, the stern would stick up out of the water, and the props would spin faster making a *whop whop whop* sound that made it even harder to sleep."

American commanders were determined to avoid another Tarawa, and so this time around they devoted much energy to intensified aerial bombing and shelling from offshore, to soften up the Japanese positions. Estimates are that this softening up killed several thousand Japanese on Kwajalein Island alone, although it didn't knock them out, because several thousand remained to fight on. Finally it was time to go ashore, with a two-pronged assault on either end of the atoll that began on January 31, 1944. As the weeklong battle wore on, Japan was able to stage a counterattack with bombers from Saipan, setting off ammo explosions on the northern island that killed some Americans. Meanwhile, both there and to the south, the Americans were forced to clean out Japanese bunkers one by one, and it took until February 7 to secure the whole atoll. In the end, Japan lost nearly 8,000 men, with less than 1,000 surviving. The U.S. lost fewer than 400.

The next stepping-stone to be taken was Enewetak Atoll, on the far northwest end of the Marshalls, as close to the Carolines as it was to the Marshalls. But Truk Lagoon, farther west in the Carolines, and Ponape Airfield, at the far eastern end of the Carolines, would have to be knocked out to weaken

Furred by marine growth, a Japanese bomber rests on the floor of Truk Lagoon. Once featureless, the lagoon's bed now bristles with protuberances—the scraps of war. Scientists have used them to study undersea flora and fauna and how they adapt to artificial reefs.

Japan's ability to stage naval and air counterattacks as the U.S. extended its forces westward. Truk was a major naval and air base for Japan, and it was now too close for comfort.

Truk in some ways was as important to the Japanese Combined Fleet as Pearl Harbor was to the U.S. At any one time, there were major naval forces sheltered there, but when the U.S. finally attacked on February 17, most of the combat vessels had departed. Still U.S. fliers found more than 50 merchant ships and almost 400 aircraft there, and began to pound away. Three quarters of the Japanese air arm there was smashed. The ships were sitting ducks, just like the American vessels had been at Pearl, but the water in Truk Lagoon was a little deeper, and Japan's ability to bounce back was fading fast. One Japanese combat ship, the light cruiser *Agamo*, was sunk by an American submarine as she tried to escape. On the perimeter of the atoll, the destroyer *Maikaze* and light cruiser *Katori* also went down.

Truk is a true underwater graveyard. Some call it the graveyard of the Imperial Japanese Navy, although that is an overstatement, since most of the wrecks are noncombatants. But all those transport and merchant ships were not lost without causing Tokyo great pain. As we saw with the Tokyo Express coming down the Solomons slot, massive logistical operations, though not nearly as glamorous as for front-line combatants, keep armies, navies, and air forces alive. With that many ships and that much tonnage lost, Japan could not sustain its shrinking Greater East Asia Co-Prosperity Sphere for long.

As many as 60 Japanese merchant ships and 2

Continued on page 189

Facing little opposition, Marines wade ashore on Enewetak, another strategic atoll in the Marshall Islands. Adm. Chester A. Nimitz, commander of U.S. forces in the central and north Pacific, coveted Enewetak for its lagoon, the second largest in the Marshalls; here he planned to shelter the ships he would need to make his final thrust against Japan's inner empire. Success by the Allies here helped crack the Japanese outer defense ring.

Following Pages: A gentle surf quietly washes across a fallen Marine at Enewetak Atoll. Later, death of a different sort would visit here: In 1947 Enewetak was designated by the U.S. Atomic Energy Commission as a permanent mid-Pacific proving ground for atomic weapons.

Like an underwater shrine, the mast of the *Fujikawa Maru*, an aircraft transport, rises from the bottom of Truk Lagoon. Oceanographer Sylvia A. Earle glides above the mast, now host to thriving sealife.

Continued from page 183

destroyers rest on the bottom of Truk (now Chuuk) Lagoon. In relatively shallow water of less than 200 feet, the wrecks, covered with coral and sponge, are attractions for sport divers. In fact, in that shallow tropical water the ships have become islands of life, habitats for marine plant life, and of course whole ecosystems of fish and those that feed on them.

Larry Shelvey has done extensive diving at Truk and has found some interesting wrecks, which he's written about on the Internet. One is the Japanese tanker *Shinkoku Maru,* which was sent down by torpedo bombers. He points out that the ship was one of eight oilers that helped refuel the Pearl Harbor Striking Force. The wreck, which is about 40 feet deep at the bow and 130 at the stern, has live shells sitting by a large deck gun. Shelvey has found Japanese uniforms there, covered with silt, and a large torpedo hole on the port side. He's also dived on the *Heian Maru,* a submarine tender that he says is the largest wreck in the lagoon. She's on her port side, and there's quite a debris trail around her, including torpedo bodies, machinery, and tools.

Shelvey's also explored the armed merchant cruiser *Aikoku Maru,* one of the deeper wrecks in the lagoon at about 200 feet. He says the foreship was blown apart in the final explosions, and it's sitting upright, but there's no ship left forward of the bridge. He actually came across some human remains on this one, but this is unusual. Several hundred Japanese died, he says, when the ship's munitions exploded. In the midst of all this carnage, he found an unbroken china teacup sitting upright in one of the bridge compartments.

The transport *Fujikawa Maru,* he reports, is sitting intact and upright with no list. The ship holds aircraft parts, including Zero wings. It is heavily encrusted with coral, and he warns divers that blacktip sharks cruise the wreck.

Shelvey has also visited two downed Japanese aircraft, a Betty medium attack bomber in 60 feet of water and a Zero only 35 feet down. The Betty, he reports, is missing a right wingtip and most of its tail, but the fuselage is in good shape, with not much marine growth. The plane's engines came off when it hit the water, and they rest about 150 feet away. The Zero is so shallow at 35 feet that it can be snorkeled. The paint is still on its skin, though it's upside down, with landing gear visible.

That's what evidence we can see today of Japan's painful losses at Truk. As for the flavor of the American victory at Truk and the other atolls, I'm sure that while the victors felt initial elation at getting such sweeping revenge on the attackers of Pearl Harbor, such feelings were tempered as the American counteroffensive turned into something more akin to slaughter. Total war can be disgusting, and had I been there, I would have continually wondered why it had to be this way. Wasn't it somehow possible to convince a whole nation of the error of its ways without having to kill everyone?

If there was an answer, it wasn't to come for at least another 18 months. Reports of the Imperial Army and the Combined Fleet being thoroughly routed, and of young men being exterminated, was not a strong enough message to be heard in Tokyo. Japan would fight on.

The next battle would be Enewetak. Though not as large as Kwajalein, the bell-shaped Enewetak Atoll and its enclosed lagoon measured nearly 30 miles from end to end. Major islands in the atoll included Engebi in the north and Parry and Enewetak in the south. Engebi was severely pounded by American bombs and shells in the pre-invasion softening up, and was easily taken from its 1,000 defenders. But U.S. intelligence learned on the eve of the southern attack that Parry and Enewetak held more than 2,000 men, camouflaged and well entrenched. Shelling and pounding couldn't go deep enough to appreciably weaken the defenders, and the invasion was set for February 22, 1944. As always, the lesson of Tarawa was foremost in the minds of American planners. How would they clean out these hidden nests on Parry and Enewetak, without subjecting their own men to unacceptable risk?

Eugene Beck's LST 226 was part of the operations at Enewetak. LSTs had an internal ballast system that shifted forward to the bow once on the beach, to enable beaching and unloading, and then shifted to the stern to lift the bow off when the unloading was over. While beached, double doors and a ramp would open into the surf, and out would come men and tanks, as well as the smaller amphibious alligators and ducks, carrying men, supplies, and even single Jeeps. "The drill was that we would come to within a few hundred yards of shore, and drop our stern anchor. Then we'd move forward, but a special device always kept tension on the stern anchor line. If something went wrong and we turned breach, we were dead in the water, and we'd have to abandon ship. So we'd have to make sure we were always perpendicular to the shore."

Was Beck afraid during this massive operation? "I remember being down in the engine room during the start of it," he says, "and I had my radio earphones on and heard the reports of Japanese planes coming in to hit us. As it turned out, we never got hit. And although I was uneasy, I remember feeling more concerned about the older guys on the ship. We had guys in their forties with children back home. You could really see the war wearing on them. You could see them go gray before your very eyes.

"We came under some small-arms fire at Enewetak," Beck recalls, "but nobody on my LST got hit. Later in the day I actually went up on land. I found a downed Zero and pulled a piece of aluminum off the wing, which I ended up making into a strap for my cigarette box. The Japanese aluminum was amazingly thin and tough, like thin stainless steel. I also saw lots of Japanese bodies, up in the caves there."

As the invasion progressed, tanks were unloaded by ships like Beck's, and moved onshore. The terrain on the island was particularly forbidding, because it had been heavily mined, making the advance more difficult and running up the U.S. casualty tally beyond what had been expected. Often the Marines and GIs had no other recourse to clean out the Japanese emplacements than to torch them with tank flame-throwers. As the fight wore on, the Americans finally overran the hill emplacements, leaving the only Japanese resistance in flatter terrain. The final engagement was a more one-sided slaughter, with all the Japanese ending up dead. Around 300 Americans died at Enewetak, but Japan lost almost 3,000.

Beck and his LST remained at Enewetak for weeks, ferrying just about everything that needed to go ashore to support the continuing American expansion westward toward Japan. He remembers transporting medicine and food and ammo. Meanwhile the mopping up on adjacent islands went on a little longer, because the Japanese were scattered throughout the atoll. From Enewetak, Beck and his LST group would move westward, ultimately supporting the U.S. invasion of Saipan. Aside from surviving the war, he and his mates

would make it through three typhoons and, in May 1944, the second worst disaster to hit Pearl Harbor, as his LST group prepared for the next operation, the invasion of the Mariana Islands, including Saipan, Guam, and Tinian.

But before I describe that disaster and the little-known second graveyard that resulted at Pearl, what victory had been won in the Gilberts and the Marshalls? More important, what did this latest set of American victories at Truk and Enewetak mean in a strategic sense? In the eyes of military analysts and historians, these Japanese defeats represented the biggest breach yet in Japan's defensive line.

The Japanese wall was now starting to crumble, and the task for the Americans was to keep up the pressure and move so quickly that the Japanese couldn't adequately regroup. They had to move forward as fast as possible, taking note not to waste time and energy on cleaning out every nest of Japanese—only those essential to helping extend American power at optimum speed and safety. For example, while taking Enewetak and Truk, the U.S. commanders leapfrogged lesser atolls in the region even though Japanese forces were stationed there.

But for whatever reason, the American forces elected to seize tiny Bikini, which would figure later in the war, not as a strategic theater but as a testing ground for the atomic weapons that would present the next step in the evolution of warfare, the same atomic weapons that would finally convince Japan to surrender in August 1945.

The American victory that had seemed so doubtful in early 1942 was now taking shape. But in war, tragedy can occur, even at the height of victory. We'll see that later in this book, in the case of *Indianapolis*. Eugene Beck of LST 226 would see it vividly demonstrated one night in May 1944, when death and carnage would again visit Pearl Harbor—not from another surprise Japanese attack, but from human error.

"Our LSTs were stacked up in West Loch at Pearl in advance of the Saipan operation, side by side," he says. "All kinds of ammo was stored up on the tank deck of the LSTs, while gasoline and Marines were up on the foredeck. It turned out that one of the gasoline drums had been leaking, and it caught on fire. Suddenly six LSTs were engulfed in fire and started

Dangling cables on the *Fujikawa Maru* once relayed commands from the flying bridge, at top, now a skeleton. Since the precise age of Truk's artificial reefs is known, Earle collected important clues to the growth rates of marine life that congregates around submerged reefs.

exploding. To save the other LSTs, our commanders made the decision to torpedo those burning LSTs as fast as possible. Hundreds of guys were killed in that mishap, and although I was about half a mile away, I could see the flames and hear the explosions.

"The next day," he recalls, "I expected to see a huge story in the newspaper. Instead, there was a tiny little clip that said something like, '6 landing craft sunk' and nothing more. Nothing about what a disaster it was. I guess they were trying to keep morale up. But then, in the next few days, bodies started to float up from the sunken LSTs. We had ships dragging that area with hooks, to catch the bodies."

One hundred and sixty-three Americans died, and 396 were wounded, in that terrible accident. It was not until decades later that the Navy Department declassified documents related to the tragedy.

So as the story moves on toward further American victories in the westward push, a moment of silence for those who died on the *Liscome Bay* and in the shallows at Tarawa and elsewhere in the Gilberts and Marshalls. And for those who died, unsung and unhonored, in that second Pearl Harbor tragedy, in West Loch. They fell so that others could go on.

And also for the brave Japanese who died, fighting against the turning tide, fighting for the lost cause; the men burned in their cave bunkers, shot from the sky in their Zeros, and sent to the bottom of Truk Lagoon.

Let us hope that some reward came to all of them in the silence of those lost Pacific graveyards.

KA10-7

KAIO-8

Battle for Leyte Gulf, October 23-26, 1944

Philippine Sea, Saipan, Leyte Gulf, June–December 1944

EVEN AS THE UNITED STATES WAS EVICTING JAPAN FROM THE GILBERTS, Marshalls, and Carolines on the central highway to Tokyo, big things were happening farther south. By spring 1944 the U.S. had begun a relentless advance northwestward, up the north coast of New Guinea. Dense jungle and forbidding terrain made land advances virtually out of the question, but by summer 1944 General MacArthur had pushed his troops, through amphibious operations, all the way up to the northwest tip of New Guinea. It had taken two full years and many thousands of deaths since the U.S. had lost the Philippines to turn the tide of war in the South Pacific and get back within striking distance of the islands MacArthur loved so dearly.

But the major naval battles and graveyards of 1944 would remain farther north, in the central Pacific islands. The next central campaign would be for the Marianas: Guam, Rota, Tinian, and Saipan, where the central highway turns due north and heads for the Japanese home islands. The first target was Saipan, to be invaded on the morning of June 15, 1944. To pave the way, the Fifth Fleet softened up Saipan and the other Marianas with offshore bombardments and carrier-based planes. U.S.S. *Indianapolis* had a major role in the bombardment, beginning June 13. The overall commander of this

Doomed by a successful kamikaze strike, U.S. escort carrier *St. Lo* billows black smoke in Leyte Gulf minutes after a Zero on a suicide mission crashed through the carrier's flight deck, igniting torpedoes and bombs. The term kamikaze—"divine wind" in Japanese—refers to a saving typhoon that dispersed a threatening Mongol fleet from Japan's shores in 1281.

huge operation, Admiral Spruance, was reportedly especially eager to take Saipan because his Pearl Harbor and Midway nemesis, Admiral Nagumo, was headquartered ashore, sheltering in a mountain cave with the local commander of Japanese ground forces, General Saito. Nagumo's star had fallen just as Spruance's had risen, for after the loss of his carriers at Midway, Nagumo had been relegated to commanding smaller surface ships based at Saipan.

Saipan was a more substantial piece of ground than the atolls and islets that the Marines had taken at Kwajalein and Enewetak; it also had a mountainous interior. But after the lessons learned at Tarawa and the more efficient invasions of the later islands, American commanders believed they could take Saipan in three days. The workhorses of this invasion, on a series of beaches stretching over several miles, would be LSTs, more than 60 of them, filled with Marines and tanks and amphibious half-track vehicles called "amphtracs."

Eight thousand Marines landed before 9:00 in the morning of June 15, and subsequent waves of another 12,000 Americans came ashore throughout the day, amphtracs churning the shallows. But then things began to go wrong. Instead of advancing, the Americans faced their worst amphibious nightmare, as at Tarawa: Pinned down on a shallow beachhead, their advance stalled, with night falling. The Japanese defenders shelled them mercilessly throughout the night, and then, at the ungodly hour of 3:00 a.m., sent a screaming attack force to drive the Marines back into the ocean. It wasn't until dawn that the Americans were able to turn back this counterattack.

Eugene Beck was on *LST 226* at Saipan, and he remembers it well. "Saipan," he says, "was bigger than the others we'd seen. It had hills and mountains. We unloaded our tanks and smaller boats out in the deep ocean that first morning, and they went in, wave after wave. Later our guys brought the wounded back out to the LSTs. Being a flagship, we had doctors on board. Among other things about Saipan, I remember the flies. The blowflies were terrible. They came out from the island. Poor guys trying to eat up on deck were covered with these blowflies.

"One night later on," he says, " we had a whole bunch of wounded guys on cots on deck. I remember coming up from my engine room duty that night. The moon was up. I was leaning over the rail, watching our battleships out at sea firing their 16-inch shells from back over the horizon as they shelled the Japanese positions onshore. The shells went off to one side toward the island, and they all had tracers. It was spectacular to watch."

From his vantage point offshore, with the flow of casualties and reports crackling in, Beck could tell it was bad on the hilly island. When he finally could go ashore, even as the fighting raged in the interior, he saw dead Japanese on the ground who had been there for days, and found abandoned Japanese maps and weapons in some of the caves.

Americans might easily have recovered their balance after that rough first day but for ominous reports now streaming in that a massive Japanese fleet was coming to relieve the island defenders. Admiral Spruance was torn between supporting his beleaguered invaders (as well as sticking to a schedule that called for the invasion of Guam on June 18), or going to meet the Japanese fleet. He elected to postpone Guam, knowing that he had nearly twice the ships his opponent did and could reallocate some of them to meet the Japanese threat. But it was more than a matter of doing two difficult things at once. Almost spontaneously, the biggest carrier battle of World War II began to take shape. On the American side were old warhorses like *Enterprise,* together with the new *Hornet* and *Yorktown,* while on the Japanese side were Pearl Harbor veterans *Shokaku* and *Zuikaku,* as well as other newer ships.

The Combined Fleet's renewed carrier strength gave confidence to the late Admiral Yamamoto's successor, Admiral Toyoda, and his leading subordinate, Admiral Ozawa; confidence that they might turn the tide of war back in their favor. Throughout May the Japanese had been reassembling their fleet to once and for all lure the Americans into that elusive Great All-Out Naval Battle. And if any Japanese commander was up to pulling it off, it was Admiral Ozawa, for he had many of the same tactical skills as Admiral Spruance.

Spruance, meanwhile, had assembled an even larger fleet, more than 500 ships, more carriers than Japan, more than twice as many destroyers, more than 900 American aircraft to Japan's 500-plus. But Ozawa believed that, just as the outnumbered Americans had rallied at Midway, he could rally in the Philippine Sea west of the embattled Marianas. Ozawa truly thought he could win, and perhaps if every card in the battle had come up in his favor he might have. He believed his edge would come from several sources: He had about a hundred land-based planes in the Marianas, his carrier-based planes had longer range than the Americans, and he knew he had a single clear objective—to destroy the American fleet. Additionally, the nearest American land facility was more than 1,000 miles away, at Enewetak; Pearl Harbor was more than 3,000 miles distant. The American supply lines, theorized the Japanese, were now becoming as overextended as their own had been in those heady days of early 1942.

In fact, the real stakes in the coming battle were control over the 1,000 miles of ocean between the Marianas and the Philippines. Control of that water opened up all sorts of possibilities for the Americans, creating new highways to the Philippines, to Japanese-occupied Taiwan and China, and to Japan itself.

On the morning of June 19, the Japanese sent more than 430 planes in four waves against Spruance's fleet. But all too quickly for Ozawa, dreams of Japanese revenge for the debacle at Midway turned into yet another American revenge for the attack on Pearl Harbor. Repeatedly, advancing Japanese fighters and bombers went down before they found their targets, unable to penetrate walls of American Hellcats from the big carriers like *Essex, Cowpens,* and *Hornet,* while American subs and Avenger torpedo aircraft pummeled Japan's ships. On that first day alone, called the "Great Marianas Turkey Shoot," the Japanese lost around 300 planes and two carriers, including the *Taiho,* Japan's biggest. Torpedoed in a vulnerable spot, *Taiho* sank in minutes with two-thirds of her crew. Carrier *Hiyo* also went down. But the sweetest revenge came in the sinking of *Shokaku,* also from torpedoes. This great ship, whose name meant "Heavenly Crane," would never again threaten U.S. ships or sailors. Stunned by his losses, Ozawa retreated north, toward Okinawa. But still the slaughter went on: He lost another carrier and nearly 100 more planes. The final tally for Japan was about 400 carrier aircraft lost and its three largest carriers sunk. The theoretical advantages that Ozawa had counted on literally went up in smoke.

While it's hard to say just what contributed most to this massive Japanese defeat beyond the numerical superiority of U.S. attackers, perhaps the single largest

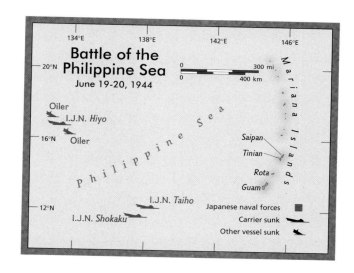

Sho-Go—Japanese for "Operation Victory"—led instead to disaster with the battle of Leyte Gulf. Three Japanese battleships, one large aircraft carrier, three light carriers, six heavy cruisers, four light cruisers, and 11 destroyers went to the bottom, while the U.S.'s losses were light. Allied victory here meant the Philippines could once again be occupied.

factor was the inexperience of Japan's pilots and crews. After a cumulative series of ship and aircraft losses that began at Midway, Japan's replacements were just not trained to the degree that the Pearl Harbor attackers had been. You might say that Japan was now down into her second- and third- and even fourth-string players, depending on men who were just not as able or as well trained as those who had fallen in battle. To compound this, Japanese losses of men and materiel in every encounter were averaging twice, three times, even ten times what the Americans were losing.

Two other factors also worked against Japan. First, its aircraft, while lighter and longer range and more maneuverable than the American planes, were poorly armored. Once hit, they were more likely to go down. Also, U.S. submarine forces had greatly expanded their effectiveness. They, more than any other force, were responsible for the high Japanese loss of carriers.

The implosion of Japan, its once mighty war machine, and the Greater East Asia Co-Prosperity Sphere, was well under way. But the Japanese fought on, even though the commanders in Tokyo could see that they now needed a miracle or an act of God to save them.

Steaming in tight curves, Japanese ships desperately try to evade carrier-based U.S. planes. In the foreground, a heavy cruiser throws up a curtain of flak while circling counter-clockwise; beyond, a Kongo-class battleship suffers two direct hits while narrowly avoiding collision with a zigzagging carrier. This, the Battle of the Philippine Sea, took place over two days in late June, 1944. Japanese commander Jisaburo Ozawa had hoped to lure American forces into a trap west of the Marianas; but Adm. Raymond Spruance, with enormous resources in his Fifth Fleet and good reconnaissance from submarines, delivered devastating losses to the enemy.

If victory were to come, it would not be from anything in their arsenal but from something more akin to the original kamikaze or "divine wind," the typhoonlike storm that had saved the home islands from a Mongol invasion so many centuries earlier.

We can say that the Philippine Sea is primarily a Japanese graveyard, a graveyard of many brave Japanese pilots who went down in the hail of superior American antiaircraft and fighter fire, a graveyard of carrier crews on *Taiho, Hiyo,* and proud *Shokaku,* which merits some special mention. Some analysts believe that if she and her sister ship *Zuikaku,* whose name meant "Lucky Crane," had not been temporarily put out of action at Coral Sea, these two experienced carriers could have made Midway a more evenly matched encounter and maybe even a Japanese victory, instead of the debacle that resulted. Whatever the truth, her sinking and the loss of more than 1,000 of her crew on June 19 was one more mortal wound to the Japanese Combined Fleet.

Anthony Tully, Jon Parshall, and Richard Wolff have done an interesting job in analyzing rather sparse war records and applying some mathematical modeling to speculate on just what took *Shokaku* down. Depending on whom you believe, three or four of the six torpedoes that the submarine U.S.S. *Cavalla* got off that morning hit *Shokaku* while she was busy refueling, preparing to launch another wave of attackers against Spruance's fleet to the east. These authors draw some interesting parallels between how *Shokaku* was damaged and sunk, and the sinking of *Titanic,* a graveyard I know something about. They see *Shokaku*'s bow damage compounding other injuries caused as torpedoes ignited the aviation fuel being pumped into her waiting aircraft, pulling her down bow first, just like *Titanic.*

One Japanese work that they've translated in their research, *The Tragic Marianas Turkeyshoot,* describes in vivid detail the final two-and-a-half hours of *Shokaku*'s life. Apparently when the torpedoes came in at about 11:20 a.m., the carrier and her destroyer escort were as oblivious to the presence of American submarines as American crews had been on June 7, 1942, when *Hammann* and *Yorktown* were torpedoed. By the time the Japanese spotted the incoming torpedoes, it was too late to do anything. Several hit on the starboard side, most forward but one amidships—which threw spray and burning fuel onto Japanese aviators waiting for their planes to be refueled. Then a massive explosion in the hangar blew *Shokaku*'s flight elevators upward. The damage was so serious that engine power and electricity were lost. Pumps wouldn't work; bucket brigades began desperate efforts to put out the fires. *Shokaku* had been hit hard twice before, first in the Coral Sea and then in the Battle of Santa Cruz Islands in the Guadalcanal campaign. If any Japanese carrier crew had experience with successful damage control, this one did. The ship began to list to starboard, and so counterflooding began. But the crew so overcompensated that *Shokaku* rolled sickeningly to port.

Fires and explosions from aviation fuel wracked the interior, particularly the hangar, and began setting off the ammunition being loaded onto bombers intended for the American fleet. The fuel itself was especially deadly, more so than normal aviation fuel because Japanese refineries, falling behind schedule, had delivered to their fliers a cruder form called *tarakan,* which gave off more volatile vapors. As much as anything, this contributed to the death of *Shokaku,* and perhaps the other carriers lost that day.

With all the explosive power now unleashed, Japanese sailors were blown apart by their own ammo and torched by their own fuel. On deck, some men fell into the open, flame-filled flight elevators as the bow gradually went down. When the order to abandon ship was given, some units insisted on a roll call, which must have seemed an eternity to those lucky enough to still be alive. While some jumped into rafts or the water, others stood their ground for the count.

Next came the most horrible part for *Shokaku.* As water began to pour into No. 1 elevator around 2 p.m., the ship suddenly stood up on its bow, causing hundreds of loyal Japanese sailors, still awaiting completion of their roll calls, to lose footing and slide screaming and clawing all the way down the flight deck into the yawning mouth of a fiery flight elevator No. 3, where they were incinerated—just before their remains would be carried to the bottom forever.

Finally, just after 2:00 p.m., the ship "stood straight up" and with a "groaning roar" plummeted to the bottom. A few more than 500 men survived, but nearly 1,300 were gone, exceeding the huge loss of life on *Kaga,* sunk at Midway. The psychological shock for the survivors was so great that even though there was ample

"Off to the Turkey Shoot"—a painting by artist Stan Stokes—celebrates a victory so one-sided that Americans called it "the great Marianas turkey shoot." In the final tally, the engagement cost Japan three carriers, two oilers, about 410 aircraft, nearly 200 land-based planes, and hundreds of men.

space on board *Zuikaku,* their sister ship was too much a reminder of the lost *Shokaku,* and so they were put on a destroyer and sent home.

Shokaku is variously recorded as having gone down at 11° 50' N or 12° 00' N, 137° 46' E or 137° 57' E, southwest of Guam in the West Mariana Basin. My charts show the ocean depths there are comparable to where *Lexington* rests in the Coral Sea, perhaps 10,000 feet down, unless she slid into a trench. What shape would we find her in? She might be intact, like *Yorktown.* But the severity of her death throes and the blasts that opened her bow and starboard side give me pause. Some accounts of her final plunge say she was "corkscrewing." If she kept that up as she sank into the depths, it could complicate how she hit the bottom, whether she stayed in one piece, and how she rests today. However, more than a thousand souls rest there too: young

Japanese sailors and their commanders, who had gone into war thinking they were fulfilling divine destiny. On that awful afternoon, they must have been questioning the very foundations of their world.

June 19, 1944 was the end for those men, for *Shokaku,* and for the battle to control the Philippine Sea and the air above it. The result was a perilous situation for Japan, because just as the U.S. was turning up the pressure, Japanese men, ships, and bases were increasingly left naked to American attacks from the sky. Just as everything had seemed to go in Japan's favor on December 7, 1941 and in the six months afterward, now everything was turning against it.

That was small comfort to the U.S. Marines still fighting their way across Saipan. Even as the air and naval battles were being won, the campaign on the ground was agonizingly slow and bloody. The flagship *Indianapolis*

Continued on page 207

Like deadly waterbugs, Allied landing craft steam toward the beaches of the Mariana Islands. After days of bombardment, Guam, Tinian, and Saipan were invaded by Army and Marines in the largest transoceanic invasion ever launched. More than 100,000 assault troops were supported by 29 carriers, 14 battleships, 25 cruisers, and 152 destroyers. Within months, heavy American B-29s—flying out of air bases here—were pounding the Japanese mainland.

Apparent clutter and confusion mark D-Day on Saipan, as an armed amphibious vehicle burns beyond these Marines. Initially pinned to the beaches, U.S. forces expanded their beachhead to 2,000 yards by the invasion's second day. Just 14 miles long and a little over 5 miles wide at its widest, this 47-square-mile island harbored thousands of determined Japanese soldiers. The Marines systematically rooted them out, helped in part by Navajo-speaking troops whose language served as a "code" the Japanese were never able to crack.

Continued from page 201

returned to Saipan on June 23 to give fire support there, afterward heading on to Tinian to soften up Japanese shore fortifications. After that, she would support the delayed invasion of Guam and become the first American ship to sail into Guam harbor since the Japanese had seized the island on December 10, 1941.

The Japanese troops on Saipan fought on valiantly until the second week in July. Once the island was lost, Admiral Nagumo, the commander of the attack on Pearl Harbor and the loser of the battle of Midway, committed suicide; so did General Saito, commander of the ground forces. U.S. deaths in the vicious Saipan shoot-out totaled more than 3,000. But for Japan, the deaths numbered around 24,000. And the shock of that loss was felt all the way back to Tokyo.

After Saipan, Tinian was taken very easily, but the attack on Guam was held off a few more days to add another infantry division that might lessen the chance of another Tarawa or Saipan. To add extra insurance, Guam was subjected to a relentless pre-invasion shelling that lasted a full two weeks. By mid-August 1944, the U.S. reigned supreme on the biggest islands of the Marianas, islands like Saipan that had been major Japanese bases. The U.S. also ruled the waters to the west of the Marianas, which served as the central gateway to the Philippines themselves.

As the American star rose ever higher in July and August of 1944, Prime Minister Tojo, the ruling hawk in a cabinet of militarists, submitted his resignation. He, who more than any other had embodied Japan's imperialist dreams and had overseen Yamamoto's plan of surprise attack on a more powerful country, was now history, together with most of his colleagues.

Parliamentary logic dictates that after such a powerful admission of error and defeat, Japan would have sued for peace. But Japan was not really a parliamentary democracy. It remained a militarist monarchy, with a culture built on insecurity and mortal fear of disgrace

---

Amid surrounding death, life struggles on: Somewhere on Saipan, a Marine cradles an infant found wedged beneath a rock. The island's Japanese defenders, tenaciously hidden in caves and ravines, fought to the last. Even after American forces declared Saipan secure, another 1,972 enemy soldiers were killed.

and embarrassment. Its society stressed the importance of saving face, of glorifying the victorious warrior, and of heaping shame on the defeated. While such a system conceivably could bring itself to dismiss the architects of a failed policy, it was another thing to admit that the culture itself had taken the wrong road—even if the road was going to end in holocaust.

Even with Tojo gone and the Americans probing Japan's inner defense perimeter with forces so overwhelming that only a miracle could defeat them, the remaining Japanese leadership went into denial. In quiet gardens of the Imperial Palace it was still possible to ignore the returned paraplegics, the terse reports of defeat, and the increasing signs of an island economy beginning to choke. Japan, bloodied and doomed, would continue to fight on.

Its next big naval battle would be the series of engagements in and about Leyte Gulf in October 1944, on the western edge of the Philippine Sea. General MacArthur had returned, as he said he would. But it had taken him and his colleagues two years to fight their way back through the Solomons, up New Guinea, on through the Admiralties. The Philippines were not unfortified, and the Japanese were still prepared to fight to the death. After all, hundreds had leapt to their deaths in Saipan rather than surrender.

The date to invade the Philippines through Leyte Gulf was set for October 20, only two months after the Marianas had been secured, and following American infighting about whether the Philippines should be dealt with before or after the defeat of Japan. MacArthur, of course, wanted to make good on his vow to return; despite opposition, he won the debate.

Before Leyte was invaded, several islands to the east of the Philippines, including Peleliu, Ulithi, and Morotai, would be secured to provide more stepping-stones for the push to the northwest. A devastating bombardment of Japanese-held Taiwan (then called Formosa) was undertaken from American carriers to make sure that the Japanese could not send Formosa-based planes to attack the American invasion force farther south.

On the heels of their huge aircraft losses in the Philippine Sea campaign, the Japanese suffered another terrible defeat at Taiwan, where the U.S. destroyed about 500 aircraft in three days. U.S. losses, while not insignificant, were nothing in comparison.

The Japanese did undertake a few innovations in these final days before Leyte. They finally changed their island-defense tactics, because the technique of trying to pin down American invaders on beaches had not worked. Japan had lost every island battle since Guadalcanal. Now they decided to really dig in and fortify their inland cave defenses, which were highly resistant to traditional assault, offshore shelling, and aerial bombing. Such tactical changes, however, were only stopgap blocks on the road to the inevitable defeat of Japan. Look at the fleet the U.S. was assembling for the Leyte invasion: more than 800 ships, including 32 aircraft carriers. More than

1,700 American aircraft were poised against Japan's 100plus. The world had never seen a fleet of such size.

Sadly, the Japanese public and much of the leadership believed propaganda that claimed many U.S. ships had been sunk in the battle off Taiwan. So, in those middle days of October, they could not see the handwriting on the wall. Many, including those in military positions, believed the Americans had been so badly hurt that the Philippines were out of danger. Imagine their shock when, on October 17, Japanese outposts on the Philippines first detected the approaching American fleet of liberation. They sent their reports to Admiral Toyoda, who though equally surprised, was not totally unprepared. The Japanese had long been planning for a possible American return to the Philippines, and the Combined Fleet had been part of those plans.

Admiral Toyoda would, in such an eventuality, again try for that Great All-Out Naval Battle, even though it had usually produced disaster for Japan, not the U.S. The problem was that Toyoda's ships were scattered about, many of them a week away. And after all those turkey shoots, he didn't have the air cover he needed. But no matter; he really had no choice but to engage the monstrous American fleet. What else could he do? Drop back to Tokyo Bay and await the inevitable?

The actual U.S. landing on Leyte was the easy part. Not that it was easy to bring 130,000 men ashore in

two days, onto land that had been held by the enemy for two years. But the area was lightly defended, and what could have been fiercely contested was not. At least not on land. Admirals Toyoda and Ozawa would attempt to settle the score on the ocean. While they couldn't muster anything like 800 ships or 32 carriers or 1,700 aircraft, they would build a fleet around the lone surviving Pearl Harbor carrier *Zuikaku,* together with three other carriers, and the battleships *Yamato* and *Musashi,* the biggest in the world. In fact, the only category where Japan was roughly equal to America's surface fleet at Leyte was in battleships and cruisers. Japan assembled 29 to America's 36.

The Japanese decided to subdivide their force and attempt another samurai naval display of feints and dodges. Their almost impotent carriers would serve as decoys to lure American ships into the open ocean; meanwhile, the Japanese battleship force would sweep in to destroy the unprotected American amphibious fleet still at Leyte. A smaller force would come through the Surigao Strait and attack the Americans head on. But the more powerful group, including *Musashi* and *Yamato,* would cross the Philippines north of Leyte, through the San Bernardino Strait, and then sail south to enter Leyte Gulf from the northeast, cutting off the Americans and creating a pincer.

In retrospect, it seems as desperate a strategy now as it would prove then. What desperation for Japan, in a war dominated by aircraft carriers, to have no other use for its remaining carriers than as lures. But then, what use is an aircraft carrier without aircraft?

And yet there was one remaining advantage for Japan to exploit, even if unknowingly. The very size of the American surface force created the potential for American confusion.

Consider the fact that the U.S. landing force was the Seventh Fleet, commanded by Admiral Kinkaid under the overall command of General MacArthur, while the force covering them was the Third Fleet, commanded by Admiral Halsey under the command of Admiral

A younger generation splashes among Leyte's larger-than-life statues depicting Gen. Douglas MacArthur's triumphal "I shall return" moment. Forced to abandon the Philippines early in the war, the "great liberator" made his return in 1944 (opposite). His dramatic walk through the surf was in fact an accident, made necessary when his landing craft ran aground short of the beach.

Nimitz. MacArthur and Nimitz had a joint command, which in most endeavors can be as effective as a two-headed dog. In combat, however, it multiplies the potential for error and accident.

The American and Japanese forces did not make contact until October 23, when U.S. submarines met the Japanese far to the west of Leyte, in the Palawan Passage adjoining the South China Sea. Two subs, *Darter* and *Dace*, torpedoed the unprotected Japanese heavy cruisers *Atago* and *Takao*. The *Atago* sank, but *Takao* limped away to the west. Then *Dace* hit the heavy cruiser *Maya*, which went to the bottom. It was not an auspicious beginning for a Japanese comeback.

After these sinkings, *Dace* and *Darter* planned to continue attacking the Japanese fleet that night, as it sailed east toward Leyte and the American amphibious force. But *Darter* ran aground just after midnight. Despite round-the-clock efforts to free her, *Darter's* crew couldn't get her off a formation known as Bombay Shoals. *Dace* joined *Darter* to assist, and the decision was made to abandon *Darter*. All the men and classified equipment from *Darter* were transferred to *Dace*. Then *Dace* tried to torpedo *Darter* to make it useless to the Japanese should they come upon it. But the torpedoes kept hitting the shoal and leaving the stranded sub untouched. Later the U.S.S. *Little Rock* also fired torpedoes, but once again they hit the shoal and didn't destroy the sub.

About a week later, U.S.S. *Nautilus* came along and scored dozens of hits on the abandoned submarine

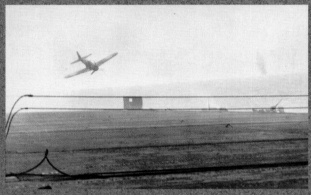

Despite the tightening Allied noose, Japanese forces continue to inflict casualties even as they lose sea battles. A U.S. carrier flight deck (left) burns after a direct hit by a Japanese bomb. Fire-fighting crews struggle to contain the blaze with water and chemicals. Sequential photos (above) chronicle the approach and crash of a kamikaze on the carrier *White Plains* in Leyte Gulf. First used effectively here, such Japanese suicide missions would continue to harass the Allies until the end of the war, resulting in the sinking of 34 ships and damage to hundreds of others. At Okinawa, they killed nearly 5,000 men.

with six-inch shells. But the hull of *Darter* survived on that spot until at least the 1960s.

Despite its advantage on paper, the American fleet was divided, its assorted elements not well positioned enough to deliver a decisive strike against the Japanese coming into Leyte. The survivors of the Palawan submarine encounter steamed ahead, and the only American group in position to counter them on October 24 was the smallest—centered around the carrier *Intrepid.*

Another American group, farther north, came under surprisingly heavy air attack from Japanese land-based planes coming out of Luzon. One dive bomber hit the light carrier *Princeton,* and later explosions damaged her so badly that she had to be abandoned. The cruiser *Birmingham* was alongside *Princeton,* helping with salvage and rescue, when *Princeton* exploded. Both vessels were heavily damaged and suffered high fatalities.

Much like the sinking of the brand new *Hornet* at Guadalcanal in October 1942, the loss of the almost-new *Princeton,* in what is called the Battle of Siboyan Sea, seemed another case of tragic bad luck, although it didn't constitute a strategic loss of the same degree for the U.S. By October 1944 the U.S. had so many carriers it could afford to lose a few. They were more expendable, particularly the light ones. But that was no comfort to the poor crewmen of *Princeton.*

While U.S. carrier fighters had done a pretty good job of holding off Japanese air attacks that day, a lone "Judy" dive bomber made it through, and about 9:00 in the morning managed to plant a bomb right in the middle of the flight deck of *Princeton.*

According to young *Birmingham* crewman Harry Popham, the bomb didn't appear to have done fatal damage at first glance, as it dropped belowdecks and left only a small hole. But as the morning wore on, power failed and gasoline dripped into the fire belowdecks. An assortment of destroyers, as well as the cruiser *Birmingham,* tried to pull aside and help the ailing ship, but rough seas kept slamming them against *Princeton.* At times it seemed like they were doing more damage than good. One destroyer even had its mast torn off in the process. Frantic firefighting efforts focused not only on hard-to-reach flames belowdecks, but also on pouring water over huge American bombs, sizzling with heat yet miraculously unexploded.

Finally, in the afternoon, when it seemed that the damage-control efforts might succeed, a second, much more horrific explosion ripped through the ailing light carrier, also pulverizing the cruiser *Birmingham,* which was alongside giving help. Popham, who while off duty had been watching much of the salvage effort on *Princeton* from his vantage point on *Birmingham,* lost his leg below the knee in the second explosion. But *Princeton* and *Birmingham* suffered even more. As Popham writes, "One hundred and thirty feet of *Princeton's* stern blew off, as well as 180 feet of her flight deck.... Official tallies of casualties on *Princeton* were 347 killed, 552 wounded, and 4 missing. Aboard *Birmingham,* the tally was 230 dead, 408 wounded, and 4 missing." Other sources claim a lower death toll on both ships.

Even as this drama was playing itself out on the water, American pilots were able to fly several hundred sorties against the advancing Japanese force, and the Japanese had virtually no air cover to protect them. All they had were antiaircraft guns, manned by very green crews. While nearly 20 American planes went down, that loss was not enough to save the Japanese supership *Musashi,* which absorbed nearly 20 torpedoes and almost that many bombs before she sank the night of October 24.

Late that same day, Admiral Halsey received reports of the Japanese carrier group that intended to decoy him away, hoping he would leave the Leyte landing force exposed to the other two Japanese forces converging there. And in one of his worst mistakes, Halsey took the bait. He ordered all three of his carrier groups and all their escort vessels to pursue the enemy carriers. In the words of historian C. Vann Woodward, "Everything was pulled out from San Bernardino Strait. Not so much as a picket destroyer was left."

Halsey did so on the assumption that the Japanese central force had been fatally wounded by American subs and planes at Palawan and Sibuyan. In fact, they were still very much in business and were heading for their rendezvous and their attack on the Americans. In later attempts to justify his actions, Halsey said that he had feared he was wasting his time just waiting for the Japanese central force to appear through the straits, and thought it more likely they might never appear. He wanted to put his forces to work where they would be most useful, as soon as possible.

What made Halsey's decision especially bad was that he chose to ignore for most of October 25 a nearly continual stream of pleas and reports indicating that the arriving Japanese battle flotilla had much more strength than expected. Moreover, the remaining American defenders were low on ammunition and totally outgunned, to the extent that the Leyte invasion itself might have been jeopardized. But Bull Halsey steamed on, until finally Admiral Nimitz, reading all the anguished pleas, sent his own urgent communiqué questioning what Halsey was doing. It was only at this point that Halsey sent a task force back south to relieve the endangered Americans at Leyte.

While Halsey chased the carrier decoys, the naval forces he left behind made contact with the advancing Japanese southern force, in what came to be known as the Battle of Surigao Strait.

It began not long before midnight on October 24. The Japanese, commanded by Admiral Nishimura, were harassed but unharmed by American PT boats as they moved through the straits. But then they met a more powerful American destroyer group. The destroyers executed beautiful maneuvers, firing torpedoes at the advancing Japanese ships. The battleship *Fuso* was hurt and pulled out of the fight; the destroyer *Yamagumo* exploded and went down; *Michishio* was also sunk; and the bow of the destroyer *Asagumo* was blown off, causing her to sink later.

Oddly, Admiral Nishimura still plowed on, even as his ships exploded or went to the bottom. The remnants of this force, including the battleship *Yamashiro,* advanced undeterred, not knowing that an even more formidable American flotilla awaited them. Early on the morning of October 25, *Yamashiro* was hit by torpedoes from U.S.S. *Newcomb,* and exploded and sank around 4:00 a.m. Much of her crew, including Admiral Nishimura, went down with her. The rear echelon of the Japanese force came through later, but seeing the trend of battle, quickly reversed course and began to retreat. The Americans pursued, sinking the heavily damaged *Asagumo* and the light cruiser *Abukuma,* as well as roughing up the cruiser *Mogami.*

Just as this one-sided battle was coming to an end, another was just beginning off the east coast of Samar Island, to the north of Leyte. While Halsey had charged north, the still formidable Japanese center force of battleships and cruisers had made its transit of San Bernardino Strait, steaming for many hours undetected down the coast of Samar and heading right for Leyte.

When the Americans and Japanese finally made contact about dawn, in what would become the Battle of Samar, it was between a formidable armada commanded by Admiral Kurita and an American "Taffy Group 3," consisting of only six escort carriers with tiny guns, three destroyers, and a few destroyer escorts. For the first time in a long time, the Japanese held the edge; Kurita had four battleships, half a dozen heavy cruisers, and assorted destroyers. While American carrier aircraft from two other light carrier groups would later help to even the odds, that early morning surprise struck fear into the hearts of Taffy Group 3. Outnumbered and outgunned, it was commanded by Rear Adm. Clifton Sprague, who soon found himself in the fight of his life.

The first stroke of good fortune for Sprague was that Admiral Kurita misidentified the U.S. light carriers as heavy carriers, then ordered his ships to meet the enemy in "general attack," which dissolved a coherent battle plan and let individual ships fight as they judged best. Such an order was better suited for a panic situation than for one where the Japanese held the edge. But Admiral Blunder was the winner here, turning Japanese advantage into Japanese confusion and eventual defeat. It was the last real chance for the Combined Fleet to remind the Americans of those dark days in late 1941 and early 1942, when Japan could do no wrong.

Not that the Japanese didn't cause pain. After all, they had the largest collection of naval firepower they had assembled since the Battle of Midway. Indeed, as the mighty Japanese ships got closer and closer to the "expendable" baby flattops, their huge shells started blasting through the lightly armored and smaller American ships like bricks thrown into a toy box. Admiral Sprague rightly feared that he couldn't last five minutes under direct assault.

And his fears began to come true. His first ship to go down was the destroyer *Johnston,* beaten to a pulp. The destroyer *Hoel,* fighting valiantly, took shells as big as 18 inches from the monster battleship *Yamato* and others. The shells were so huge and the target ship so lightly armored that they punched right through her like bullets

Continued on page 222

Exploding shells flicker like stars against the dark clouds over Leyte Island as dawn breaks. American ships are preparing to invade Leyte, the island where MacArthur will famously wade ashore in a few days. Eighth largest island in the Philippine chain, Leyte guards the eastern approaches to the Visayan Sea and is bisected by a heavily forested central mountain range. U.S. forces landed successfully here on October 20, 1944, expelling the Japanese.

Crewmen fight valiantly but in vain to save the American light carrier *Princeton* after a lone dive bomber emerged from cloud cover and dropped a single 550-pound bomb on her flight deck on October 24. The bomb crashed through *Princeton*'s thin deck and penetrated deep into its innards before exploding, igniting gasoline stores there. Then torpedoes mounted on the ship's planes began to go off, as did other munitions aboard. The resulting conflagration blew the ship apart, causing injuries even on the cruiser *Birmingham*, which had come alongside to help.

As *Princeton* burns behind them, survivors in a rubber boat approach the destroyer *Cassin Young* to be rescued. Doomed *Princeton*—the last U.S. carrier to be lost during World War II—refused to sink until scuttled by American torpedoes. Her loss was unusual in that, in effect, it resulted from a single bomb.

Workhorses of the invasion fleet, LSTs—
landing ship tanks—nuzzle the beach of
Leyte Island like nursing puppies (below).
Troops build sandbag piers (right) out from
the beach to the gaping maws of the 300-
foot-long ships; each could carry as many
as 20 tanks. Making landings usually
caused some damage to an LST's hull, so
they could be used only about ten times
before becoming useless. The behemoths
were so vulnerable to attack that their
hundred-man crews complained that LST
really stood for "large slow target."

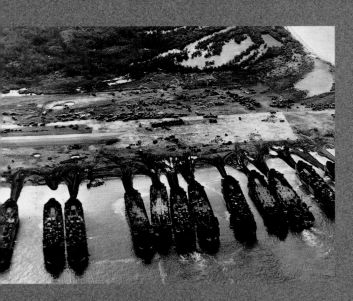

Continued from page 213

through tin foil. Meeting so little resistance, the shells often didn't explode but made so many holes that *Hoel* finally gave up the ghost and sank anyway. So did the destroyer *Samuel B. Roberts*.

Mercifully, by about 8:00 in the morning, American carrier planes from Sprague's group and two other Taffy groups began to dull the Japanese assault. One valiant and successful American effort at ship salvage was on *Kalinin Bay*, a light carrier riddled by huge artillery hits. Her men patched her holes underwater and kept her afloat. But the American sinkings weren't over. The next U.S. ship to go down was *Gambier Bay*, at about 9:00 in the morning. It was Japan's turn when *Chokai* and *Chikuma* sank, killed by aircraft hits. The heavy cruiser *Suzya* also went down. Symbolically, Japan desperately turned to its final, most tragic weapon of last resort, suicidal kamikaze attacks on Taffy Groups 1 and 3. The biggest kamikaze hit was on Group 3, where *St. Lo* was squarely hit and sunk. Finally, Admiral Kurita, having received reports that his southern colleagues were no more, decided to withdraw.

The Americans had lost more than 1,000 men, and nearly that many wounded, but they had won the battle and saved the day. And they had won the Battle off Samar with an unlikely defender, Taffy Group 3.

One more chapter had to be played out in the Battle of Leyte Gulf. Known as the Battle off Cape Engaño—Engaño being Spanish for "trick," and appropriately so, because Halsey had been tricked—it was the culmination of his bull-headed pursuit of the decoy aircraft carriers that hardly had any aircraft left. Needless to say, Halsey had the edge when he finally caught up with the decoys. He commanded five dozen ships and nearly 800 planes, to Japan's 29 aircraft and fewer than 20 ships. This final battle, which was really more of a slaughter, was a U.S. vengeance match, settling old scores that went all the way back to Pearl Harbor. No matter that the Rising Sun was sinking fast; that terrible morning three years earlier still burned in everyone's memory.

The biggest kill for Halsey was the carrier *Zuikaku,* the Lucky Crane that had helped launch those two bomber waves north of Oahu. By October 25, 1944 it was the lone surviving carrier from that day of infamy. It held up under three waves of American air attack, but finally *Zuikaku* was torpedoed and went to the bottom. Then the carrier *Zuiho* went down forever. The carrier *Chitose* also sank, as did *Chiyoda*, although later.

Halsey's victory, which he had thought would be the biggest of the day, was strangely hollow. The real heroes had been Sprague and his battered but victorious fleet of baby flattops. Halsey could take brief pleasure in the sinking of four Japanese carriers and the avenging of Pearl Harbor—until he received a stinging communiqué from Admiral Nimitz, asking about the task force that was supposed to be helping poor Admiral Sprague and Taffy Group 3 back at Samar. Finally Halsey sent his warships off in pursuit, far too late to catch what was left of Admiral Kurita's flotilla.

What was the final tally after four days of naval fistfights in and about Leyte Gulf? The U.S. had lost the light carrier *Princeton,* two escort carriers, a pair of destroyers, and one destroyer escort. But Japan had taken a near-fatal licking: It had lost four carriers, including the mighty *Zuikaku;* the supership *Musashi and* two other battlewagons, and almost two dozen heavy cruisers and destroyers.

As Maj. Gen. J. F. C. Fuller has written, "The Japanese fleet had [effectively] ceased to exist, and, except by land-based aircraft, their opponents had won undisputed command of the sea. When Admiral Ozawa was questioned on the battle after the war, he replied, 'After this battle the surface forces became strictly auxiliary, so that we relied on land forces, special [kamikaze] attack, and air power.... There was no further use assigned to surface vessels, with the exception of some special ships.' And Admiral Yonai, the Navy minister, said that he realized that the defeat at Leyte 'was tantamount to the loss of the Philippines.' As for the larger significance of the battle, he said, 'I felt that it was the end.'"

Indeed, the naval war was over. The greater tactical flexibility, massive war production capacity, and larger population of the U.S. were all grinding Japan down. Although the Philippines were far from secured, the rest of the Pacific War would be fought on land and in the air.

What a massive burial ground is Leyte Gulf. Not only is the ocean bottom off the Philippines littered with the lost ships and aircraft of a great war. Not only are thousands of men from both sides forever at rest there, having made it this far in a race against death, but no farther. You could also say that the imperial dreams of Japan are buried there. While Japan would fight on with a dark stolidity, the awful tide of vengeance was washing back toward the home islands, a tidal wave now gathering force. What could have been the mood back at headquarters in Tokyo as the news trickled in? It must have been like a graveyard there too. The last hopes of the air force gone, the last hopes of the Combined Fleet gone, the great ships *Zuikaku* and *Musashi* only memories now. No more grand plan, no more hopes of a Great All-Out Naval Battle.

And yet, even as the Americans surged forward, they experienced tragedy and irony. As the fight for the Philippines wore on into December, the U.S.S. *Ward*, the plucky old destroyer that had fired those first shots on the morning of Pearl Harbor day in 1941, probably sinking midget sub *16-A* off the mouth of the harbor, had made it as far as Leyte Gulf too. She and her cook Will Lehner had fought their way across the Pacific, good supporting players in theaters like New Guinea and Bougainville and Rabaul. The *Ward* had seemed almost divinely protected throughout her long transpacific journey. Ships and men and aircraft fell all around her, typhoons took others down, and still she sailed on, as she had for almost 30 years.

The only omen of a change came on October 20, 1944, when two crewmen fell overboard while *Ward* was supporting the Leyte invasion. One was saved, but one, Edward Duchin, utterly vanished and was presumed dead, the only life lost on *Ward* in all her naval career.

Weeks later, on December 7, 1944, *Ward* was in Ormoc Bay on the western side of Leyte Island, carrying a load of American troops to be landed there. Just after dawn she unloaded those men, then began anti-submarine patrols between Leyte and Ponson Island. Some time around 10:00 that morning, as Japanese aircraft continued their largely futile but nonetheless deadly strafing runs against the American victors, Will Lehner found himself at general quarters as he had so many times before, "shoving shells in No. 4 gun. I saw a kamikaze coming in at us, and I was afraid he'd hit the deck and slide straight down and kill everybody on it. As it turned out, he hit us on the port side, crashing into the side of the ship."

The plane, an ailing bomber perhaps fatally wounded rather than crashing deliberately, sent one engine boring all the way though the ship and, bursting out on the starboard side. "Gasoline exploded through the quarterdeck," says Lehner, "starting a fire amidships and in the troop compartment. One electrician was showered with gasoline, and burned badly. A lot of guys jumped in the water at

that point. But I was afraid of sharks, so I stayed on until a minesweeper came and picked me up."

The old ship lost power as the fires spread. Ammunition began to explode. By 10:24, less than half an hour after that bomber crash, the order was given to abandon *Ward*. Once all the men were off, U.S.S. *O'Brien* was given orders to fire on *Ward* and sink her, and so she did. The last sight Lehner and the rest of the rescued crew saw after the smoke cleared was *Ward*'s bow sticking up in the air. Then she went down.

"She sank exactly three years to the day after she fired those shots on the minisub at Pearl Harbor," says Lehner. "After she went down, we were taken that night to Leyte, then on to New Guinea, and then to San Francisco. Once I was there, I was diagnosed with shell shock and put in the hospital. I'd been through three years of battles, two typhoons, 26 engagements. I got my medical discharge in May 1945, with 50 percent disability. I considered myself very lucky."

And so, in a strange irony of war and retribution, the *Ward* also rests in Leyte Gulf. The same ship that started my Pearl Harbor search and was the genesis of this book rests in waters that are relatively shallow, although the deep abyss of the Philippine Trench is only a few miles west. Proud, lucky *Ward* met the same fate as midget sub *16-A*, three years later to the day. Is there some meaning in this kind of symmetry? Much as I've pondered these things, I can't find any lessons to impart, other than clichés. Let her sinking serve only to remind us that in modern naval war, even the victors are chastened by tragedy and loss. The only lesson I can draw is that war should be chosen as a last resort.

Even as U.S. Marines and GIs poured across the Philippines in late 1944 and early 1945, Japan refused to surrender, despite the loss of most of her South Pacific empire. This left the Americans only two choices: Let Japan escape, unrepentant and suicidal and unreformed. Or pursue total war, in hopes of a more lasting peace afterward. The choice was no choice. The war would have to go on until there was no doubt in any Japanese mind who was the victor and who was the vanquished.

If only that truth and that mutual acknowledgment could have been established at Leyte—but it was not to be.

More Pacific graveyards would need to be created to end this awful war.

CHAPTER SEVEN

BIKINI ATOLL

Indianapolis and Bikini Island, July 1945–July 1946

BY NEW YEAR'S DAY 1945, THE STRATEGIC POSITION OF THE UNITED STATES in the Pacific had completely reversed itself from December 7, 1941—that day when the U.S. had been completely outgunned and outmanned by Japan's surprise attack. Three years later, despite the deaths of thousands of American servicemen and the loss of a wealth of ships and aircraft, the defeat of Japan was only a matter of time and of blood.

With the Greater East Asia Co-Prosperity Sphere more of a misnomer than ever and millions of Asians under Japanese control eager for her overthrow, Japan still fought on. Even if her navy was long gone and even if she would surely be defeated, she would make the American victory as costly as possible on land and in the air.

From strongholds in caves and redoubts from Luzon in the Philippines to Iwo Jima and Okinawa, Japanese soldiers would fight on. And thousands of her pilots were now being trained for suicidal kamikaze missions. As evidence of Japan's fatalistic determination, even though the Japanese commander in Luzon recognized by Christmas that Leyte was lost and had been mostly written off by Tokyo, his abandoned men kept on fighting Americans on Leyte until May 1945.

Ironies abound as members of the press and the military, urged not to smoke or pilfer, tour the site of an atomic bomb test on Bikini Atoll shortly after the blast. Some 80 obsolete naval vessels, among them battleships and aircraft carriers, were the target of the first bomb. The painting (above) depicts the nuclear test explosion on Bikini Atoll after the war.

Despite costly mopping-up operations to the south, the American focus now was on bringing pain to Japan itself. Island bases were needed near enough to Japan to facilitate an aerial softening up of her home islands, and Saipan and Okinawa would do. But since Saipan was a good 1,500 miles from Tokyo, Iwo Jima was selected as the intermediate stopping point. Unfortunately, taking Iwo Jima would prove to be perhaps the hardest land campaign the U.S. fought in the Pacific. Why? Because at Iwo Jima, Japan was fully able to exercise her last-ditch ground strategy of making America pay in soldiers' lives for every inch of land captured. This previously unfortified island might have been easily taken in fall 1944 after the collapse of Saipan and Guam, but it hadn't been done then. The intervening months until the February invasion allowed Japan to turn the island into an underground redoubt of multilayered tunnels and almost invisible gun emplacements. Even though the U.S. had bombed Iwo Jima almost constantly since fall 1944, Japan's fortification went ahead largely unimpeded because construction was done underground, mostly invisible from the air and impervious to anything but a direct hit.

Some Americans predicted the island would be taken in four days. But reality set in from the first moment of the invasion on February 19, when the American landings began to founder. The beach was in reality a low lava cliff, difficult for men and amphtracs to climb. On that day more than 2,000 Americans died, out of the 30,000 who landed. Then the campaign crept along yard by yard, taking a full six weeks to stabilize. The U.S. lost more than 5,000 men overall, while Japan lost more than 20,000. And like a monster that wouldn't die, Japanese soldiers, starving but armed and ready to kill, kept popping up from hiding until summer 1945.

Okinawa would be the next step, in April. Seven days after the invasion of Okinawa, on April 7, one final naval battle took place just off the southern coast of Japan, sending the massive battleship *Yamato*, sister to *Musashi,* to the bottom with nearly 2,500 men on board. She was on a suicide mission, since she didn't have enough fuel on board to return to port.

So the two "super-sisters" rested on the ocean bottom by April 1945. What many don't realize is that there was a third, newer, and even larger, super-sister, *Shinano,* which had been converted in 1944 to an aircraft carrier, the largest in the world. In late 1944, on her maiden voyage out of Tokyo Bay, this carrier was sunk by U.S. submarine Capt. Joseph Enright before the U.S. even knew she existed. In fact, U.S. naval intelligence discounted Enright's reports of the torpedoing, and it wasn't until years later that his spectacular kill was confirmed by Japan. I liked the Enright story so much that I wanted to go find *Shinano*. Through a Japanese colleague at Woods Hole, I approached the Japanese government but was denied permission to enter their waters and look for her off Tokyo Bay.

After the sinking of *Yamato,* the prospect of kamikaze attacks would become a potential obstacle to the American advance, since Japan still had several thousand aircraft scattered about the region, even if little fuel. And in early April, kamikaze attacks were carried out, doing damage to the new carrier *Wasp,* the *Franklin,* and the old *Saratoga,* and totaling the destroyer transport *Dickerson* and killing her skipper. Samuel Eliot Morison calculates that 3,000 kamikaze attacks were carried out in the Okinawa campaign, exacting a psychological and materiel toll in the process.

When the invasion of Okinawa began on April 1, the U.S. had assembled a vast armada of amphibious and support ships, and by April 9, had brought 160,000 men to shore. Kamikaze attacks on ships wore on, sinking more, including the destroyer *Mannert L. Abele,* which went down in a record five minutes, and the destroyers *Pringle, Luce, Morrison,* and others. Morison calculates that 90 American ships were sunk or destroyed in the Okinawan campaign, making it the largest American naval graveyard in the war. More than 12,000 American sailors and soldiers would die at Okinawa by the time it was declared secured in early July 1945.

Even though the U.S. was paying a terrible price for its advances, it was advancing, and Japan was paying an even higher price as it retreated. The home islands were now being subjected to fierce aerial bombing and even offshore shelling for the first time in the war. A B-29 bombing of Japanese cities on March 9–10 reportedly burned more than 80,000 Japanese to death, a precursor of what would come in late summer at Hiroshima and Nagasaki. And still Japan fought on, despite the war now touching her own shores and her own civilians, despite the loss of Okinawa and Iwo Jima. In fact, Japan was moving men, aircraft, and materiel to defend the southern island of Kyushu, where she thought the U.S. would first come ashore.

As this grand drama was playing itself out, the cruiser *Indianapolis* was once again on the front lines, taking part in the pre-invasion bombardment of Okinawa begun on March 4, 1945. For seven days, she had hurled huge shells onto Japanese shore defenses. Then on March 31, the day before the invasion, a Japanese fighter on a kamikaze mission appeared out of nowhere and took aim at the ship's bridge. From only about 25 feet up, the pilot released his bomb, then crashed onto the main deck. The crash itself did little damage, but the bomb burrowed deep into the ship, blowing holes through the bottom and killing nearly ten crewmen caught in sudden flooding. But the ship didn't sink and made it back to San Francisco under her own power for repairs.

After the overhaul, the next mission for *Indianapolis* was to proceed at high speed to Tinian in the Marianas. Her cargo: parts and fissionable material to be used in atomic bombs destined for Hiroshima and Nagasaki. Leaving San Francisco on July 16, she reached Pearl Harbor in three days. She then proceeded to Tinian in record time, ten days after leaving San Francisco, and unloaded her secret cargo. With the war now reaching its horrendous conclusion, *Indianapolis* was next dispatched to further duty off Okinawa. The crew of *Indianapolis* would have been justified in thinking that their greatest mission had just been completed. In fact, their worst test was yet to come.

According to public records, *Indianapolis* Capt. Charles B. McVay III requested a destroyer escort to cross the Philippine Sea, but was denied this because his superiors deemed it "not necessary." He also was not informed of the earlier sinking of the destroyer *Underhill* on his planned route of travel. One small comfort: to protect against potential submarine hazards, the captain was authorized to "zigzag" at his discretion, visibility permitting.

Indianapolis left Guam on July 28. While she did zigzag when visibility allowed on those two days, limited visibility the night of July 29–30 prompted the captain to put her on a straight course. Just after midnight, as he and much of the crew slept, disaster struck. Japanese sub *I-58* exploded two torpedoes against her starboard side. As fire and flood scourged the proud ship, her crew would have 12 minutes to get off before she went down.

Bikini Atoll encircles a nuclear graveyard. Atomic bomb tests here in 1946 sank 12 large vessels, including—for revenge— prizes of war: *Nagato,* the Japanese battleship that coordinated the Pearl Harbor attack, and Germany's *Prinz Eugen.* Another 21 tests through 1958 rendered the isles of Bikini uninhabitable but the waters finally recovered; today sport divers flock to Bikini to explore the underwater sites.

Those 12 minutes must have seemed like an eternity in hell. Captain McVay and many of those who survived stumbled straight out of a deep sleep into a face-to-face confrontation with death. About 400 men never left the ship. They went to the bottom, as *Indianapolis* capsized and sank. Another 900 men made it into the water, some in rafts, many swimming or clinging to debris. They considered themselves lucky to have survived. But as the next five days wore on, many more would join those who had already died. And those who lived would come to envy those who were dead.

Why? The sinking of *Indianapolis* was perhaps Admiral Blunder's finest hour in all the Pacific War. This was not even blunder in the thick of battle. This was disconnected bureaucratic stupidity, laziness, and fatal negligence. The first blunder was sending the ship out unescorted, and not warning the captain of what lay ahead. The second was ignoring an Army pilot's report of flares from the life rafts seen that first night. The third was ignoring the fact that *Indianapolis,* not known for being slow, failed to arrive at port as scheduled. The fourth was ignoring an intercepted message from the captain of *I-58* bragging about his kill of an American cruiser.

Eager for action, *Indianapolis* crewmen will enact one of the great dramas of the war: After delivering the first operational atomic bomb to Tinian in 1945, the *Indianapolis* headed for Guam. Two Japanese torpedoes sent her to the bottom in 12 minutes—and 900 of her crew into the water. They spent five days there, under nearly constant shark attack, suffering from hunger, thirst, exposure, and wounds before being rescued. The few who survived reach safe haven (above). The captain of the submarine, Mochitsura Hashimoto, died in 2000, age 91, having spent the last years of his life as a Shinto priest in Kyoto, Japan.

As a result of all these blunders, for five days 900 men were left in mid-ocean to be savaged by shark attack and dehydration. Not until the morning of August 2 were the survivors, mostly held afloat by life jackets, sighted by an aircraft on routine patrol. Once that discovery was made, a radius of 100 miles was combed, but it was much too late to serve any purpose. The final tally was that only 316 of the *Indianapolis* crew were saved, out of 1,199 men.

Captain McVay was later court-martialed for the loss of his ship. Coming from a Navy family including a father who was an admiral, Captain McVay later committed suicide. It wasn't until October 1999 that he was exonerated by an Act of Congress. As survivor Paul Murphy testified before a Senate committee on September 14, 1999, "Of the hundreds of Navy captains who lost their ships to enemy action during World War II, our captain was the only one to be court-martialed. Admiral Spruance, for whom the *Indianapolis* served as flagship, was opposed to the court-martial. Adm. Chester Nimitz was opposed to the court-martial. Their recommendations were ignored.

"Mr. Chairman, the loss of the *Indianapolis* remains the greatest sea disaster in the history of the United States Navy. This was an embarrassment to the Navy because they never even noticed we were missing until survivors were spotted quite by accident four days later. Someone had to be blamed . . . so they made our skipper take the blame to avoid admitting mistakes which were not his."

In the Philippine Sea northwest of Guam, the cruiser *Indianapolis* rests somewhere on the bottom. As a naval officer for more than 30 years, and having spent more than 40 years at sea, I have kept the story of this tragic sinking in the back of my mind for as long as I can remember. I can't think of a more frightening death than to be eaten by a shark, even if I were already dead. I've told my wife that the last thing I want is to be buried at sea. Cremation with my ashes poured safely on land is what I want done.

I remember vividly the opening scene of *Jaws,* when the young girl is violently pulled beneath the waves, and later, when the sea captain tells of his hatred of sharks, having himself survived the sinking of *Indianapolis.* I've read Dan Kurzman's book *Fatal Voyage,* about the *Indianapolis,* more than once, considering whether I should become a hunter of that ship just like the sharks

were hunters of her crew. The moment after I discovered *Titanic,* I started receiving letters from surviving crew members of *Indianapolis* asking me to find her.

But the more I thought about such a hunt, the more improbable it seemed. To begin with, she was sunk in a remote stretch of the Philippine Sea between Guam and the Philippine Islands, which meant that logistics would prove difficult. And the ocean floor in this area is deep and rugged, some of the most difficult underwater terrain in the world. A sonar could easily mistake a rock formation for the ship. And what if she had broken up on the way down? But I've been up against those obstacles before, and have been successful.

What continued to bother me was the length of time that elapsed between the ship's sinking and the rescue of her surviving crew. Five days they drifted in the water as many were eaten by sharks. No logbook survived from either the *Indianapolis* or the Japanese sub, for the latter quickly left the scene. There were no other ships nearby to verify the site of the sinking. So the search area would be large, far larger than any previous search I'd undertaken, far larger than for the *Yorktown.* My best estimate is the search area would approach 1,000 square nautical miles, ten times the area for *Titanic.*

No, I would sit this one out. At least, until some new technological innovation came along that gave me an edge, a better chance for success.

Horrible as the sinking of *Indianapolis* was, there were greater stupidities and horrors to come before this war was over. Perhaps the greatest blunder in history was Japan's refusal to surrender, even as the American Navy was surrounding and shelling her home islands, and her ports and cities were being pulverized by B-29s. The second prime minister to succeed the fallen Tojo took office in April 1945. Baron Suzuki was supposedly in favor of peace, but because the army and its militarists still dominated Japan and its government, he could not utter the word. Instead, according to Samuel Eliot Morison, he and his government tried to save face by having Stalin serve as a mediator. And even worse, they did not prepare their people for the price they would have to pay for staying in the war. By late July 1945, just about every Japanese city was now at risk of being bombed to rubble. But the stream of surreal propaganda announcements from Tokyo did not stop. Even the loss of Okinawa somehow became a "great Japanese strategic victory."

U.S. submarine *Pilotfish*, among the vessels sunk during atomic tests in 1946, rests on the bottom of Bikini Lagoon. Islanders, relocated to Kili Island some 500 miles away before testing began, now mark some wrecks with buoys and actively promote sport diving in the waters of their former home.

On July 26, the Potsdam joint declaration issued by President Truman, Prime Minister Churchill, and Gen. Chiang Kai-Shek called on Japan to proclaim its unconditional surrender, or face "prompt and utter destruction." The Japanese were given a week to respond. But even as the kamikaze kept up their attacks, even as Japan began to build bomb shelters to protect its people, Prime Minister Suzuki responded only that Potsdam was not worth responding to.

This brings us to the biggest Pacific graveyards of all, Hiroshima and Nagasaki. And it brings us to the time-worn issue of whether the use of the atomic bomb could or should have been avoided. And whether its use was moral or not. Granted the incineration of tens of thousands of misinformed and oppressed Japanese civilians was a wretched tragedy. In a perfect world, even

if the Japanese government and military refused to give in, it would have been preferable to find some way to circumvent and overthrow their leaders without killing any more Japanese people.

But 1945 was a far from perfect world. So without the cooperation of the Japanese government and the military, the only American alternatives to using the atomic bomb were 1) to let Japan escape judgment by stopping the war then and there; 2) blockade Japan and starve the country into submission, while accepting the constant threat of kamikaze retribution upon our ships; or 3) rely on conventional bombing and a land invasion to occupy Japan, multiplying the horrors of Tarawa and Iwo Jima by a thousandfold, and losing tens of thousands more American and Allied men in the process.

Nuclear horror engulfs Hiroshima, Japan, on August 6, 1945. A single atomic bomb dropped from a U.S. B-29 destroyed most of the city and killed upward of 70,000 Japanese. While the decision to use the bomb has remained controversial, it hastened the end of the war and made the invasion of the Japanese homeland—a military exercise that would have cost thousands of Allied lives—unnecessary. Reconstruction of the city began about 1950, and today Hiroshima resembles many other Japanese cities. It has become a spiritual center for the movement to ban the use of nuclear weapons.

Those "what ifs" could entertain us for years. But the fact was that the U.S. had fought a conquering, totalitarian, racist aggressor inch by inch all the way from the front yard of Australia and the central Pacific to the doorstep of Japan. The U.S. and the Allies had paid in blood to liberate Asia. And even in these final days the enemy was unrepentant and unconciliatory, suicidally aggressive and still dangerous, with a million men under arms on the home islands, huge stores of ammunition, and 5,000 aircraft left. Other seemingly less brutal methods could have prolonged the war indefinitely, or cost thousands more innocent American and Japanese lives.

I don't think President Truman had any choice. I don't see any other alternative that would have so quickly shocked the deluded Japanese leadership into unconditional surrender. It is the curse of war that the innocent often suffer more than the guilty. A new Japan would have to be built on the consensus and participation of an informed, empowered people, not on feudal dreams of grandeur that benefited only a chosen elite. The tragedy is that the people would have to pay such a price to get there.

And so at 2:25 in the morning of August 6, the B-29 *Enola Gay* took off from Tinian with what was code-named "Little Boy" in its bomb bay, a device assembled from parts delivered there by the ill-fated *Indianapolis,* whose few survivors had just been rescued a few days before. The four-ton, 12.5-kiloton bomb was airburst at about 1,500 feet above the Japanese Second Army Headquarters in Hiroshima at 9:15 a.m.

Within seconds, the fireball generated temperatures of 300,000° C, the top of the atomic cloud soaring above 50,000 feet. The blast itself created a 1,200-mile-an-hour wind that leveled all wooden houses within a mile of ground zero, and even collapsed concrete buildings or blew out windows and doors. Bare skin suffered thermal burns as far as two miles away, and most creatures exposed to thermal rays within a half mile of the explosion died instantly. People exposed to radiation within 1,500 feet of ground zero also died, while others were blinded by the thermal wave. Survivors within three miles later developed cancer, keloids, cataracts, leukemia, low white blood cell counts, anemia, loss of hair, and bloody discharges.

To put a wrapper on this day of horror, a black rain fell that really was the settling of airborne radioactive debris. The final death toll at Hiroshima was put at 140,000, or between one-third and one-half of the city's population, according to official figures given to the United Nations in 1976.

Three days later, on August 9, "Fat Man" was dropped on Nagasaki. The physical and human consequences were the same, although the death toll there was put at 70,000. Among survivors, 350,000 Japanese would qualify for government-funded treatments for aftereffects of the nuclear blasts.

It was only after these twin horrors were visited upon the country that the Japanese government began to come apart. The emperor and the Imperial family finally emerged as advocates of surrender, while the diehards, including Admiral Toyoda, believed that to save face the country should fight on until annihilation, or at least one final battle. Even as the emperor's unconditional surrender was being sent to the Allies, militarist plots to kidnap him and kill the prime minister almost succeeded. It was not until August 14 that Japan's definitive surrender was communicated and then announced by the Allies. And it was not for a few more days that the Allies felt confident that the surrender would really be respected. Members of the Imperial family had to visit key military posts to make sure no diehards subverted the peaceful surrender.

It's ironic how as World War II finally ended, we can see how much it has changed the shape of the world and the nature of war. The world in 1941 and 1942 was one where totalitarianism looked like the wave of the future. Great chunks of the globe were under the heel of goose-stepping warlords. The U.S. was just emerging from two decades of isolationism. Britain was the world's leading colonial power. But by 1945, all that was turned upside down. The U.S. for at least a year would be the unchallenged superpower, and the British Empire would begin to shrink radically. And warfare had changed so much. So many terrible lessons had been learned. But all those transformations were to be overshadowed by the beginning of the nuclear era. A terrible new weapon had been developed that would almost cancel out everything else, shifting the theater into the realm of esoteric theory, into the study of blast waves and kill ratios and radioactivity. This awful weapon, which has been used only twice in combat—at Hiroshima and Nagasaki—would redefine foreign policy and military tactics and strategy.

At war's end, the horror of nuclear incineration was tempered by the fact that only one nation owned the bomb, the victorious United States, and it had no challenger on the horizon. American military leaders and scientists wanted to publicly demonstrate their new weapon, which had been exploded secretly for the first time on July 16, 1945, in the New Mexico desert. Everyone wanted to know more about the weapon that ended World War II.

If our leaders had known in July 1946 what they know now about the impact of radiation, they might never have undertaken any tests. But they were blissfully naive, and so exactly a year after the bombing of Hiroshima and Nagasaki, the U.S. staged a pair of nuclear bomb tests in and about Bikini and Kwajalein Atolls, ostensibly to gauge their effects on naval forces.

There was such hope at the end of World War II and the dawn of the nuclear age. For a brief moment, it seemed as though the United Sates and its democratic values might shape a new, safer, more democratic world. And to deter any who might think otherwise, the United States, the only nuclear power, could back up its ideals with a powerful bang.

Indeed, the innocent Bikini Islanders were asked at a church service one Sunday morning if they would agree to "temporarily" relocate from their homeland, so that this terrible weapon that might bring an end to all war could be thoroughly tested. Their leader Juda agreed to the move, but little did he or the Americans know that the consequences of this test would drag on for decades and tarnish America's good name in the region, as well as cause the nuclear contamination of what had been, until the arrival of war, one more serene Pacific tropical paradise.

This test to end all tests was called "Operation Crossroads," because it signified the intersection of conventional and nuclear war. "Crossroads" involved 42,000 men, more than 250 ships for support, more than 150 aircraft, and thousands of tons of materiel.

Three tests were scheduled: "Able" on July 1, "Baker" on July 26, and "Charlie," which never happened. "Able" was a 2.3-kiloton airburst detonation about 500 feet up in the air, dropped from a B-29. "Baker" was the same size weapon suspended about 100 feet beneath one of the target vessels. There were 90 targets riding at anchor, with all their valuable contents stripped, but loaded with fuel,

water, and ammo to replicate their normal displacements, as well as instruments to measure the effects of the blast.

"Able" did not go quite as expected. For one thing, the bomb landed about 500 yards off target. And while it did sink the heavy cruiser *Sakawa*, the destroyers *Anderson* and *Lamson*, and the attack transports *Carlisle* and *Gilliam*, the audience seemed to have been expecting something more dramatic. Most of the ships stayed afloat. In fact, the damage was so light and the radiation levels appeared so low that American crews were climbing aboard the surviving ships only a day later.

"Baker's" underwater blast was a bit more spectacular, sinking eight ships, including the battleships *Arkansas* and *Nagato,* the carrier *Saratoga,* and the submarines *Apogon* and *Pilotfish. Saratoga* was hit first by an awesome 90-foot wall of water, then another, and she sank in several hours. But "Baker" also generated a spray of radioactive water and debris from the bottom of the lagoon that bathed most of the surviving ships. They were judged too radioactive to work with, and so began a very dangerous and time-consuming process of "scrubbing" the vessels.

Now out of the bottle, the nuclear genie began to show its even darker side. Researchers realized the support fleet itself had become contaminated from low-level radiation in the algae and other marine growth on the ships' hulls, and in the support ships' seawater piping systems. So in August and September, the surviving ships were towed to Kwajalein Atoll, where the water was uncontaminated and where they could be scrubbed without as much risk to support crews and ships. Work continued on target ships at Kwajalein into 1947.

To put it bluntly, military researchers in those early years were flying blind when it came to the risks of radiation. The initial learning process involved no more than the usual dose of trial and error, but unfortunately, the consequences of error when it came to radiation were probably more grim than anything known before. Radiation and its attendant systemic and genetic damage—as increasingly apparent at Hiroshima and Nagasaki—somehow seemed more insidious than being injured or killed in a conventional way.

The unsuspecting researchers and Navy crews at Bikini were only the first in a long line of people who would be exposed to radiation risks much higher than

Ghostly in the underwater gloom, *Pilotfish* attracts a diver. The 240-square-mile lagoon of Bikini Atoll opened for diving in 1966 and, supporters hope, may one day be a marine park.

anyone knew. On that morning in 1946 when the Bikinians consented to "temporarily" relocate, they had expected to be back in a matter of months. As radiation data became clearer, they were instead shuttled to a series of vastly inferior islands, where starvation, lack of water, and poverty were chronic problems. And in 1954 the "Bravo" H-bomb test utterly scorched Bikini again, and seems to have blown radioactive material over their new temporary home at Kili. Finally in the 1970s some islanders began to resettle on Bikini at their own risk. A U.S. government trust fund of reparations payments

was later established, and as of this writing, with radiation down to acceptable levels, Bikini has established itself as a leading nuclear dive site.

What was an unfortunate blight on the history of the Bikini people, and also on postwar American conduct in the Pacific, has finally become an asset to tourism, albeit 40 years too late to make up for the initial pain. Divers, researchers, photographers, and historians now come to chronicle the sunken nuclear graveyard at Bikini. Luckily, the depths are such that the sites are accessible to scuba divers, both sport and professional.

I haven't had the chance to explore Bikini Island, but many others have. In 1989 and 1990, Dan Lenihan's Submerged Cultural Resources Unit from the National Park Service, the same group that had mapped Graveyard Pearl Harbor prior to my own expedition, studied 9 of the 21 vessels sunk in Kwajalein and Bikini Atolls during Operation Crossroads. My friend Jim Delgado also took part in the expedition. The dives they did were mostly decompression dives of 100–180 feet, and even those depths made the work difficult enough. They started the documentation of each wreck by first having an illustrator draw the ship from its original plans. Then they would watch video footage of the dives, and make adjustments. They also rigged up a face mask with a microphone inside that was connected to the video cameras, so that the diver's comments tracked with the visuals of the wreck as he examined it.

The National Park Service report speaks for itself:

"U.S.S. *Saratoga,* the most accessible site to divers and therefore of primary interest for evaluation, became the principal focus of the documentation project. Prior to the test, its armament was stripped and fixtures removed; blast gauge towers and other instruments designed to measure the effects of the blast, as well as aircraft, vehicles, and radars, were mounted on its decks. The blast from Baker blew the vessel 800 yards from its position and inundated it with a 94-foot-tall blast wave, sinking it to the bottom.

"Investigation of the site revealed a virtually intact vessel sitting upright in 180 feet. Sections of *Saratoga* rise within 40 feet of the surface, with its mast and island visible from the surface. The worst damage, aft on the starboard side of the hull, is where the blast ripped loose shell plating and exposed frames. The flight deck also suffered extensive damage. The blast wave and the thousands of tons of water that rained down from the blast column smashed the wood decking and ruptured the steel deck. The vessel's superstructure remains recognizable, although the ship's funnel was toppled and crushed onto the flight deck. *Saratoga*'s island and mast remain standing, though various components were shattered or blown off. All five of the aircraft secured to the deck for the test were swept from the ship by either the blast or the waves. The four aircraft stowed in the hanger remained at their stations. Five 20mm antiaircraft guns were observed on the site, two on the lagoon floor near the sheared off stern sponson gun platform. Test equipment installed prior to the blast still remains. NPS divers penetrated several of the *Saratoga*'s interior compartments, including the flag plot bridge, navigation bridge, pilothouse, and aerological office."

"The group also examined the attack transport *Gilliam,* which ended up at "surface zero" for the airburst detonation of "Able." Understandably, it suffered more than any other ship that was looked at. As the NPS report says, *"Gilliam* sits upright on the bottom at 180 feet. It suffered severe hull damage, its successive decks compressed into the hold and hull sides above the waterline bent inwards up to ten feet."

The NPS expedition also had a Navy ROV take a look at *Carlisle. Carlisle* stood more than 400 yards from "Able" surface zero, but it took some hits as well: "The blast moved the vessel approximately one hundred and fifty feet, knocked down the stacks and mainmast, pushed the superstructure to the starboard, and damaged the foremast. Although *Carlisle,* an identical sister ship to *Gilliam,* was farther from surface zero, it too suffered considerable damage. Its decks were also compressed down and its shell plating buckled, dented, and dished."

The NPS document notes that *Nagato,* the one-time flagship of the Imperial Japanese Navy, endured both "Able" and "Baker." The investigators "found the *Nagato* inverted in one hundred and seventy feet of water. The vessel appears to have capsized stern first, the transom striking the sea bottom, causing the hull to fold across the aft deck. Aft of the rudders and screws is a major break in the stern hull. Torn plates reveal twisted and splayed frames in the interior, a result of the deadly force that struck the vessel."

Jim Delgado says that Lady Sara fascinated him the most of all the wrecks at Bikini. *"Saratoga* is my favorite ship," he says. "She taught the Navy how to fly, and had a bad time during the war, with kamikaze and other hits at Guadalcanal and Malaya. She played a leading role at Iwo Jima. At Bikini, she was sunk fully loaded. She still has aircraft on her hangar deck. The researchers really didn't think she would sink. But the nuclear blast reverberated off the bottom. She went up on a 90-foot wave, then a smaller one, and sank in several hours. I was able to check out Admiral Halsey's day cabin on *Saratoga.*

"As for the submarines," he says, "they are shrink

Continued on page 244

Bizarrely nonchalant, military and civilian VIPs watch a test explosion on Enewetak Atoll, another of the Marshall Islands, in 1951. They are just 12.5 miles from ground zero. Unaware of the danger from radiation, observers in earlier tests routinely boarded targeted ships just hours after a blast.

Following pages: A man-made dawn breaks over Bikini in 1954. The camera is about 50 miles from ground zero. This was Bravo, the largest of the U.S. tests, a 15-megaton hydrogen blast a thousand times greater than the Hiroshima bomb. After the test, cesium 137 fallout blanketed Bikini, making the atoll unlivable.

wrapped around their frames. They were exposed to 5,000 pounds per square inch of pressure in a millisecond. In the case of *Apogon,* a bubble of air was forced through her, shot from stern to bow, and peeled her right open.

"The *Nagato* is also amazing," Delgado says. "Here is the ship that was Yamamoto's command ship at Midway, a piece of living history parked on the bottom. Another great ship is the *Anderson*; she carries a lot of history. *Anderson* screened the *Yorktown* at Midway, the *Lexington* at Coral Sea and Guadalcanal, and she provided close support at Tarawa. She's intact, on her side, 130 feet down, lying on her port side. *Anderson* was very close to the "Able" burst. She was in the fireball, and you can see some washboarding on her hull, either from the heat or the blast wave. Her five-inch gun barrel is bent back at the bridge. She took a 9,000° heat blast."

I asked him about *Prinz Eugen,* because she was *Bismarck's* escort on her fatal maiden voyage, an earlier search that brings me a lot of memories. It turns out she survived both Able and Baker, and then was going to be decontaminated and towed away when a storm drove her aground at Kwajalein Atoll and sank her, upside down. Her stern is above water, sticking up for all to see. One of her props was later cut off and given to the West German government.

Despite all the men, equipment, and publicity surrounding Operation Crossroads, the scientist in me questions the value of this very large and expensive experiment. Delgado agrees, and directs me to the report that he, Lenihan, and Larry Murphy wrote, which NPS published in 1991:

"Crossroads was a demonstration to the world, particularly the Soviet Union, of the United States' wealth and power at a time when the nation, in the aftermath of the war, was assuming the role of the global leader. The Los Alamos National Laboratory's archivist and historian notes that the prevalent attitude of the lab's weapons scientists then, as well as now, was that Crossroads was not a true scientific test. Rather it was 'purely a show.' Such a demonstration is critical when a new leader assumes the stage. The demonstration of this fact, given the nuclear apprehension of its own citizens, was of paramount importance to the U.S. government, and as early as April 1946, Admiral Blandy, speaking in a live radio broadcast, stated that Cross-

roads would 'help us to be what the world expects our great, non-aggressive and peace-loving country to be ...the leader of those nations which seek nothing but just and lasting peace.' More bluntly, commentator Raymond Gram Swing noted that Crossroads, 'the first of the atomic era war games...is a notice served on the world that we have the power and intend to be heeded.' Several factors support this view. The concept of the United States as the richest nation on earth was implicit at Bikini. Vannevar Bush, writing in 1949, noted that the production of atomic weapons 'requires such major expenditures and such major effort that they cannot be afforded at all except by countries that are very strong economically and industrially.' Such a nation was the United States, for we 'paid the bill' for developing such weapons. By expending two of these extremely expensive and rare weapons at Bikini, the United States was demonstrating its wealth, a fact underscored by the sacrifice of a tremendous fleet of target ships. All in a destructive display that echoed the potlatch ceremonies of Northwest Native Americans who proved their wealth by purposeful destruction of valued and valuable items."

And so with Bikini, we come to the end of the great Pacific War. If only our naive expectations about nuclear weapons had proved true. If only we had been able to build a peaceful community of nations that had outgrown war. About the best thing that can be said about nuclear weapons is that they appear to have prevented a conventional war between the U.S. and the Soviet Union. And yet, take a look at the sad roster of the surrogate wars that were fought between 1946 and now—in Korea, Vietnam, Afghanistan, Angola, the Horn of Africa, and elsewhere. I wonder if the nuclear standoff didn't just displace conventional warfare into the laps of those nations least able to endure it.

It was uncharacteristic of the straight-shooting, slow-talking Americans to be staging global nuclear theater in front of hundreds of foreign journalists and dignitaries just to make foreign policy and strategic points. But you could say that is what we have been doing ever since. That is what much of nuclear strategy was, and is, for everybody. It was theater, and it was all theory. The U.S.S.R. showing off that they could make a 100-megaton H-bomb. Or President Reagan's Strategic

What Japanese torpedoes and kamikazes couldn't sink, nuclear fission did: 500-pound bombs,
still live, lie 130 feet down on the carrier *Saratoga*'s hangar deck. Divers can reach her bridge at
40 feet, her deck at 90. Even complete Helldivers survive. Not so her aft flight deck: Falling
seawater and debris created there a canyon 200 feet long, 70 feet wide, and up to 20 feet deep.

Defense Initiative showing the Soviets that we could out-design and out-spend them in a new weapons race. Or the Indians and Pakistanis each showing that they could incinerate the other, without actually doing it. And then all the doctrines and theories and scenarios that emerged, like Mutual Assured Destruction, first strikes, trading cities as sacrifices, accidental launches, underground testing, the SALT and START treaties and attendant signing ceremonies.

If these strange weapons prevent real killing and war, then so be it. Let's just hope that the line is never crossed between nuclear theater and reality. Hiroshima and Nagasaki were enough of a taste of nuclear reality. We learned that these weapons only have value as deterrents.

Once they are actually used, as President Eisenhower reportedly mused, it all becomes absurdity. Victory and defeat become hard to distinguish, and so nuclear war itself becomes an absurdity, a very nasty and expensive way for us to commit suicide.

And so at Bikini, not only do we come to the graveyard of many of the great ships that fought the Pacific War, we come to the graveyard of our national innocence. Because by the end of the 1940s, we were no longer the lone beneficent custodians of a biblically righteous weapon. We were beginning a sinister global competition that would go on for 40 years and would keep the world on constant nuclear alert for much of that time.

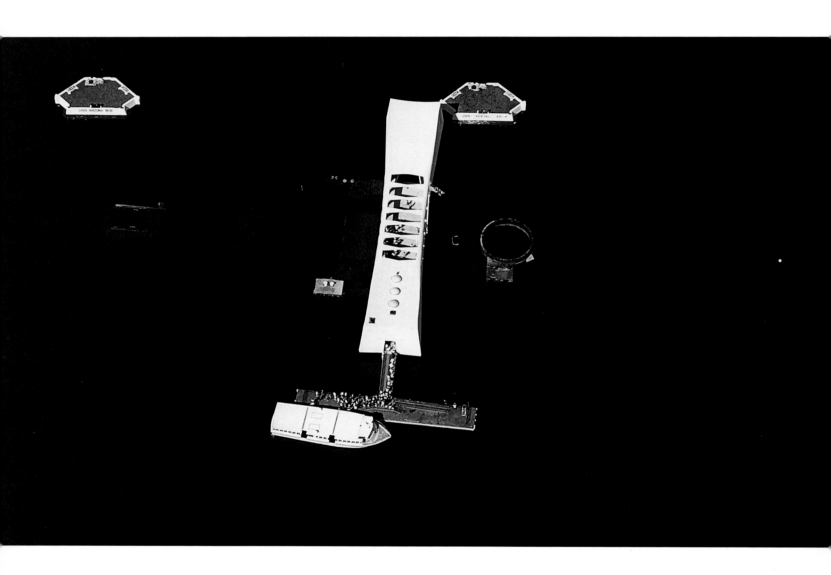

Arizona Memorial, Pearl Harbor, Hawaii

Robert D. Ballard

AND SO THAT BRINGS US TO THE END OF MY TOUR OF UNDERSEA PACIFIC graveyards. But I owe you a final report on where we started in this book—my two-week exploration of graveyard Pearl Harbor in November 2000, searching for the lost Japanese midget sub that triggered the first American shots of World War II.

In those two weeks we turned up many things of interest. One teaser we found that made us think we might be on the right trail was some Japanese torpedoes. We couldn't be sure if they were Type 91 or Type 97. Type 91s were the air-launched variety thrown at our helpless ships on that December morning of 1941, and 97s were submarine-launched versions.

However, a closer look showed us that the torpedoes had had their warheads removed and the access ports on their sides opened, suggesting that the Navy had examined these and dumped them on the bottom. It is possible that they were taken from the midget sub that beached on Oahu, but our experts at the Air and Space Museum believed they could see mounting lugs on the sides of one of them, indicating that it may have been air-launched and would have had no link to midget subs.

We also found a 1920s-era seaplane, probably a PD built by Douglas, of the kind that served at Pearl Harbor until 1935, when it was replaced by the more modern PBY Catalina. As far as we can tell, this PD with beaching gear and wheels attached is the only one of its type still in existence. But it's not in perfect condition, since it has no engines or wings. That tells me the Navy stripped it for parts and dumped it, probably toward the end of the 1930s.

And we found a Grumman F6F Hellcat, or possibly an F6F-5. Its landing gear is retracted and its propeller blades are bent backward, which points to a crash landing in the water. It seems to have rocket-launching stubs under the wings, and is painted in a manner that suggests it was lost between 1944 and 1947.

We also found amphtrac LVTs—amphibious tractors—like those that helped power the invasions of Tarawa and Saipan. They seem to be early versions that had hand-operated machine guns and no turrets. On at least one of them, the gunner's circular opening can be seen in the top of the driver's compartment.

And last of all, on our final day out, we took a close look at what our preliminary data suggested might be a conning tower, and a periscope lying nearby. This was the moment of truth for all of us. You could have heard a pin drop as we gathered in the cabin of *American Islander* to watch the video that a one-man sub had just brought back from the bottom. My heart was pounding as we were brought closer and closer to the ovoid "tower" and the rusted pipe, or "periscope." I looked good and hard, and swallowed, knowing that I'd have to tell everybody the bad news. What we were looking at wasn't a midget submarine. It was just more UUOs—unidentified undersea objects.

I'm very sorry to report that we closed down our expedition in search of the lost Japanese midget sub without finding it. The only other time I have done that was in my search for the Loch Ness monster in Scotland. And somehow, that one didn't hurt as much, for we don't even know if Nessie exists. We do know that five midget subs existed, and they tried to break into Pearl Harbor. I do not like to fail. And yet, the prospect is always there in underwater exploration.

Why no success in the midget sub hunt? I think the most likely explanation is that the sub, wounded or not, strayed beyond the confines of where she was last seen. If indeed she still had power late the night of December 7, when she sent that last radio message, she could have traveled miles away from the encounter with the *Ward*. She could have made it three or five or ten miles out to sea, and then gone down forever, sliding silently down the submerged volcanic slopes of Oahu Seamount.

Others remind me that she could have disintegrated into little pieces when she was shelled. Or been covered over by dredging outside this busy harbor. Maybe. But I think it more likely that she made a good try to get back to the mother ship, a few miles out. And that increases the size of the search area, beyond what I have the time and money to undertake right now. But I like the one that got away. It keeps me coming back.

As we've taken the reader on this tour of Pacific graveyards, you will have become aware of just how much is still out there waiting to be found. The mighty *Lexington,* and the proud Hornet, and the plucky *Wasp,* the super-sisters *Musashi, Yamato,* and *Shinano, PT-109* and *Indianapolis,* not to mention the hundreds of other ships and aircraft from both sides that went down.

They are scattered far and wide and deep beneath this vast ocean that takes up a huge chunk of our planet's surface. I and a few others have been lucky enough to explore only a few of them. Most of these Pacific graveyards are still beyond our reach, existing only in the memories of those who were there more than half a century ago.

But there is one Pacific graveyard that is accessible to us all, with or without sonar or minisubs or ATVs. I'm thinking of U.S.S. *Arizona,* that great battleship that became a fiery tomb only about 90 minutes after *Ward* fired on the lost Japanese midget sub.

Arizona is a graveyard that has become a public memorial, her keel resting on the bottom 40 feet down, but her deck and turrets are clearly visible just below the shimmering surface of Pearl Harbor. You can still see the iridescent rainbows caused by leaking fuel and oil, bubbling up to the surface as it has for the last 60 years. Most of the crewmen who were killed or trapped below decks went down with her, and there they rest to this day. Some 400 were removed in the 1940s. About 700 remain.

Dan Lenihan and Jim Delgado have done subsequent research at *Arizona.* They tell me it's like a moment frozen in time—a firehose dropped on deck, a broken teacup, an unbroken bottle. A young man's comb. A shot glass. The forward area where the killer explosion happened, they say, looks like a volcanic crater.

You can stand in the open-air memorial that straddles the sunken ship and read the names of those who went down. And you will stand there with tourists from the U.S. and Japan and many other places. You will feel the quiet reverence of this place, and you will wonder what secrets it holds to this day. If there is one lesson I would like readers to draw from my latest hunt, it is this: The secrets of the sea are the secrets of our history. The ocean bottom can serve as our memory when real memory fails. There is nothing like physical evidence to correct arguments that have gone on for decades. And even though the conventional story and the message of Arizona is that America was caught unawares at Pearl Harbor that awful morning—that's not quite the total story. Because the case of the *Ward* and the midget subs shows that we were more aware than we remember. We were more aware than we knew at the time. In fact, America fired the first shots at Pearl Harbor, though we didn't see the greater significance of what we were doing. But the historical fact is that we fired on the Japanese before they fired on us. Not that that diminishes their treachery, or the loss of *Arizona*. It just paints the full picture.

We fired the first shots that plunged us into the greatest war of all time, even if we didn't know it then. We didn't understand that we were making history, when we were. But that's the kind of history I like. Just like the bottom of the ocean: mysterious, contradictory, multilayered, one veil of secrecy pulled away only to reveal another.

And so, I leave the graveyards of the Pacific, still wanting the one that got away. And wanting to find all of those that have never been found. Wanting to uncover the histories of many people now turned into memorials at the bottom of the sea, living museums that tell the secrets of the dead.

What secrets did I uncover on this latest trek? That's a fair question. It's a long way from Pearl Harbor to Bikini Atoll. Four and a half years and 3,000 miles, to be exact. What do these places have to do with one another, except that they are graveyards? And my answer is, I think they are deeply connected. Pearl Harbor and the midget sub attack gave rise to the nuclear theater of Operation Crossroads.

How so? To distill everything down to its most simplistic, the surprise attack on Pearl Harbor taught us that complacency could invite aggression. The nuclear theater at Bikini taught everyone that a terrible weapon would deter those who were tempted to attack the United States.

And so it has been ever since. Deterrence—the military version of prevention—has been more important a doctrine than combat tactics for more than 50 years now. The objective since our fathers and grandfathers fought the Pacific War has been to deter war, so as to avoid the heroics needed to win such a losing war ever again. It is so much easier to deter than to find another MacArthur or another Spruance or another two million heroic men and women who could take back what had been lost, who could fashion victory from defeat.

Deterrence, in other words, is better than graveyards. Having seen so many of the latter, I could not agree more. There is no better way to honor the graveyards of the Pacific, the Atlantic, and everywhere else, than to remember one beautiful morning in December 1941, a glorious morning in paradise, when the green mountains of Oahu and the cobalt expanse of the Pacific suggested that ours was a world of beauty and light, and no darkness could ever change it—only to have this shattered by sky-borne messengers of death and unseen enemies beneath the sea.

That is the mystery of us as a people. Capable of such beauty and such nobility, we can also deliver evil. I cannot tell you why, other than we are steeped in ambiguity. You could say that a human life, and even human history, is the ebb and flow of this struggle between nobility and evil. I would like to think that the noble side of humanity is winning out, even if incrementally. But ours is a work in progress. To make the best of our future as a people, we must understand our past.

The exploration of our past is the search we all must make. Though we may fail in our quest to understand, we will surely fail if we don't undertake the search at all.

I made my commitment a long time ago. I would rather fail while exploring than fail by never having tried. And so I go forth from the disappointment of Graveyard Pearl Harbor to the next hunt. Because I'm in this for the journey—as much as for the destination.

After all, that's what exploration is.

WORLD WAR II: PACIFIC THEATER OF OPERATIONS

TIME LINE OF MAJOR EVENTS

1941

December 7	Japan attacks Pearl Harbor
December 8	United States declares war on Japan
December 9	China declares war on Japan
December 10	Guam surrenders to Japan
December 23	Wake Island surrenders to Japan
December 25	Hong Kong surrenders to Japan

1942

January 2	Manila falls to Japan
January 11	Japanese forces invade Netherlands East Indies
Febuary 1	American carriers raid Marshalls and Gilberts
Febuary 27	Allies lose the Battle of the Java Sea
March 7	Netherlands East Indies surrenders to Japan
April 9	Bataan surrenders to Japan
April 18	American carrier-based B-25 Mitchells bomb Tokyo
May 4 to 8	Allies win Battle of the Coral Sea
May 6	Corregidor surrenders to Japan
June 4 to 6	Allies win Battle of Midway
August 7	Allies land on Guadalcanal

1943

March 2-5	Allies defeat Japanese in the Battle of the Bismarck Sea
March 13	Japanese troops retreat across the Yangtze
May 30	Attu surrenders to the Allies
October 2	Allies capture Finschhafen
November 1	Americans land at Bougainville
November 20	Americans land at Tarawa and Makin
November 22	Allies meet in Cairo

1944

January 31	Americans land at Kwajelien
Febuary 17	U.S. carriers destroy Truk
Febuary 29	Allies land in the Admiralty Islands
March 22	Japan invades India
April 22	Allies invade Hollandia
June 15	Americans land at Saipan
June 15	First B-29 raid on Japan
June 19 to 20	Americans win the Battle of the Philippine Sea
July 21	Americans land at Guam
September 15	Americans land at Peleliu
October 20	Americans land at Leyte
October 23 to 26	Americans crush Japanese fleet in the Battle of Leyte Gulf

1945

January 9	Allies invade Luzon
January 22	Allies reopen land route to China
Febuary 19	U.S. Marines storm Iwo Jima
April 1	Americans land on Okinawa
August 6	Americans drop the atomic bomb on Hiroshima
August 9	Americans drop second atomic bomb on Nagasaki
August 10	Japan opens peace negotiations
August 14	Japan accepts allied surrender terms
September 2	Japan signs surrender
September 8	Japanese forces in China surrender
September 12	Japanese forces in Southeast Asia and Southwest Pacific surrender

Source: http://www.geocities.com/Athens/Crete/7962/timeline.html; accessed March 1, 2001.

ACKNOWLEDGMENTS

Although this book is entitled *Graveyards of the Pacific* and it was written in memory of those brave souls that were lost at sea during World War II, it is also about those who survived and it is these people I want to thank. Were it not for their willingness to open their hearts and bring back memories difficult to retell, this book would not have been possible.

Bob Ballard

I would first of all like to thank the late historian Adm. Samuel Eliot Morison for providing an insightful, vivid, and critical road map to the enormity of the great Pacific graveyard in his works, including *The Two-Ocean War.* If not for his in-depth research and vivid writing, I might not have been able to cover as much tactical and historical ground.

My thanks also to Donald M. Goldstein, Katherine V. Dillon, and J. Michael Wenger for research and insights in their work, *The Way it Was: Pearl Harbor* giving a moment-by-moment, blow-by-blow accounting of that terrible day in December 1941.

My special appreciation to fellow Santa Fean and writer Dan Lenihan at the Submerged Cultural Resources Unit of the National Park Service Southwest Division, for supplying background material, library access, and insight into his personal exploration of several of the key sites that this book covers. I would also like to thank Dr. Steven Ewing of Patriots Point Museum in Charleston, South Carolina, for directing me to survivors of key Pacific battles who were able to give their own firsthand accounts of some of the key events of this huge Pacific war.

My special thanks also to U.S.S. *Ward* survivors Russell Reetz and Will Lehner, who gave of their time and their memories during the short time we were together on *American Islander* off Pearl Harbor. They were there when the first U.S. shots of World War II were fired, and they may have seen that elusive Japanese midget sub go down to the bottom at dawn on December 7, 1941. Also to Kichiji Dewa, crewman on Japanese mother ship and submarine *I-16*, who knew the crew of the lost midget sub, and who to this day still loves submarines and the submariners' life; and to Japanese military historian Katsuhiro Hara and interpreter Makoto Uchino, for providing context to the brief encounter on Pearl Harbor Day between U.S.S. *Ward* and the lost midget sub.

I am equally indebted to all the interviewee-survivors of all the other battles in this book, who gave me their own memories and perceptions of times and places that most of us will never experience. My final salute to one of those interviewees, *Arizona* survivor Carl Carson, who died in January 2001, while I was writing this book. His death is a reminder that our World War II survivors are a precious and dwindling national resource, joining on a daily basis those heroes who went to their Pacific graveyards in 1941-45.

My appreciation to Tria Thalman of National Geographic Television for helping me maximize my time with Bob Ballard's November 2000 expedition and for providing me with transcripts of never-before-published interviews with Pearl Harbor survivors who were taken to Hawaii by the Navy in summer of 2000 to reflect on their memories of the Day of Infamy.

My thanks to Cathy Offinger of Bob Ballard's staff, for making Bob's far-flung expeditions come together, and for helping me understand the process; and to underwater photographer Kip Evans, for giving me a taste of a 1,200-foot dive.

And finally, my special appreciation to veteran master-editors Walton Rawls and Marian Gordin and researcher Winfield Swanson, for helping this non-Navy writer navigate some strange new waters without running aground; and to National Geographic illustrations editor Sadie Quarrier and designers Bill Marr and David Seager for their inspired work. My thanks also to Kathy Walburn at the Institute for Exploration, for helping me keep in touch with Bob Ballard as we both wrote and traveled. And my appreciation to Kevin Mulroy and Johnna Rizzo of National Geographic Books, for enabling this big project to come together.

Michael Hamilton Morgan

PHOTO CREDITS

INDEX

BIBLIOGRAPHY

Ballard, Robert D. and Rick Archbold, *Return to Midway.* Washington, D.C.: National Geographic Books/Madison Press. 1998.

Ballard, Robert D. with Rick Archbold. *The Lost Ships of Guadalcanal.* New York. Warner/Madison Press, 1993.

Burlingame, Burl. *Advance Force: Pearl Harbor.* Pacific Monographs.

Delgado, James P., Daniel J. Lenihan and Larry E. Murphy. *The Archeology of the Atomic Bomb.* Santa Fe: National Park Service Southwest Cultural Resources Center Professional Papers. 1991.

Fuchida, Mitsuo and Masatake Okuyima. *Midway: the Battle that Doomed Japan.* Annapolis: Naval Institute Press. 1955.

Fuller, Maj. Gen. J. F. C. *Decisive Battles of the Western World, Vol. 3.* London: Eyre & Spottiswoode. 1956.

Goldstein, Donald M., Katherine V. Dillon and J. Michael Wenger. *The Way it was: Pearl Harbor, The Original Photographs.* Washington: Brassey's. 1995.

Hammel, Eric. *Guadalcanal - the Carrier Battles.* New York: Crown Publishers. 1987.

Hoyt, Edwin P. *Japan's Way: The Great Pacific Conflict.* New York, McGraw-Hill, 1986.

Hoyt, Edwin P., *Blue Skies and Blood: the Battle of the Coral Sea.* New York: S. Eriksson. 1975

Johnson, William L. C., *The West Loch Story.* Seattle: Westlock Publications. 1986

Kurzman, Dan, *Fatal Voyage: the Sinking of the USS Indianapolis.* New York, Pocket Books. 1990

Layton, Edwin T., with Roger Pineau and John Costello. *And I Was There: Pearl Harbor and Midway - Breaking the Secrets.* New York, William Morrow & Co. 1985.

Lott, Arnold S. and Robert F. Sumrall. *USS Ward Fires First Shot WW II.* St. Paul, MN: First Shots Naval Vets. 1983.

Morison, Samuel Eliot. *The Two-Ocean War.* Boston, Little, Brown. 1965.

Popham, Harry. *"Eyewitness to Tragedy: Death of USS Princeton".* The History Network. May 1997.

Prange, Gordon W., with Donald M. Goldstein and Katherine V. Dillon. *Pearl Harbor: the Verdict of History.* New York: McGraw Hill. 1986.

Prange, Gordon W., with Donald M. Goldstein and Katherine V. Dillon. *Miracle at Midway.* New York: McGraw-Hill. 1982.

Regan, Stephen D. *In Bitter Tempest: The Biography of Admiral Frank Jack Fletcher.* Ames: Iowa State University Press. 1993

Roland, John. *Infamy. Pearl Harbor and Its Aftermath.* Garden City, NY: Doubleday, 1982.

Samuel Eliot Morison *"History of United States Naval Operations in World War II" Volume XII "Leyte"* (Little, Brown & Co., Boston 1963)

Stinnett, Robert B., *Day of Deceit - the Truth about FDR and Pearl Harbor.* New York: The Free Press, 2000.

Tregaskis, Richard. *Guadalcanal Diary,* New York: Random House. 1943.

Tully, Anthony, Jon Parshall and Richard Wolff. *"The Sinking of Shokaku – An Analysis".*

Woodward, C. Vann. *The Battle for Leyte Gulf.* New York: MacMIllan. 1947.

United States Submarine Losses – World War II. U.S. Navy Department, Office of the Chief of Naval Operations, Naval History Division, Washington, D.C.

Operation Crossroads, 1946. Washington: Defense Nuclear Agency, 1984.

"Statement of Paul J. Murphy before the Senate Armed Services Committee in support of Senate Resolution 26". Congressional Record. September 14, 1999.

Tully analysis of Shokaku sinking is on www.combinedfleet.com/shokaku

PT109 info from www.ptboats.org

JFK info from www.historyplace.com/kennedy/warhero

Leyte Gulf info from www.odyssey.dircon.co.uk/Leyte_Gulf

Guadalcanal battle info from redrival.com/carrierbattles

Coral Sea info from members.nbci.com/_xmcm/mkirkwood/coral

Larry Shelvey Truk dive accounts from www.bclinks.net/~sshort/shipwrecked/truk

Hiroshima/Nagasaki info from File://c:My%20Documents\atomdamage

**PUBLISHED BY THE
NATIONAL GEOGRAPHIC
SOCIETY**

John M. Fahey, Jr.
President & Chief Executive Officer

Gilbert M. Grosvenor
Chairman of the Board

Nina D. Hoffman
Executive Vice President

**PREPARED BY
THE BOOK DIVISION**

Kevin Mulroy
Vice President and Editor-in-Chief

Charles Kogod
Illustrations Director

Barbara A. Payne
Editorial Director

Marianne R. Koszorus
Design Director

STAFF FOR THIS BOOK

Kevin Mulroy
Editor

Walton Rawls
Text Editor

Sadie Quarrier
Illustrations Editor

Bill Marr
Art Director

David M. Seager
Assistant Art Director

Johnna Rizzo
Assistant Editor

Marian K. Gordin
Copy Editor

Martha C. Christian
Tom Melham
Barbara A. Payne
Contributing Editors

Winfield Swanson
Researcher

Carl Mehler
Director of Maps

Matt Chwastyk
Joseph F. Ochlak
Map Research & Production

Ron Fisher
Picture Legends Writer

R. Gary Colbert
Production Director

Meredith Wilcox
Illustrations Assistant

**MANUFACTURING &
QUALITY CONTROL**

George V. White
Director

John Dunn
Manager

Phillip L. Schlosser
Financial Analyst

The world's largest nonprofit scientific and educational organization, the National Geographic Society was founded in 1888 "for the increase and diffusion of geographic knowledge." Since then it has supported scientific exploration and spread information to its more than eight million members worldwide.

The National Geographic Society educates and inspires millions every day through magazines, books, television programs, videos, maps and atlases, research grants, the National Geographic Bee, teacher workshops, and innovative classroom materials.

The Society is supported through membership dues, charitable gifts, and income from the sale of its educational products.

Members receive NATIONAL GEOGRAPHIC magazine— the Society's official journal—discounts on Society products, and other benefits.

For more information about the National Geographic Society, its educational programs, publications, or ways to support its work, please call 1-800-NGS-LINE (647-5463), or write to the following address:

National Geographic Society
1145 17th Street NW
Washington, D.C. 20036-4688 U.S.A.

Visit the Society's Web site at
www.nationalgeographic.com

Library of Congress Cataloging-in-Publication Data

Ballard, Robert, D.
  Graveyards of the Pacific : from Pearl Harbor to Bikini Atoll / Robert D. Ballard, with Michael Hamilton Morgan.
    p. cm.
  Includes bibliographical references and index.
  Contents: Pearl Harbor -- Coral Sea -- Midway -- Guadalcanal -- Truk Lagoon -- Philippine Sea -- Bikini Island
  ISBN 0-7922-6366-9 -- ISBN 0-7922-6387-1 (hardcover deluxe)
  1. World War, 1939-1945--Naval Operations, Japanese. 2. World War, 1939-1945--Naval Operations, American. 3. World War, 1939-1945--Campaigns Pacific Ocean. 4. Naval battles--Pacific Ocean. 5. Operations Crossroads, 1946. 6. Shipwrecks--Pacific Ocean. 7. Underwater archaeology--Pacific Ocean. I. Morgan, Michael Hamilton. II. Title.

D777.B34 2001
940.54'5952--dc21

2001030792

Printed in the U.S.A.

Composition for this book by the National Geographic Society Book Division. Printed and bound by R. R. Donnelly & Sons, Willard, Ohio. Color separations by Quad Graphics, Martinsburg, West Virginia. Dust jacket printed by the Miken Co., Cheektowaga, New York.